It's Critical!

Classroom strategies for promoting critical and creative comprehension

David Booth

Pembroke Publishers Limited

© 2008 Pembroke Publishers
538 Hood Road
Markham, Ontario, Canada L3R 3K9
www.pembrokepublishers.com

Distributed in the U.S. by Stenhouse Publishers
480 Congress Street
Portland, ME 04101
www.stenhouse.com

We acknowledge the financial support of the Government of Canada through the Book
Publishing Industry Development Program (BPIDP) for our publishing activities.

We acknowledge the assistance of the Government of Ontario through the Ontario
Media Development Corporation's Ontario Book Initiative.

Library and Archives Canada Cataloguing in Publication

Booth, David W. (David Wallace)
   It's critical! : classroom strategies for promoting critical and creative comprehension

Includes index.
ISBN 978-1-55138-228-9

   1. Reading comprehension — Study and teaching (Elementary). 2. Reading
comprehension — Study and teaching (Secondary). 3. Critical thinking — Study
and teaching (Elementary). 4. Critical thinking — Study and teaching
(Secondary). 5. Creative thinking — Study and teaching (Elementary).
6. Creative thinking — Study and teaching (Secondary). I. Title.

LB1050.45.B665 2008   372.47   C2008-903753-7

Editor: Kate Revington
Cover Design: John Zehethofer
Typesetting: Jay Tee Graphics Ltd.

Printed and bound in Canada
9 8 7 6 5 4 3 2 1

Printed on 30% recycled paper

13 trees were saved for our forests

Preserving our environment
Pembroke Publishers chose to use recycled paper
to print this book and saved these resources[1]:

energy	water	greenhouse gases	solid waste
61 million BTUs	113,691 L	4189 kg	1608 kg

Printed by **Webcom Inc.**
on Legacy TB White 30% post-consumer waste.

FSC

Mixed Sources
Product group from well-managed
forests, and recycled wood or fiber

Cert no. SW-COC-002358
www.fsc.org
© 1996 Forest Stewardship Council

[1]Estimates were made using the Environmental Defense Paper Calculator.

Contents

Introduction: The Deep End of the Pool

This book grew out of a project, where a group of teachers, administrators, and academics, including myself, came together to examine the methods and strategies for deepening the understanding of our students about the themes, issues, and concerns of every area of the curriculum.

As teachers concerned with literacy development, in every grade and in every subject, we want our students to enter deeply into the world of each text they engage with, to make the most meaning possible from their experiences with it at this time in their lives.

How deeply we enter the world of a text, with all its layers of meaning, is influenced by a combination of factors. The understandings we develop will depend on our backgrounds; our knowledge of the topic; our attitudes towards the text and the author; our interest in the text; the skill of the author; our energy level; the others involved; our ease with the genre, format, language, syntax, and style; and the required expected responses. We need to recognize and interpret these factors in the context of preparing, planning, and implementing the literacy events in our classrooms.

Traditionally, the process of meaning making has been called "building comprehension." Too often, though, we have been uncertain of our goals and desired outcomes. Did we want the students to find particular answers to specific questions? Did those answers add to their growing knowledge of the complexities of the text? Did they help the students connect this text to the other texts of their lives? Were the students able to question the text, the author's intent, and the choices the author made? Did we help the students to work with the genre and the form in which it appears, to know the features of this text form and how it functions, to build on their background information, to predict, infer, and summarize as they read? Making meaning is more than completing comprehension exercises.

In seeking to deepen our students' understanding of the texts they meet, everything matters — it's all critical. For example, reflective and enriching response activities can deepen and extend the students' meaning making; conversely, simplistic and routine worksheets and activities can dampen exploration and minimize the worth of a text and the experience.

Think of a child in a pool, feeling at one with that medium, as a caring instructor holds him afloat or suggests how to move his arms more effectively: that is my image for teaching kids with different types of texts. With swimming, you are always *in* the medium, always interacting with the water in a real way. With a text, it is not a matter of having a guidebook or later finding out what you should have thought; we want our students *in* that story — and as mentors, we will help them swim inside it.

I think that a swimming pool is a great metaphor for school as a whole. Our children will practise and grow more skillful if they are somehow "with the water," diving deep into the pool again and again. I hope teachers will see themselves as strong mentors, caring and believing in how children live and breathe and work and learn. We as mentors have to jump into the water as well. We have to know what the deep end means and possess the necessary skills and behaviors so that our children can swim safely and grow as human fish, unafraid to risk leaving the shallows.

Years ago, I saw a mentor at work in a swimming pool. When I enrolled my four-year-old son in swimming classes at the University of Toronto Olympic-sized swimming pool, we supervising adults were asked to leave and move up to a gallery away from the instruction. Out came the instructor, a woman with long flowing hair to her waist. She jumped into the water and said to the shivering children: "Come on in. The water's fine today!" And every child jumped into the cold water of that giant pool. Then she called out: "Who wants a ride to the deep end on my back?" And there was my son, first in line, on the back of an Amazon, heading into the unknown depths beyond . . .

Mentoring by wise and experienced others: a definition of literacy education.

More than 35 fine, professional educators, many of whom sometimes let me borrow their children for an hour or two, have joined me in developing this book about supporting and encouraging our students from Grades 1 through 8 to engage with different types of texts as deeply as possible. They share a variety of teaching techniques and activities, all designed for increasing the students' understanding, for expanding their meaning making. Some of these writers have years of teaching experience, some are acting as resource teachers, and some are college educators working alongside their new teacher colleagues in mentoring roles. All of them are involved in moving students into deeper understanding.

They are representative of the teachers I meet in my travels who work alongside their students as true mentors. They are just as interested as the youngsters in what can happen as they explore a text. Sometimes they work with the class all together, sometimes in small groups, and sometimes with the children reading and writing independently. I notice that these effective teachers always find time and opportunity for bringing the class together after a series of hands-on activities, where projects are shared, more questions are raised, responses are read, and problems are handled cooperatively.

These educators all understand that we want our students to explore every text they meet with all of their capabilities and energies, to be stretched beyond simple expectations into unknown and uncharted territories of thought and feeling, to be so completely engaged in acts of meaning making that they don't want to leave to catch the bus at 3:45 in the afternoon.

The children they teach seem to know how inquiry works, what research really means, which texts are most useful for which activity, and who can assist them in meeting the learning expectations established together. They reflect on what has happened during the experience, notice and articulate their personal learning strategies, and plan their next literacy event. They are integral to the classroom structure and dynamic: their thoughts matter and they welcome challenging and complex learning situations.

I marvel at the quality and the wide variety of literacy events these educators have recorded for this book (see Part B), and I find myself inside each of the units described, thinking about how I would have participated, excited by the prospects inherent in the new approaches to learning represented by these contemporary classroom practices. I notice their students engaged in so many of the thinking processes that we hope for in our schools — brainstorming, researching, interpreting, problem-solving, discussing, presenting, composing, conducting inquiries, publishing reports, writing poems and scripts, critically examining issues and concerns, and reflecting on their learning. For my part, I have added bits and pieces from my teaching life of researching and working with teachers in developing literacy programs. Like all teachers, I value best practices, and these teacher-writers have demonstrated so many of them that we could create a book.

Which we have done.

Jump in the pool — try the deep end!

1

"Just Tell Me What It Means!"

"If a democracy is to survive and prosper, it must have responsible citizens capable of creative and critical thought, with free access to information and story."
— National Children's Book and Literacy Alliance

During a lesson on poetry, a frustrated student in a Grade 12 English class raised his hand in response to a complicated question. "Just tell me what it means!" he cried. For too many older students, comprehension has become a question-and-answer activity, without much time to enter into a dialogue with others to unpack and discover meaning.

Driven by test scores and busy schedules, we sometimes fall victim to the Right Answer syndrome, but literacy is about meaning making, negotiating with a text for deep understanding in order to develop as a proficient reader and writer.

In March 2006, the *New York Times* published a front-page article on the tendency of schools to push reading and math at the expense of all other subjects. At one high school in Sacramento, 150 students out of 850 spend five of their six class periods on math, reading, and gym, leaving only one period for all other subjects. Those students doing poorly are prohibited from taking any classes other than math, reading, and gym. This pressure comes from state test scores, and raising those scores is the single goal for many schools.

What does "illiterate" mean in the 21st century? Many different forms of texts —manuals, schedules, guitar magazines, sheet music, and almost anything with numbers in it — I cannot read efficiently. Does that make me illiterate?

What kinds of citizens will emerge from this "basic" education is beyond me, but what interests me most is *what* the kids are reading. Are there no selections on topics related to the rest of the curriculum? Are they mandated to read only one genre? Who are the authors who seem to speak to these students? What care is being taken to develop independent, thinking individuals? What do students do with what they have read? Are writing and technology inherent parts of the program? Are these students beginning to believe that this is what reading as adults will look like?

Rethinking Literacy

As teachers, we are confronted with the pragmatics of teaching literacy every time we meet our students. There are so many issues to think about. Are we using inappropriate texts with our limited readers? Are we beginning formal literacy teaching too early? Are we so bothered by disruptive behaviors that we ignore the miscreants? Are we losing too many boys and many girls because of our choices of suitable literacy experiences? Do we assess, but then not use the data to build our teaching methodologies? Do we have enough support personnel? Are government curricula too rigid, too complex, and too many?

Effective teachers enrich their programs with texts that are new to the youngsters or different from their standard reading materials, while at the same time building opportunities and respect for the resources "owned" by the students. I think it's a matter of negotiating the literacy territory. We recognize that every child has a right to read what he or she wants to read at some time during the day, but also know we require the strength to ensure that the students experience texts that can change their lives in different ways, scenes that can make them laugh and cry, novels that portray lives so like or unlike their own, articles about science and geography and health that move them further into ideas and issues. We need ways of helping them meet these texts actively, as full participants in the literacy event, rather than only as recipients of teacher wisdom.

I want the children we teach to know the possibilities that rich literacy processes can tap into, to know they can alter their futures, see the world from different viewpoints, transform their world pictures, own their lives, resist manipulation by corporations or governments, find pleasure and laughter and satisfaction in all types of texts, feel worthy as readers who make important choices, risk and fight for valued beliefs that will benefit all, be awake to the imagined possibilities that surround them. We aren't what we read; we read what we *are* — and what we can become.

If we create a place for all types of texts, shared in engaging and significant ways, we can enlarge the literacy sphere of every child we meet. As teachers and librarians, we have magical powers that parents lack; they are weighed down by hopes and expectations and dreams and responsibilities and the demands of daily life, quite different from our professional approach to child care in the widest sense.

All of us need to think about the texts we experience by interacting with others, for we know what we think only when we try to articulate or represent our thoughts. That is why school can be such a powerful force in teaching literacy: we have a built-in community for exploring our text-generated ideas. We bring our own life needs to every experience with text, whether those in charge want us to or not.

Students need to *do* something with what they read. When we explore a text, when we respond to it through discussion, role playing, or art, we add to our understanding, we alter our perspectives, we create a new text that lives alongside the original, both adding to our grasp of the issues or of the people we began to explore. We change ourselves as we rethink, retell, and re-imagine the original text. We read it again — and we find it has become a whole new experience.

The meaning making at the heart of reading and writing texts grows from engaging with the ideas that are being read and written about. When students are inside the experience, needing to read and write in order to come to grips with the issues and concerns being discussed or examined, when texts are being interpreted or constructed as part of learning, then I can sense that a literacy event is happening. The young person needs not only to inhabit the words and images, but to see herself as a performer, representing and owning the learning. The student *becomes* the literacy. She reads and writes with her whole self, with her body, with her emotions, with her background as a daughter and as a student and as a citizen; she sits in school beside her family members, and she reads every text she meets alongside them, inside her cultural surround. Literacy is constructed through identity.

For ways to respond to a text through discussion, see especially Chapter 3: Deepening Understanding through Book Talk. For ways to respond through role playing, see especially Chapter 9: Deepening Understanding through the Arts.

To us, reading is an invisible process that allows us entry to a thousand thoughts, whenever we want or need to read a text. We can choose what and when to read, how to skip the sections that hold no interest for us, when to stop reading an unsatisfying book and move to another text, when to find another website, which magazine to read, depending on our mood and interest. We can read anything and everything while waiting in the doctor's office, read something others may scoff at, drift through a bookstore and browse the shelves, reread a book that our psyche cries out for, read while watching our children play hockey, become lost in a fictional world and lose track of time, spend hours searching on the Internet for health information. Reading in these ways happens as part of how we live our lives. We have learned the magic word: choice.

Can we let reluctant, dormant readers in on this secret? Learning to choose, to select, may be the truth we have been seeking in our literacy teaching. The libraries are vast, the bookstore has two or three floors full of shelves, the racks hold hundreds of magazines, and the Internet goes on forever. We must help young people become readers who know what they need and what they want, aware of personal choices that can free them from past fears of failure and disappointment.

For me, if the inquiry is significant, if the exploration of the topic is authentic, if the student is connected to the issues or themes or ideas under consideration, then the learning will be woven together smoothly. If the need to discover is strong, reading as a process goes unnoticed. Whether we read a book, a newspaper, a film, or a computer screen, we read for a reason.

See especially Chapter 8: Deepening Understanding through Inquiry for more on inquiry.

Yet readership of newspapers and books, especially of fiction, has declined, and the literary culture loses more young people every year. There has been a retreat from complex and deeply structured modes of printed texts.

How do we nurture in our young people a love and need for the printed word? If they aren't literate in a variety of texts, they are cut off from so much. About one-third of the population in North America lacks basic literacy skills to function successfully. Look among the dropouts, the soaring prison populations, and the homeless to find the most visible functionally illiterate, but know that there are many more invisible illiterates, too.

How do we build a culture of literacy that is inclusive of the multitude of text forms, so that intensive and extensive experiences are part of the continuum of literacy? How can we enhance literacy and expand competency with electronic texts? Being literate means being able to choose where to go in life — education is about having many choices and making wise ones.

We need to rethink literacy and how to go about supporting our students in becoming literate.

The New Literacies: Shifting Definitions and Perspectives

Our traditional way of thinking about and defining literacy is not enough if we hope to provide youngsters with what they will need to be full participants in the world of the future.

For young people, learning will require opportunities to explore meaning making with many text forms and in new combinations of forms, such as the visual text literacies found in our electronic, computer-filled world. Although images have not replaced the alphabetical code, children live in the age of television and computer screens. Yes, we continue to read and write printed text, but even our relationship with printed text is altering and mutating: the page form lives alongside text that rolls vertically, with forms of e-mail and text messages that are multi-modal.

A future literate culture will be determined not only by its literature — fiction or non-fiction — but also by newspapers, magazines, television, computers, networks, films, CD-ROMs, hypertext, e-mail, and other forms yet to be created.

What constitutes literacy has changed throughout history. Today, we understand that there are multiple literacies. This shift from *literacy* to *literacies* has created possibilities and reconsiderations of pedagogies that look at literacy in multiple ways, through a variety of media and approaches. The term **new literacies** points to multiple linguistic systems within literacy. Literacy practices, which are multiple, shift based on the context, speaker, text, and function of the literacy event (e.g., doing a Google search). Yet schools often do not reflect this. As Jim Cummins (2006) puts it:

> In urban contexts across North America and Europe, the student population is multilingual, and students are exposed to and engage in many different literacy practices outside the school. Within schools, however, the teaching of literacy is narrowly focused on literacy in the dominant language and typically fails to acknowledge or build on the multilingual literacies or the technologically mediated literacies that form a significant part of students' cultural and linguistic capital.

Even definition of the term **text** has gone beyond the traditional acts of reading and writing using an alphabetic code or symbol system, to include digital technology, images, sounds, and oral discourse. Now we refer to a text as a medium with which we make meaning through a variety of modes — written, visual, tactile, or oral. Texts span audio books, magazines, paintings, films, computer screens, narratives, graphics, information, opinions, poetry, songs, scripts, instructions, and procedures.

Here are some other related definitions:

- **Multitexts** occur when one text form is transformed into multiple texts (e.g., a popular cartoon is also seen on lunch boxes and bed spreads).
- **Intertextuality** refers to the interconnections of multiple texts and multiple textual meanings within one text. For example, Japanese graphic novels, called manga, make you think about Japanese lore and popular culture.
- **Modes** represent the materials used to create an effect in texts: visual, written, oral, tactile, performative, or animated (e.g., a teenager's blog).
- **Genre** indicates a type of text that can be thought of in three ways: (1) by form (as in novels, scripts, manuals), (2) by function (persuasion, narrative, exposition), and (3) by the types of language used (e.g., a computer manual, a dictionary). Writers/speakers draw upon these forms of cultural resources or cognitive tools as ways of framing their thoughts and ideas for readers/listeners.
- The **structure** of a text refers to its physical organization. For example, Facebook has a profile and then a wall where you can write comments.

The textual features of a genre can help us structure our thoughts, but we need to be able to adapt the form to our goals. For example, within a novel there may be photographs, graphics, maps, lists, diary entries, definitions, descriptions, or transcripts inside the general category.

Literacy no longer presupposes print, and comprehension extends past printed text to any messages that have permanence. Due to the accessibility and high level of exposure to various forms of visual media, such as television, cinematography, and printed magazines, many people have developed and internalized a form of visual literacy that allows them to read and comprehend the narratives of such media almost effortlessly. It is, therefore, easy to forget that these media have various basic components and communication techniques that their creators learn and deliberately utilize. Likewise, the readers or audience for these media also initially master and internalize the required "reading" strategies.

Our definitions of reading and reading instruction are changing, as is the way we see the world. The new literacies are profoundly shaping the ways in which we view and use language. Just as the telephone altered communication strategies, our students will encounter a wide and perhaps unthought-of variety of information and communication technologies. Just think of video cameras, web editors, spreadsheets, list servs, blogs, PowerPoint, virtual worlds, and the like. Our youngsters will require technological expertise in their home, work, and civic lives. They will need to be plugged in (or wireless) for survival.

Today we should be concerned less with understanding one type of written text than with mastering multiple texts and modes, and the practices implied in each. We need to concentrate less on the purely linguistic and more on the multi-modal. Our students are dealing with a greater network of meanings, so our literacy curriculum needs to match that in order to set them up for the future. There may be a pronounced difference between the literacies students are developing at home and the literacy of schools. This divide must be understood and explored. We need to rethink the way we learn to be literate and the way we regard literacy and literate behavior.

Print does not hold prominence over visuals, or combinations of both. While the literacy inherent in each mode involves composition, decoding comprehension, and response, changes in how text forms function will alter or expand our definition of literacy. Think of the multimedia in a website: as the mouse clicks, meaning-bearing icons, animations, and video clips may appear, along with graphics of all types, pop-ups — an entire sign system dependent upon the "reader's" tool kit.

Isn't it paradoxical that as we invent universal symbol systems, we also find a growing diversity of cultures and languages with all the nations and groups involved? We will need to help readers develop multiple perspectives if they are to communicate successfully.

Technology and Literacy in Context

Everyone I know working in the areas of education and literacy spends hours each day reading and writing on the computer, while celebrating the book as the most important centre of the child's world.

Schools are trying to give their students opportunities to become computer literate — to learn about technology, but more important, to use technology to support and enhance their own learning. Youngsters at all levels are now working with word processors, chat lines, blogs, e-mails, text messages, web searches, image editing software, and so on. And all of these activities are literacy events. Boys and girls are reading — and especially writing — more than ever in the world's history. Despite that, we can consider the quality of the literacy events in which they are engaging, the kinds of learning processes they are exploring — and the options they may be minimizing or even missing.

Chapter 3: Deepening Text Understanding through Book Talk describes virtual literature circles and discussing text through blogs.

How can we build on students' digital literacies so that they can learn to read and write in ways that will help them value the intertextuality of the many different literacy experiences in their lives? We can be plugged in at times and still gather together and sit in a circle, to listen to a tale 2000 years old. The texts that students read and enjoy at home are print and electronic: with computer programs, they can not only adapt visual information, but also transform it. Our choice of texts in the classroom needs to reflect the multi-modality seen on the Web and in CD-ROMs to appeal to students' reading behaviors.

By the same token, computer use can be balanced by programs involving print resources that connect the students to the worlds they inhabit, while stretching their abilities and interests: we can include novels, biographies, poems, columns, and articles that represent the best writers of life-enriching works we can find. Print texts are artifacts that carry assumptions about readers, their gender, their culture, the way they will read books, and even the type of message they are expected to receive — they are important tools in children's burgeoning development of literacy skills. Resources that touch the emotions and the intellect have a much greater opportunity for moving readers into deeper frames of understanding. Aesthetic knowledge lets us see further and sense the *as if,* "the hallmark of thoughtful, mindful citizens," as education philosopher Maxine Greene puts it.

Bill Gates has stated that the only thing necessary for successful interactions with computers is literacy, something that makes teachers more significant than ever. We are mandated to ensure that students can make sense of the different codes they will encounter in life, the many modes and forms of communication, and that they will have the strategies and behaviors necessary for literacy success. A tall order, but schools are working hard to achieve it.

The *Toronto Star* reported on a sociolinguist's two-year study of more than one million words of text messaging between 71 Toronto teens. Sali Tagliamonte found that their unique shorthand not only forms just 2.4 percent of their online dialogue, it also shows a versatility and adaptability that may strengthen their command of the language.

In a technological world, where two-year-olds are working at computers, the mode and content of literacy have altered. In my years of teaching, I have had to adapt my own behaviors, rethink policy and pedagogy, learn new techniques for making and interpreting print and image, re-examine cultural agendas, and continue to experience the world through what we can call "multi-literacies" — the page, computer screen, cell phone screen, television, and so on. We need to see literacy as a series of processes that can offer us a means, a pathway, to deeper, more complex understandings and constructions of our own worlds.

The traditional foundations of literacy remain constant: word and vocabulary recognition, decoding knowledge, comprehension, critical analysis, the writing process, and spelling. Yet the new literacies will demand other skills, new competencies, in order for people to function as literate citizens. And, of course, speed has become an adjunct literacy tool with computers. Limited readers need help learning to skim websites containing enormous amounts of information, to link web pages, and to evaluate text in all its forms. We need to consider how we can best assist them in becoming competent literacy participants.

Technology does not necessarily improve the acquisition of literacy. It requires carefully crafted learning programs focused on creating dynamic opportunities for interpreting, manipulating, and creating ideas in the classroom. The rapid development of the Internet is a little like a gold rush: some miners find gold, but many find failure. Have we changed how we help youngsters move towards deeper literacy? We need to.

In 1992, there were 50 websites. As I write this, in 2008, there are over 100 million.

The value of literacy education, both inside and outside schools, involves what we do with what we learn, and with whom we live. If teachers do not prepare students for the literacies required in their future lives, what should they be teaching? Business spends millions of dollars training employees in the literacies required for effective practice and will continue to do so as the needs of the workplace change. What literacy strengths do students leave school with? What do they see as the functions of literacy in their lives?

The way we incorporate texts into our schools' curricula can lead to limitations in the lives of the students. In today's world, literacy is far more than the ability to sign one's name. Social and work considerations present severe challenges to youngsters with strong literacy deficits. But now to the difficulties of reading manuals, newspapers, and novels we have added the immensity of the functions of the Internet and its permutations and combinations.

Literature or Literacy?

Males may choose to read other kinds of texts, such as *The New Yorker* and *Sports Illustrated*, both of which include the work of fine writers. Remember, too, that many novels are not necessarily included in the literature canon.

Many people are confused about literature and literacy. The first definition of *literature* in the *Canadian Oxford Dictionary* is "written works, esp. those whose value lies in beauty of language or in emotional effect." Too many parents and teachers regard only novels, poetry, and "literary non-fiction" as reading, and many boys and men think that they are not readers because they don't choose one of those genres.

The thinking that "novel" is the magic word for literacy is unfortunate for many readers. Today, even in Grades 3, 4, and 5, the whole-class novel is the main reading strategy. At least a third to half of a class likely can't handle that text. Yet it is mandatory methodology, chapter by chapter. Is the goal literacy or literature? We need to examine how we can have both.

We want our students to work towards independence, to develop into lifelong readers who see books as friendly objects. How can we help students to think carefully about the texts they read, to become aware of how literature works, so that they can become critical and discerning readers who understand the literary techniques that authors use, recognize the multiple perspectives that literature generates, and value their own emotional responses to the heart of a powerful story?

We can begin by providing students with a large quantity of novels, a wide range and a great variety of experiences with the genre of story — all kinds of narratives, including fiction and non-fiction. By supporting extensive reading and nurturing thoughtful personal responses to both what has been read and the views of others in the literacy community, we can help developing readers to build new understandings.

As teachers, we have all experienced the disappointment that comes from a student revealing boredom or dissatisfaction with something we had judged to be a wonderful piece of literature. Finding appropriate and interesting books that represent quality literature for our students is a complicated task, but it is at the centre of our struggle to help them become critical and creative readers.

Learning to appreciate literature is a developmental, lifelong process, dependent on many variables — background, skill, experience, familiarity, life and text connections, purpose, situation, and so on. We need to move towards supporting readers' decisions about the print resources they select — their newspapers, novels, magazines, their work and organizational materials, and their choices of reading for fun and games. We then need to consider in our teaching how to increase the options that print resources can offer and explore with students how different texts work — what to look for and what to expect — so that they can make informed choices and select the resources that will give them the most satisfaction.

We need to help young people, regardless of background and ability, to look at their responses to different texts, to reflect on why they feel as they do, and to consider the author's role in determining how they respond to the ideas and words in texts. Not surprisingly, reading the texts we want or need to read in search of deeper understanding may be the answer to many of the common problems teachers and parents face in promoting books to their young people.

To be open enough to have your perspectives and interpretations change because of your participation in a discussion about a shared text means that you are engaged in truly learning about yourself and your world.

Many readers still enjoy the classics, but as reading tastes and writing styles change, readers may make alternative choices. Students can find in the classics a different life from their own in language, custom, place, time, or circumstance; for some, the differences can make the reading difficult. Independent readers may relish the depth of language and content that characterizes classics.

The literature canon for youngsters has not altered much over the last 50 years. The same novels are used throughout most school districts in North America, without much awareness of equity or gender issues. The books are often read and analyzed chapter by chapter, with too little attention paid to the impact of choice and the teaching strategy on the future literacy lives of the students.

Teachers and reluctant readers, in particular, have different criteria for texts. Teachers, it seems, favor elegance of story structure, sophistication of character development, complexity of description, irony, and references to other literature. But reluctant readers tell us they want action, raw humor, familiarity, and complex illustrations. How can the two be reconciled?

How can a text full of long, uninterrupted print passages compete with the visual and aural sensations that beat upon young people and catch them in the media net? Young people are inundated with so many texts from television, cereal boxes, advertising, and computer games. Can we draw on the range of powerful literature we have access to for motivating reluctant readers to explore the ideas, the other worlds, the information, the surprises, the sense of imagination contained inside the very books they too often disdain? What if these readers could find themselves engaged in a book they couldn't put down? What would change in their reading lives? Would they forget their reading problems and simply read?

Reading a book is a solitary act, a private affair in which we are walled off from present life, from the concerns that grab our attention, yet school is a public place. And so the conflict begins: How do we engage 25 students in the silence of the reading moment and what are we to teach them?

Talk is a bridge. Often, I as a reader am altered by my conversations with another reader of the same text, even if the responses are in print form; I hear the voice of someone who has shared my text, and I rethink my experience. I see the film based on the book, and my thoughts about the story move in another direction. School can do this for youngsters, as long as we keep in mind that we are not teaching the book, but the understanding of how books work, how story lives, how artists create characters out of words, how our own lives are enriched by the new pathways that open between the pages.

As a teacher, I will teach as many literary terms, works of art, and icons of literature as I can make matter to my students — that is where the negotiating, intervening, motivating teacher comes into play. Teachers are mentors for youngsters in exploring how our literature works, but it is best if we guide and model, teach rather than test. Eventually, it is the reader's responsibility to be aware of the writer's craft and the conventions that writers use, in order to have rich and fruitful experiences with literature.

One answer to meeting the needs of our students is to offer options so that their text selections can become more varied, even more challenging. We can show them possibilities, without demeaning their present literacy lives and choices. Formulaic books, series books, or books by an author who follows the same structure in each book are magnets for many readers and build reading power and fluency. We should not overlook their value.

Remember that we can make people read what they don't want to read only as long as they are in school. We often judge the literacy worth of individuals by the place that one particular art form, literature, has in their lives. When we begin listing the various forms of print that fill up students' lives, we notice that they read many types of texts: computer screens, sports pages, comics, game manuals, TV guides, and school textbooks. The list goes on.

Those of us who spend our leisure time among books want to pass on our love. We want others to join us in the book club, to enter a bookstore or a library with excitement and to leave fulfilled even before reading our selections. We read the reviews, wait for the Saturday newspaper section devoted to books, talk to our colleagues about book gossip, and hoard our new purchases for holiday reading. Can we reconcile students and books as they grow into adulthood? We can; we do with many. But we will have to rethink our goals, our values; to see texts as filling the world, so that we can select those few that will change us, fulfill us, surprise us, validate us, and connect us to our families, friends, and fellow citizens. Some texts will be print, some image, some both, most electronic, a few on papyrus or pulp.

How do we balance the immediacy of visual images with the power of printed texts? We will not overcome illiteracy by ignoring the media in students' lives and pushing books and magazines, nor will we build literate citizens by excluding reflective, aesthetic, and informative printed texts. It is more difficult to read a book than to watch a film, but much depends on the nature of the experience and the context and the text itself. Did the student choose it alone or with classmates? Is there a test on it? Is there time to accomplish the "reading"? Does it require the student to interpret and reflect and rethink assumptions? Is the student changed by what is seen, heard, or read?

We want our students to meet books, to discover the options they can bring to their choices in life, but our definition is about to change. The year 2009 will see the launch of the Sony Reader, a portable device for digital books and documents, along with digitized titles from major publishers. The Reader is the size of a thin paperback and weighs 250 grams. Writing in the *New York Times*, Kevin Kelly of *Wired* magazine creates a fascinating manifesto for the coming change to our definition of books. "The world's texts are being electronically copied, digitized, searched and linked. The force of the web lies in the power of relationships. Search engines create a trillion electronic connections through the web."

Books and screens will co-exist for the near future. Book people are strong-willed proponents of the paper-print media, and technology will continue to expand as young people are born wireless. But students will need teachers, librarians, and friends to promote and provide choices to extend and enrich their literacy options with different texts, along with time and places and opportunities for adding new ones to their crowded lives.

To teach the canon, you must believe in the canon; not only that, you must add to it, find new texts, celebrate them with the students, and read joyfully. The enthusiasm of the teacher is catching, and at least your students will know what you stand for, what you value. Seeing this will help them to develop their own text needs, not just now in class, but throughout life, as they study, work, marry, and parent.

Re-visioning Comprehension

Rather than assess students' literal understanding, we need to teach them specific strategies for better comprehending what they read.

Reading is far more than attempting to second-guess the intent of the author; it is a process of interpretation and negotiation from the locus of our lived and vicarious experiences at a moment in time. We need to constantly expand our abilities to process print, from a single word on a billboard to a dense novel translated from Russian. From our first beginning steps in reading, texts present challenges to us — the words and language patterns, the structure and organization of different kinds of texts, our purpose in reading a particular text, and especially the content and our connections to it.

Comprehension, then, is the process of constructing personal meaning as a reader focuses on a particular text: the reader makes sense of the author's language, considers the information and ideas, and somehow synthesizes the data and integrates it into his own background, culture, and world of understanding. As teachers, we need to understand how reading works, how meaning making with print is developmental and can expand exponentially over time. As supportive, wise mentors, we can guide attempts at meaning making so that students will be in the company of others considering similar issues and ideas generated by the text — classmates, critics and reviewers, and authors whose writing connects to this work or adds to background knowledge.

How do worksheets filled with comprehension exercises change us as readers? In the past, many novel study units incorporated dozens of questions to be answered by the reader. Few seemed to interest or pique reader curiosity, or, much more important, arouse an emotional or connecting response.

Our comprehension alters as our life goes on, and our response to a text is never frozen. The landscape of our minds is constantly shifting as we read, when we reflect on what we have read, when we consider the ideas and opinions of others. In the quest for deep understanding, we don't teach a particular book; we use the book as a stimulus for exploring ideas and issues. Gordon Wells (1994) says: "As the learner appropriates the knowledge and procedures encountered in interaction with others, he or she transforms them constructing his or her own personal version. But in the process, he or she is also transformed."

Years ago, reading expert Charles Reasoner taught us to help readers *reveal their comprehension*. As we assist students in growing as readers, together we could reveal our thoughts, our ideas, and our feelings about a selection we have read. Then, together, we could enrich and extend each other's perceptions and perspectives about the text, deepening our understanding of how the writer and we readers made meaning together. We are part of the process of comprehending a text. We matter; *everything* matters.

As readers, we interact with texts (and authors), each reader and text forming a relationship integral to the meaning making in a particular context. Always, the reader's own experiences and the textual meanings held in the code and in the way it has been constructed work together to determine the interpretation that will result. All the while, with a purpose in mind, we bring ourselves to the page, using our own personal schema to determine what we think about what we have read.

Our negotiations with a particular text float on a continuum, depending on the function of the task and the implications of the reading. Sometimes we want exact data from a text, but in literature, our lives contribute such vital information as to affect the meaning being made. We rely on the interdependent interaction of all of our resources, including our feelings and our spirits, to make textual meaning. We read a text from our complex lives. Just as the reader works in a sociological, cultural, and psychological frame, so does the author; and part of the critical understanding of a text is the reader's recognition of the choices the author has made in constructing the text and the awareness of the reader's own personal context for making meaning.

Generally, readers work in a non-linear fashion, rather than through literal levels to inferential predictions and finally to critical generalizations. They change their judgments as they glean information and discover implications, anticipating and adjusting their predictions as the context deepens. All these processes are components of higher order thinking, the guesswork that leads to broadened consciousness. Can we design classroom activities that will provide opportunities for using various thinking processes when young people engage with print and screen texts?

To understand a text means having an intellectual and often emotional response and using the learning experience to construct new knowledge so that we can move more deeply into the text's complexities. We can share our new growth, become excited about the concepts we are uncovering or discovering. We want to know more, express our insights, and search out other text types that can deepen our knowledge. We feel that we are engaged in meaning making, and we are carried along the learning path far away from where we began. What's more, we understand our own process of meaning making; we can articulate it and share our findings with others. We are mentored into more thoughtful, deeper territory.

Readers bring their unique personal concerns to interact with the text on all levels. The teacher's role is to empower students to wander inside and around the selection, to wonder about it, to make meaningful connections, to question it, to deepen their understanding of it. With the teacher as lifeguard and coach, students can safely explore the text and relate the ideas they find in it to their own lives, to the author, to the text, to what other students see, to what they see in their own minds, and to the bigger world picture.

Some story worlds are easy to enter; others less so. We have seen that mountain, lived in that city, walked through those bulrushes, or owned a dog like the one in the book. Other story worlds are more difficult to enter: we need the deft author who invites us in, the clever storyteller who draws us along, or the perceptive teacher who builds a context for us. As we hear or read the words, we transform those symbols into startling pictures that let us see into the story.

We need only to think about different readers' responses to a newspaper article, a political speech, a new CD, a religious film, or a novel to realize that text requires interpretation if meaning is to be made. The reader's encounter with a printed work is complex. Meaning making with text is a dynamic interaction, depending as well upon the format and the context of the text.

According to Allan Luke and Peter Freebody (1999, 5–8), effective literacy draws on a repertoire of practices that allow learners, as they engage in reading and writing activities, to

- **break the code of texts:** recognising and using the fundamental features and architecture of written texts including: alphabet, sounds in words, spelling, conventions and patterns of sentence structure and text;
- **participate in the meanings of text:** understanding and composing meaningful written, visual and spoken texts from within the meaning systems of particular cultures, institutions, families, communities, nation-states and so forth;
- **use texts functionally:** traversing the social relations around texts; knowing about and acting on the different cultural and social functions that various texts perform both inside and outside school and knowing that these functions shape

the way texts are structured, their tone, their degree of formality and their sequence of components;

- **critically analyse and transform texts**: understanding and acting on the knowledge that texts are not neutral, that they represent particular views and silence other points of view, influence people's ideas; and that their designs and discourses can be critiqued and redesigned, in novel and hybrid ways.

Linguistic and cultural differences that different texts present offer us a wealth of opportunities, an enrichment of possibilities. As we recognize the complexities of society's issues, we see the need for "reading" at the deepest level, for recognizing the shades of grey between black-and-white extremes. Those who read only minimal text in any form or format are susceptible to control by corporations, unethical political leaders, or charlatans. Literacy is a foundation of citizenry in any language — a right of freedom. An informed citizenry requires competency in many different text forms.

We need to help children learn what reading is for and give them strategies for making connections between the text and their lives. We need to position our teaching of reading inside the act of reading, modelling how we think when we read real texts so that students work inside the process of understanding how print works. The text furnishes the hints, the clue, the start, the framework, and the reader constructs the meaning. We need to read along with children and then talk about the reading and their lives so we can find out what they think about their reading: their questions, reactions, interpretations, opinions, inferences, arguments, and celebrations.

Students need opportunities to expand and practise their comprehension strategies (as outlined in Chapter 2). They are using their strategies for comprehension in deep and involving ways as they read and discuss complex and multi-faceted texts. When these experiences are extended and supported by their own written and artistic responses, students are moving into the field of interpretation, appreciation, and critical and creative thought, understanding the negotiation that is required in order to participate in reading what others have written. They are learning to consider the complexities involved in the relationship between text and reader.

See especially Chapter 3: Deepening Text Understanding through Book Talk, Chapter 4: Deepening Understanding through Graphic Texts, and Chapter 5: Deepening Understanding through Text Sets.

In our literacy classrooms, we can organize our resources and our schedules to support literature groups, where students participate in text talk with other readers who are enjoying the same book or sharing insights on different books. These instructional techniques allow us to increase the range of materials the students could experience — different genres, new authors and illustrators, books from different cultures and countries — and to engage them in thoughtful and critical conversations with other group members, where they share personal interpretations and expand their understanding of and appreciation for both the text and the contributions of others. As their discussions reveal the different interpretations and perceptions of their classmates, they increase their personal background knowledge and understanding of how authors work, and they begin to analyze and reflect on their new responses to the text as they "live through" these collective meaning-making sessions. Literary appreciation can't be demanded, but it can be nurtured and supported.

There is such satisfaction in watching developing readers enter a discussion with a group about a selection they have all read and begin to notice how they create meaning, wrestle with ideas, prove a point by reading a portion of the text that supports their viewpoint, ask questions about the comments of group

The book report is a testing device rather than a teaching strategy; however, if the student writes it as an outgrowth of the reading and reflection that grew from conversations about the text and from thoughtful text drawn from the student's reading journal, then the written report could help the student to consider the text in light of the experiences surrounding it.

members and the text, draw inferences from the discussion and the words on the page, and gain insights from our experience with print. They are constructing meaning and making sense of their responses to what they have read and heard, mediated by the ideas and feelings of the group members. Suddenly, reading has become a successful act, a socially constructed learning experience.

Students are part of the process called reading, sharing thoughts and concerns, modifying and extending ideas, secure in their membership within the literacy community. The participants are learning how readers work, how to talk in their heads to themselves and to the author about the ideas stimulated by the print. They come to understand that everyone reads for a purpose: to affirm, recognize, understand, argue, find out, laugh, weep, and discover who we are and who we might become.

Phonics and Literacy

I like the philosophy of the well-known children's author and educator Mem Fox, who follows the three secrets of reading:

- understanding the world (general knowledge, conversations, life experiences)
- knowing how language works (all about books, the Internet, newspapers, advertisements)
- seeing how print works (letters, meanings, upper and lower case, punctuation)

She says that good readers use the three secrets "simultaneously, rapidly and efficiently."

But what about disabled readers? Are they lost inside one of the secrets of reading, unable to weave the three parts together? Do they not have enough information to bring to the text? Do they not understand the value of the text? Are they stymied by too many words to attack with a limited knowledge of phonics? Does the whole daily reading experience end in frustration and a sense of failure? We can change their literacy futures.

Some older students tell us that they can read the words in a printed text, but don't seem to understand them or spend much time reading. We need to demonstrate reading strategies by showing the students how readers think when reading. They can better understand the text through their connections to the characters, the events, and the issues.

What happens to those students living out their literacy lives in classrooms where "words" are separated from "comprehension"? What texts do they read and write? We want to give students knowledge about words. Although phonics instruction is usually irrelevant to the proficient reader, we need to find ways of letting beginning readers in on the secrets of how words work so they can discover that this process called reading is worth acquiring. Our student readers and writers need an ever-increasing word bank of immediately recognizable words, effective ways to discover unknown words in their reading texts, and useful strategies for spelling words in their writing. They can learn to notice how letters fit together, the patterns involved in word construction, how we can take words apart to discover their inner workings. Building word power is a lifelong undertaking.

And our students need to experience real reading events alongside whatever sound/letter activities we think necessary.

Even the most conservative authorities on the issue suggest that we embed word study inside authentic, real text for the reader. The only reason to learn about the relationship between how we speak and how we represent speech is so that we can read and write more effectively. Today fine books and papers help us learn how to assist young readers in acquiring literacy strategies; word recognition, word constructing, and word-solving are vital processes in interacting with a text. But the goal is to read with as much understanding as possible, to use word knowledge to read something that matters to us.

Moving towards Critical Understanding

We want to encourage critical understanding in our classrooms, to create situations with the texts we offer, so that students engage in thoughtful, critical, and collaborative conversations about the text, their responses, and those of their classmates. We want to build a collegial atmosphere that allows for problematic issues and challenges that involve critical thinking as a way of moving towards deeper understanding. We can offer our students tools for critical understanding: the knowledge and strategies for responding thoughtfully and critically to the issues that arise from experiencing. We want critical understanding to become a habit of mind.

Consider the importance of critical understanding on the Internet. Students are surfing the Web and constructing their own individualized texts, evaluating sites, processing information, and interpreting data, so that they can connect themselves to the world. Critical understanding is now seen as a mainstream strategy. We want to encourage students to become more critical in their use of all media, including the Internet; therefore, we need to teach them to be active and critical readers who can make the most connections possible.

Philosopher Maxine Greene teaches us to let texts enter our lives, to respond to them from experience, and then listen to others responding. We can then begin to realize, for example, that other readers may have a more intimate knowledge of the material in a given text than we have. To have a single view from a teacher, taken from a manual, leaves little opportunity for the individual to consider other possibilities. Each perspective must be analyzed and reflected upon. We need to talk about why a reader feels a certain way, what is going on in the reader's mind, and why the storyteller is telling the story.

Critical literacy

Critical literacy has explicit meanings in our educational contexts today. Given that students are constantly exposed to a wide variety of texts, both in and out of school, critical literacy becomes a tool for helping them interpret the embedded messages, connecting them to their present understanding of what they know or what they thought they knew and moving them into unfamiliar territory. Critical literacy encourages them to question the authority of texts and address issues of bias, perspective, and social justice that they may contain. Many readers assume that print materials are automatically true. But, as students learn to view texts critically, they come to recognize that texts are full of the author's view-

Read, for example, "Advertisements as Texts" by Ken Pettigrew (pages 102–3).

For so many of us, how and what we read today is different from even the near past. We choose materials that can be handled easily in short bursts of time; we browse and sample newspapers, professional journals, magazines, websites — smaller snippets of text — and struggle to find time for longer items, such as novels and biographies. Many of the selections are highly visual, filled with colorful illustrations, detailed drawings, and photographs, with a variety of fonts and sizes.

points as taken in the context of their own lives, and often these need to be examined, even challenged.

With the increasing complexity of the texts in our lives, students need to go beyond literal understanding and to think deeply about what the texts say and mean. Writers of texts are influenced by their own contexts in society; their texts reflect their choices, values, and authority they assume. Students can learn to analyze these positions and come to understand that a text is the author's version of the world. Readers make their own meanings from a particular book and form the viewpoint of their own developing lives. Who they are at a particular stage in life will determine to a great extent how they interact with a particular text.

Our task is to help students make sense of the vast array of messages they encounter every day. In a school where the teacher may teach 130 students on a rotary timetable, it may be difficult to remember that it isn't the novel being taught, but what the novel represents, what an author is attempting to do, what tools the author has used to accomplish the goal, the context in which the book was written, the cultural and gender implications, why the story resonates with some readers and not others, why the novel was selected.

For those teachers who are uncomfortable with the activism aspects of critical literacy, I suggest they move with their students towards the critical *understanding* of a particular type of text — novels, poems, documents, historical recounts, television ads or programs, photography, and so on — using some of the following prompts:

"Prompts for Deepening Comprehension," on pages 147 to 150, provides an extended list.

- Who wrote this text?
- Why do you think the author wrote this text?
- What is the author's background and experience?
- Whose point of view is expressed?
- What does the author, filmmaker, or artist want you to think?
- Whose perspective is found in this text?
- Whose voices are missing, silenced, or discounted?
- Which characters in the text seem to hold all the power?
- Were characters or events portrayed in ways that were unexpected?
- Do you belong to any of the groups in this text?
- What is the world like for the people in the text?
- Did the illustrations leave out things that you thought should have been included?
- How might alternative perspectives be represented?
- How might you make the story more complete?
- Can you find some research on the author and his or her perspective?
- Is the information in the text accurate and believable?
- What do other sources of information say about these events, characters, and issues?
- How does this book help you to think about social issues and social justice?
- How did the design of the text affect you?
- What action might you take from what you have learned?

Critical literacy asks us to examine how particular texts work, the choices the author made, the intent of the publisher, the point of view expressed, the omissions, and the biases. It also calls for agency: readers are to recognize how the text is affecting or controlling them; contribute to change and to social justice; confront inequities; and see alternative viewpoints to those presented by the author. This approach requires a school culture that supports such an action-oriented process, but this attitude and way of thinking towards social change can be developed in individuals in incremental steps. For example, even when writing their life stories from personal memories, students can come to recognize how aspects of culture, power roles, and social relationships are brought to light.

Pauline Beder, an experienced school librarian, offers her thoughts on how to build an awareness of critical literacy.

Invite students to bring their out-of-school literacies into the school. Encourage them to share their expertise with their peers and teachers. Model how to ask probing questions, seek alternative points of view and challenge the obvious. Show your enthusiasm for learning and give students choices and time to engage deeply in tasks that are authentic and engaging.

Many classrooms today are global in nature, where students of conflicting cultures and religions are sitting shoulder to shoulder and expected to learn together. Today's students need to understand multiple perspectives, respect diversity, and understand a variety of social norms. They need to be able to negotiate between conflicting opinions. Do not shy away from controversy. Provide time for talk around issues, opinions, particular media texts. Teach students how to have an open mind and still stay true to their beliefs. Teach them how to take a critical stance, ask probing questions and always seek the truth . . .

Read aloud, watch, listen together and offer a taste of compelling, entertaining and thought-provoking texts. Engage students in grand conversations that explore controversial topics. Deconstruct media to understand the writer's and creator's intent and craft and then provide opportunities for students to construct their own pieces . . .

Model through think aloud and role play how you seek meaning as you read texts. Students need to be able to distinguish fact from fiction, argument from documentation, real from fake and marketing from enlightenment. New media literacies involve the ability to think across media and be able to read and write across all available modes of expression.

Give students time and choice in their exploration of all forms of media. We do not know what format information will take in their lifetime. What we need to teach them is how to look at all media through a critical lens. Not a negative lens, but one that is open-minded, curious, and not afraid to look deeply and ask difficult questions.

Students need to develop habits of mind such as curiosity, open-mindedness, persistence, and a burning desire for justice and truth. They need to feel empowered by knowing that they can make a difference. Learning about others who have had the courage to take a stand for what they believe in plants the seeds of responsible citizenship and empathy in our students' hearts and minds.

Creative Literacy

It is impossible to read fiction without imagination, without placing yourself in a created world, conjuring up in your mind a different life, identifying strongly with a character, and making all sorts of connections. The fictional lives are painted with the reader's imagination, just as the author has constructed a cosmos for the reader to seek to understand and interpret. This is the imaginative negotiation between reader and author that comprises an act of fiction.

Consider how your classroom program supports this. Are there times in the day when children are permitted and encouraged to express thoughts and feelings through the Arts, to wonder aloud in conversation about a significant text, to hypothesize about a science project they are about to begin, to take risks solving a complex math problem that may require several attempts? Are they allowed to try and try again without feeling failure, but instead, challenging their own puzzlements with imaginative efforts?

If we include ourselves as imaginative participants in the life of the classroom, then we can more easily notice and interpret the acts of imagination that enrich and extend everyone's learning.

In his books on active learning, Jeffrey Wilhelm promotes an inquiry approach that uses role-playing strategies. Such strategies allow youngsters to step inside the texts they read, to see the other sides of the words, to *really* see what's between the lines. They can thereby own the text. Through improvising and reading aloud for authentic reasons, the students gain new perceptions and often connect their emotions to the ideas represented in the texts. When teaching any type of selection, it is a good idea, I find, to move quickly into active exploration: our job becomes much easier when students own the work.

See especially Chapter 9: Deepening Understanding through the Arts.

Teaching for deep understanding means both deep understanding of the artforms and media within which we work and deep understanding of the complex world in which we live and create. Maxine Greene (2001) helps us to better understand the role that imagination must play in our encounters of teaching and learning. Aesthetic education, for Greene as for many arts educators, speaks to our efforts to look at things as if they were otherwise, to imagine a more just, a more generous, a more artful world. In classrooms, we are engaged in this work daily. Greene calls on Herbert Marcuse to support this expansive view of the arts: Marcuse said that the Arts do not change the world, but can change the living beings who might change the world (cited by Greene 2001).

In their book *For a Better World: Reading and Writing for Social Action*, Randy and Katherine Bomer say that learning through the all the varieties of aesthetic knowing — visual arts, manual arts, music, drama, dance, poetry, personal stories and plays — "are legitimate and potent ways of responding to social realities and acting on them."

Karen Gallas, in her fine book *Imagination and Literacy*, writes that "education is a process of working to master or acquire different discourses at increasing levels of complexity, and that full literacy implies an ability to work with all kinds of texts, especially those that seem unfamiliar. To be open to what a text offers depends on the action of the imagination."

I can't find a better, more inclusive definition of reading. Readers read each text they confront based on life experiences, content and context, the type of discourse, the format, and the style. The more we know about a topic, the more complex and sophisticated the texts we can manage. In this sense, reading success with a particular text is dependent on the quantity and quality of previous exposure to similar texts. If we let children read more, have more situations in which they can read, and do more with what they read, we can move them along the curriculum of texts so that they can face and handle more complex texts; we can mentor them through conferences and conversations so that they are stretching their minds and their imaginations, cross-referencing their experiences of the text with those they have lived through. We can move our students into literature with resources that matter to them and that matter to us.

The Potential for Deep Understanding across the Curriculum

We become better at working within a specific literacy as we practise using it and refining the way we use it. For example, we begin to understand how a scientist thinks and behaves as we act like one — wondering, observing, asking questions, taking careful notes, and writing up our conclusions.

By drawing attention to the features of different types of print texts, we can help our students to build background knowledge concerning how texts work, to the nature of different genres, and to the cues and text features of each. The more familiar they are with the characteristics of a text, the more accessible it will become and the more easily read. They will know what to expect when they read a novel, a science text, a poem or a letter; they will recognize the intent of a speech, an editorial, or an article; they will know how a particular author structures a novel, and why a narrative can be told through letters.

As we use a particular literacy's code and schema, we become more familiar with how it functions; we can begin to see how the bits and pieces fit together in order to make the most meaning. We notice the shape of a text and are able to make logical predictions from its structure, especially in expository texts. The text "grammar" of different genres and text forms creates an infrastructure that informs our understanding of how this particular selection is going to work.

Genres are a social entity and are constructed based on their purposes, audiences, and functions within any given society. As students become more familiar with the functional aspects of a particular genre, they will be better equipped to take a critical stance towards the genres they encounter. Students often need special support with information texts, learning to recognize the features of different genres and how to make sense of the content effectively and efficiently.

Classrooms with helpful reading and writing programs often forget the difficulties inherent in using a single textbook for mathematics or science, or the complexities involved in reading information from books in the library or on screen. There are specific tools and strategies that we can share with young readers to help them learn how to process these text types and modes.

Deep comprehension can occur in every subject or area of the curriculum. We want students to be constantly engaged in the literacy events of every discipline — discussing, reading, writing, diagramming, researching, interpreting, representing, and shaping information, and then sharing, presenting, arguing, refining, questioning, critiquing, summarizing, and responding to each other's findings and opinions, and revisiting, rewriting, revising, rethinking, reworking what we thought we knew. As youngsters begin to invest in these multiple ways of exploring the world, from Kindergarten to Grade 12, they work with the themes, issues, and concepts, along with the concerns, misconceptions, and surprises that inquiry holds. What is new learning for the students can be satisfac-

In *Writing across the Curriculum: Because All Teachers Teach Writing,* Shelley Stagg Peterson notes: "At the same time that students are playing with words to create a poem, they are also playing with ideas. This is a great place for learning to happen ... As they trim away extraneous words and replace vague words with more precise words, students refine and sharpen their understanding of the ideas."

tion, even joy, for the teacher. We will watch them gain new and deeper understandings only if the teaching/learning event has significance for their lives.

Thinking like a historian

We read history in many different genres and historical fiction can create a clear context for different times, places, and people. Carefully researched, well-written historical fiction can portray human experiences in realistic, engaging narratives that enable students to understand perspectives and ideas. Students learn to read like historians, constructing interpretations, and reasoning through new ideas and information. It is essential for students to become critical thinkers and producers of new knowledge if they are to see themselves as stakeholders in the future. Understanding that history is an act of interpretation rather than a set of facts to memorize will help them to begin the work of historians as they consider multiple perspectives and empathize with various historical groups. Asking essential questions that lead to inquiry will provide opportunities for students to read and write for authentic purposes.

Thinking like a mathematician

When we talk about "literacy" in the mathematics program in elementary schools, we are faced with different, but interconnecting questions about teaching and learning: how are we defining literacy in our practice and theory, and how should we go about implementing literacy in our mathematics program so that the students will benefit?

"Critical Talk That Matters in Mathematics," on pages 109 to 110, looks at mathematics in terms of literacy.

Learning with and through mathematics means that students are engaging in thinking processes using the codes of mathematics to test hypotheses and carry out inquiries, as well as traditional language codes that will enable them to consider, structure, and share the connections they are making. Students are thinking multi-modally, using two or more meaning-making systems (and they may be charting and diagramming their constructs along the way). Becoming literate in mathematics, then, involves new ways of learning and knowing that will give children access to the technology and structure of mathematics so that they can analyze and interpret its problems and productions.

Students require information and experience in both language and mathematical modes of meaning making, and especially in the interconnecting of these ways of representing ideas. They will need to be accomplished readers and interpreters of both types of texts — words and numbers; often, some children are unable to handle tests and exams in mathematics because their language skills are too limited, even though they may have developed the requisite mathematical abilities. We could read the questions out loud with the students until they become clear. Students could help each other by explaining difficult terms and what is required in a question, making the numeracy component clearer and clearer.

What if the problem for some students was the word sentences, not the number sentences? We will need to ensure that children's reading and writing processes are developing alongside their mathematical understandings, connecting them as often as possible in our classroom learning experiences. We can promote literacy in the math classroom.

Gender and the Literacy Club

"The Boys Club: Moving Deeply into Text Forms," on pages 61 to 64, talks about engaging boys through carefully chosen graphic novels.

If reading is about making sense of texts in every area of life, and if understanding a text demands background that can shape our interpretations and understanding, why should gender not be considered a significant factor, along with social status, age, ethnicity, subculture, and even the mood and purpose of the person reading?

Being a boy or a girl relates to how out-of-school literacy practices often go unrecognized or, more important, untapped in the classroom. What many students value as literacy texts can unintentionally be dismissed or demeaned in school. And yet their deep involvement in and dedication to computers, magazines, CD-ROMs, videos, card collections, and hobbies can offer us entry points into their lives as readers and writers.

Of course, students are decoding gender long before they are decoding print. They build up their concepts of gender right from birth, depending on whether they are girls or boys, and gender is certainly a key issue by three or four years of age. Very young children notice and respond to visible differences between boys and girls, and some recognize that these gender differences are fundamental to their lives and to how they will interact in society. Nature and nurture have become catch words, but how the brain thinks, how the unconscious works, how the affective and emotional factors relate, how the child is raised (both intentionally and unintentionally), how the social structures surround the child — all of these factors contribute to the child's perception of gender.

We know from research on gender and literacy that boys often prefer resources — books, magazines, and websites — that favor facts over fiction. What does this mean for their future literacy abilities? Will fictional stories exist for them? For boys, computers are intrinsically motivating, allowing students to set their own goals. It is easy for us, as educators, to forget how rapidly computers and technology have become a part of the repertoire of tools available to us in our schools and equally easy to forget the benefits these tools can provide. For many boys, who may have a predilection for solitary, fact-based activities, computer use is a natural and comfortable tool for learning.

People are concerned about males and literacy. Dozens of books document issues in male culture and in raising and schooling boys. Some emphasize biological differences between males and females; others take a sociological approach; still others struggle for a culturally elitist model promoting literary wonders. Before deciding on plans of action, we need to examine the issues pertaining to the literacy lives of boys, how they perceive themselves as readers, and how parents, teachers, and peers influence their literacy development. The role of gender in reading success is complex, and we need to explore many of the assumptions and stereotypes held about boys and how they handle the world of printed text. We need to listen to the voices of writers for young people, of authorities in this field, and, most important, of boys and men as they reveal their literacy challenges, struggles, tastes, and values, and offer us insights into how we can support all learners in their literacy journeys.

If we believe that all children should have access to the literacy world, how will we ensure that boys, in particular, see themselves as readers who can handle the requirements of a variety of texts? For many, confronted by worksheets and controlled readers that dictated their eye movements and caused their reading hearts to beat irregularly, books never metamorphosed into friendly objects.

No single category includes all boys or all girls, but patterns emerge. When we look at studies and reports that examine boys and girls and their learning styles and special interests, their growth patterns, and their stages of intellectual development, we do notice differences. These differences are not in all boys or all girls, but in enough of them to cause us to reflect about our demands on their young lives.

There are definite problems with the ways in which many boys view themselves as literate beings, with how they approach the acts of reading and writing, and with how they respond to assessments of their skills. At least the faltering test scores have opened up discussion on these issues that concern many teachers and parents.

Many questions have arisen. How closely are we watching and interpreting the alarmist data? Are *all* boys at risk? If not, which ones? How significant are developmental stages in boys' literacy abilities? What is "normal" literacy achievement for a six-year-old boy? Is it the same for a six-year-old girl? Which boy and which girl? Are we concerned about the girls who are doing poorly? And most important, what do we mean by "literacy"?

How we, as parents and as educators, consider these questions will determine our school policies and curriculum, but how we answer them will determine the future of our children. Those of us who are responsible for educating boys are deeply concerned over the plight of those who can't or won't enter the literacy club at school. But our rules for school entry are strict, and oddly enough, computer skills and other forms of "unorthodox" reading are seldom part of the qualifications. Many boys have joined alternate literacy clubs, just not the one we hoped they would.

Supporting a Literacy Community

What is really exciting about a literacy community is discovering that what is achieved as a group usually exceeds what individuals could have achieved alone. Students are shocked and surprised into knowing. We are aware of how the minds of our students construct and reconstruct their burgeoning world knowledge. We want them to become, like ourselves, involved in understanding the different literacy forms and requirements of the various disciplines in order to apply these learnings to their own problem-solving and decision-making endeavors.

Think of a school where the students spend a week, or even months, exploring a topic or theme that interests them as a class, or in groups, or, occasionally, as individuals. What will they read, write, construct, observe, record, paint, revise, make, critique, present? How will we organize their time and help them track their experiences? What resources, including technology, books, magazines, and films, will we search for to deepen their experiences? How will they share and reflect at the close of the inquiry? What will they remember and take home to pin on a wall or put on top of a dresser? How will we account for and represent their learning? How are they employing inside and outside school those literacy strategies we keep talking about? What have we taught them about how literacy, in all its modes and shapes, works? Good schools everywhere are looking at all of these components as basic to learning, and literacy education — in its new and wider definition, including writing — is a mainstay of every successful school program.

2

Strategies for Promoting Deep Understanding

In her book, *To Understand*, Ellin Keene says that comprehension strategies are taught for one reason: to enable readers to understand more deeply. To become thoughtful, insightful readers, they need to extend their thinking beyond a superficial understanding of text. They will need to acquire knowledge, explain information, connect it to previous knowledge, and then reapply it. Readers need to think about not only what they are reading, but what they are learning. We build up our store of knowledge to develop insight, to think more deeply and critically, to question, interpret, and evaluate what we read. We construct our own meaning as we make connections, ask questions, infer, select important ideas, synthesize, and monitor our progress.

Constructing Meaning through Strategic Reading

During the act of reading, the reader makes use of strategies that interact, intersect, and occur simultaneously. We need to stress the interrelationship of all the reading/thinking strategies involved in the act of reading. Explicit instruction with demonstrations can clarify procedures and enhance students' understanding. We need to show learners how we think when we read, guiding them in the practice of constructing meaning with text in pairs, in small groups, and as a community. We go from guided practice to the application of the strategy in real reading situations. We need to use these strategies automatically and seamlessly. Reading is an act of composition.

We use the text to stimulate our own thinking so we can engage with the mind of the writer. We need to help students think about what they read so they can know when, why, and how to use the strategies that proficient readers use. And they need to see themselves using these strategies and voicing their insights. By developing an awareness of when and how to use them, they are learning how to think about their reading and how to approach ways of ensuring deep understanding.

We hold many expectations of students as readers. They are expected to read independently and more often, to read longer and more difficult texts in a variety of curriculum areas, to read faster and more selectively, to remember more information, and to make integrative connections. There are new words and terms to learn in all the different subjects; there are challenges posed by many of the school texts because they are outdated, not accessible, or poorly written. Often, readers of widely differing abilities are expected to read the same resources without support structures.

Can we base our teaching on sharing the strategies that proficient readers use to comprehend text, showing our students how to think deeply about what they read? We can help them move beyond the superficial so that they can discover their own ability to understand more completely, to reflect on what they have met in print, and to move towards the insight that comes from connecting and considering their connections to the text, to their personal experiences, and to their lives.

Making Connections

Life experiences build the readers' contextual knowledge bank, so as they meet texts in print or on screen, they can connect to the thoughts and perceptions that emerge. In order to become meaning makers, to become readers, we must bring our lives to the text. For all of us, connecting is the path to learning.

For example, when wholly engaged with a text, we bring the sum total of our lives to the meaning-making experience: our experiences, our cultural contexts, our relevant background knowledge, our connections to the other "texts of our lives" — other books, other computer programs, or the songs that are suddenly conjured up — our emotional state as we read, and our knowledge of the nature of this particular text. We consider how the text works, the author's style, our place in the text, and the events of the world at large that are somehow triggered or referenced by our reading. We need to link what we have to the schema we already employ, making additions and changes to remember and apply what we have learned.

Our main goal as literacy teachers must be to help students build bridges between the ideas generated by the text and their own lives. We want to help them gain access to the prior knowledge that is relevant to making meaning with the text, the information that life experience has retained and remembered in the brain, sometimes accompanied by emotional responses or visual images. When we give students a framework for understanding how they can enhance their reading by activating their own connections, we offer them a reading strategy for life. Connections have been classified in these ways:

- text to self: connecting to past experiences and background
- text to text: connecting to other texts in their lives and the forms those texts take
- text to world: connecting to events in the world at large

Of course, these three general categories may sometimes interconnect and intersect, but students then have a strategy for coming at a text selection in a variety of ways. As they begin to observe, take note of, and reflect upon how these connections affect understanding of a particular text, they can deliberately use each aspect of the connection frame to increase their personal and collective processes of meaning making.

When we are engaged in reading, all kinds of connections are whizzing through our minds as we recall personal experiences, summarize what has

Although generally we want to model and support those connections that promote deeper insights into what we will read or have been reading, leftover reminiscences and queries may prove to be powerful resources for writing in response journals or during a writing workshop, where they can be developed and extended. Reading is still a powerful resource for writing; the printed thoughts jiggle and bump against our own, drawing on ideas from the head to the pen or keyboard.

happened so far, synthesize and add information to our constantly expanding mental storehouse, analyze and challenge the author's ideas, and change the organizational schema of our minds. Making connections with what we read is a complex process. We can recognize only what we have somehow met before. Our knowledge is built from and based on all we have met, and those connections are being made all the time, consciously and subconsciously.

Brazilian Paulo Freire, with his emphasis on dialogue and his concern for the oppressed, was perhaps the most influential thinker about education in the late 20th century. He gave us the expression "reading the word, reading the world." Somehow, when we read powerful, significant texts, we travel outside ourselves, exploring what lies beyond our immediate neighborhood, extending our vision, and awakening our personal and cross-cultural meaning making.

Determining Important Ideas

Traditionally, we have taught students that finding the main idea was the first step in understanding a text; however, there may be *many* ideas in a reading selection. We need to assist young readers in learning how to determine what is important, especially in reading non-fiction, what is necessary and relevant to the issues being discussed, and what can be set aside.

The question has to be: Which details matter? Rather than providing questions that ask the student to locate or remember insignificant story details, we should have the student search out only those details necessary for a deeper understanding, for supporting an idea or clarifying a point. What we use in constructing meaning are the pieces of information that add to our growing understanding of what we want to find out or need to experience; these are details we can't do without, pieces of the puzzle essential to creating the complete picture.

In fiction, the goal is to discuss the structures of stories and to help students see overarching similarities and differences in stories. We don't want to get bogged down in the specific details of illustrations and story. There is a time and place for scavenger hunts — and a time and place for attending to the big picture.

Especially with the Internet, we need to help students sift and sort information, make decisions about what they need to remember or disregard, to pick out the most important information, highlight essential ideas, and isolate supporting details. Highlighting is easy, but determining what to highlight is a challenge. In order to make sense of reading and move towards insight, students must determine important ideas and information in the text they are reading; if they are going to learn anything, they will also need to remember what is important in what they read. Non-fiction, as well as expository text, is full of features, text cues, and structures that signal importance and scaffold understanding for readers so that they can extract necessary information.

More non-fiction needs to be shared, explored, and taught in our classrooms. If the text quality matches the compelling photographs, charts, and illustrations, then non-fiction can equal fiction. Readers need to build background knowledge of the genre, to appreciate how certain features signal importance. But the writing needs to be interesting as well as accurate, even rich in voice. The first purpose of non-fiction is to convey factual information, important ideas, and key concepts. Non-fiction often scaffolds learning and enhances the understanding of the genre.

Making Inferences

As readers or viewers, we make inferences when we go beyond the literal meaning of the text, whether it is a film or a graphic novel, and begin to examine the implied meanings, reading between the lines to hypothesize about the text. When we read, our connections drive us to infer, as we struggle to make sense of the text, looking in our minds to explain what isn't on the page, building theories that are more than just the words on the page. As we conjecture while reading, the information accrues, our ideas are modified, changed, or expanded, and our world picture allows this new text to enter the constructs in our brains.

Inferring allows us to activate our connections at deeper levels and to negotiate and hold tentative until further information confirms or expands our initial meaning-making ventures. Predictions are inferences that are usually confirmed or denied, but most inferences are open ended and unresolved, adding to the matrix of our connections. Readers often need to engage in dialogue with others to further explore these expanding thoughts and to become more adept at recognizing the need for digging deeply into the author's ideas; by so doing, they increase their own abilities at constructing and negotiating meaning with text and in life.

We want readers to carefully weigh all evidence from a text in order to determine their own opinions, to combine textual information with their own background knowledge. They need to draw conclusions and apply logical thought to substantiate their interpretations. We want readers to make and to recognize informed opinions. For example, young readers need to be trained to recognize persuasive writing and use judgment as they read it.

Thinking deeply and widely requires an analytical approach involving a careful examination and consideration of the text, whether it is print or another form of media. We search for informed opinion, ideas that can take us beyond our own limitations and stretch and enrich us, so we bring more depth of understanding to our experiences. Wilhelm (2001) says we have to help students hear their own thinking about a text "out loud."

Visualizing the Text

When we read, we picture much of what the print suggests, making movies in our heads. And these images are personal, each one of us building a visual world unlike any other. Reading words causes us to see pictures, which is understandable, since words are only symbols, a code for capturing ideas and feelings. But our imaginations work no matter the surrounds, and we see the world the print suggests. We can demonstrate this strategy for youngsters and help make them aware of its strength in supporting meaning making with print texts.

See especially Chapter 4: Deepening Understanding through Graphic Texts.

Graphic novels, where text is composed of words and images, used in interesting and unusual formats, can have a positive effect on different types of readers. Not all students have equal abilities in generating images in their minds while they read written texts, and according to research findings, comprehension from such reading is negatively affected by the degree of weakness in visualization ability. Because they provide pictures in association with written text, graphic novels assist students in conjuring up images in their minds in their overall comprehension of the narratives involved.

Asking Questions

We read because we are curious about what we will find and keep reading because of the questions that fill our reading minds. Of course, good readers ask questions before they read, as they read, and when they have finished reading. As we become engaged with a text, questions keep popping up, questions that propel us to predict what will happen next, to challenge the author, to wonder about context for what is happening, to fit the new information into our world picture. We try to rectify our confusion, filling in missing details, attempting to fit into a pattern all the bits and pieces that float around our meaning making, even reflecting on our own experiences.

We continue to read because the author has made us curious — constant self-questioning causes us to interact with the text, consciously and subconsciously. As we read on, our questions may change, and the answers we seek may lie outside the print. Not all of our questions will be answered during our reading. As we continue to read or reread, we can sometimes clarify the confusion or resolve the difficulty as we gain more insight into the text.

Often, our most limited readers ask themselves the fewest questions while reading. When they have finished reading the prescribed print offering — a disenfranchising ritual — they wait for us teachers to interrogate them. They have not learned that confusion is allowed as we read: that authors count on it in order for the dynamic of reading on to occur.

As readers grow in their ability to self-question, their understanding of how authors think and of how text makers work will increase. How can we help youngsters to interact with the text as they read, to care about what they are reading, to become engaged with the meaning making that real reading requires? We can find ways to involve them in their print explorations.

The deeper and more complex the text, the more questions we will bring forward as we try to make sense of it. The deeper our interest in what we are reading, the more substantive our questions will be. Monitoring our reading means paying attention to questions that arise as we read and that remain when we have finished. We begin to make connections to what we already know, wrinkling our brows at incongruities or seeming inconsistencies, accepting that our minds work in this inquiry method while we read and that the sincere questions that remain after the reading can form the basis for our text talk, for exploring further research, or for just pondering and wondering about the complex issues that the reading has conjured up.

How will we help young readers to become independent thinkers who will choose to engage with a text if we don't encourage and guide them to predict as they read, to practise inferential thinking, to question the text when complex questions are not easily answered? When will they learn to draw their own conclusions, to seek out further information, to ask a friend for an opinion on a difficult issue that arises because of the text? How will they learn to become curious about the ideas generated by the author? Manuals for published programs sometimes offer ideas for giving the students thoughtful and deepening literacy strategies, suggesting book sets for increasing students' reading repertoires, or presenting significant background information for supporting the text.

Our questions must grow from our conversations about the text, from the honest revelations of the students' own concerns, as we try to guide them into deeper interpretations. We ask honest questions that are driven by their inquiring dialogue, just as I would in a conversation with peers during a book club session. Such questions are based on listening to interactions rather than on any scripted agenda.

We want the students to engage in thoughtful considerations about the text and its connections to their lives, not struggling to find the responses they think we want.

Synthesizing

As we read, we continually glean new pieces of information from the text, often in a random fashion, which we then add to our personal knowledge in order to construct new understandings about the issues we are exploring. Piece by piece, we develop a more complete picture as new information merges with what we already know, and we begin to enhance our thinking, achieve new insights, or change our perspective. We synthesize our learning as we begin to integrate previously experienced learning with the words and ideas discovered through reading the text, in order to see differently, to construct new, more complex ideas. Stephanie Harvey and Anne Goudvis say, "Synthesizing involves putting together assorted parts to make a new whole."

The more we connect the bits and pieces of print information with our previous experiences, the greater the chance of finding new patterns and of developing deeper insights. When we synthesize, we change what we thought we knew; we expand our personal understanding. We derive more information as we read, and we assimilate into our developing understanding of the big picture. We begin to synthesize the issues and ideas generated by our reading of the text in light of our own lives. We move from recounting the new information into rethinking our own constructs of the world. We synthesize our new learning in order to consider the big ideas that affect our lives.

Summarizing

When we read aloud a novel to a class over several days, we begin each session with a recap of the events that preceded the new reading. This is the essence of platforming: stating where the discussion has been in order to make sense of what is coming. We need to know where we have been if we are going to make sense of where we are going.

Summarizing is an organizing and reorganizing strategy that allows us as readers to categorize and classify the information we are gathering as we read; we can then add it to our storehouse of knowledge and memory. We need to constantly connect the new information we garner from the text and to find a way of making sense of it so that we can assimilate it into our ever-developing construct of knowledge. How would we ever remember the tons of data we receive as we read without systematically adding it or rejecting it in our schema of understanding?

As teachers, we need to help students learn how to abstract important ideas and then use them as tools for thought. It may help students to focus on summarizing for making sense of reading. We summarize constantly as we read, sorting out significant ideas and events and other bits and pieces of information.

If we are reading a longer selection or a complex and difficult text, we need to pause every so often, coming to grips with a means of classifying the barrage of information. We might jot down notes to help us connect and remember the details so that we can focus on the big picture; we might check the table of contents to strengthen our awareness of where this section fits into the whole; we might reread the introduction to clarify the framework for the information we are meeting. As effective readers, we summarize as we read.

Analyzing

All of us have at some time had the experience of analyzing a poem or a story to such an extent that by the end of the lesson, we had lost whatever appreciation we had for the selection. Often the teacher felt this to be a necessary building block for future independent learning, but seldom did many of the students internalize the learning so that they could use it later. Analysis and criticism are connected processes: before we provide opinions on print texts, we need to carefully analyze the many aspects of the writer's craft that went into creating them.

We can help developing readers to understand a text more deeply by providing them with techniques for considering its effectiveness as they learn to analyze its particular aspects and both appreciate the writer's craft and better understand their own responses. They can begin to step back from the initial experience so that they can reflect more clearly about the text's effect on them and how the author conveyed the ideas and the emotions embedded in it.

Whether we are reading an emotion-filled story or a resource containing information, our goal is not to dissect the selection, but to notice how it works, how the author has built the text. We can help students to discover the underlying organization, the elements that identify the genre, the format of the selection (including any graphic support), and the overall effect of the work. For me, these are opportunities for guiding readers into a deeper awareness of the text, the author's techniques, and their own developing responses. Critical reading relies on readers employing all the strategies they know in order to come to thoughtful, carefully decided conclusions about the value of the author's work. As citizens, students will have to think critically about the life issues they will encounter, and analyzing texts with a questioning eye is part of the developing process.

Monitoring and Repairing Meaning

How can we help students to monitor their own reading comprehension? They need to stay on top of their reading, keeping track of how well they are understanding it, detecting obstacles and confusions that derail understanding, and knowing how to repair meaning when it breaks down. Traditionally, however, we only assessed their reading after they finished a text; we did not help them become aware of what is happening as they read, when meaning making is interrupted, or when they lose track or become confused.

We all need strategies for repairing a breakdown in understanding during reading; otherwise, we will just plough on to the end totally confused — or rely on someone else to tell us about what we thought we read. Even excellent readers sometimes find themselves lost or their minds wandering.

Often, oral reading practice in a group results in little or no comprehension for limited or struggling readers as they wait their turn and focus only on pronunciation.

When something doesn't make sense or a problem arises in understanding, experienced readers address it. They move to repair comprehension by accessing different strategies.

- Overviewing is a form of skimming and scanning the text before reading in order to determine important ideas and information. It helps determine importance.
- Readers may need to do some work with the ideas, the words, the images, or with the structure of the text before reading. Often, a discussion before reading can present the students with enough background and terminology to make meaning with the words and images.
- Using their prior knowledge and backgrounds helps readers to make sense of new information.
- They need to monitor their reading as they go along and track their thinking by coding the text and jotting down responses — they need to choose the strategy that will help them keep track of their reading.
- Readers need to construct meaning as they go, going back and salvaging what they can, repairing the meaning making when it breaks down, clarifying their thinking, noticing when they lose focus, slowing down, rereading to enhance understanding, reading ahead to clarify meaning, questioning the text, disagreeing with information or logic, identifying and articulating what is confusing or puzzling about the text, drawing inferences, determining what is important, what really matters, and synthesizing their new learning.
- If a reader can't retell part of what has just been read, then he/she has to go back and take stock of the text, review the purpose for reading, do some more work on the text, or reread. There is little sense in continuing when the way is lost. Engaging in brief conversations about the reading with a partner, a group, or the teacher can put a reader back in action.
- If the reader has no interaction with the author or the text, it might be useful to begin predicting what could happen next and then rethink and revise the guesses as the reader finds out more information.
- Although all readers shift back and forth between the print and other ideas unrelated to the text, the proficient reader recognizes this wandering and tries to connect the ideas in the text with events in life.
- If the reader can't make any pictures from the words in the text, then meaning has been interrupted and the mind is not imagining what the words are creating. It takes practice to paint mental pictures from the text, but as the reader becomes more adept with graphic novels, in particular, this process becomes automatic; the ideas in any text can grow clearer, and new connections can be made.
- Students already with some background in strategies reread and work towards handling any confusion, considering various approaches: Should they highlight information that puzzles them? jot down questions that arise as they read? reread the introduction or the blurb on the back cover? check a difficult term in the glossary? have a brief conference with the teacher to get them back on track? Can they begin to make connections with the text as they read, relating other background experiences, both in print and in life?
- Students can use colored sticky notes to code prior experiences, thoughts, queries, and reflections while reading. Once the reading is finished, these

sticky notes can be grouped on a page so that the reading/thinking processes can be seen as a whole. Students can analyze their own patterns: Where were the difficulties? Which words or terms caused trouble? What questions arose? What connections were made? What was the author trying to say? How did I solve the confusion? What do I think about the topic now? Students can begin to see how they go about constructing meaning, identifying confusions, and monitoring their own reading.

Responding to Texts

Sometimes, students spend more time on their responses to a text than on the act of reading. We need to support them *while* they are reading, for the accumulation of positive, meaningful reading experiences will drive them forward to become proficient readers. Conferences, discussion groups, and dialogue journals (between student and teacher) can keep students on track and nudge them towards deeper understandings as they are reading. Nonetheless, through carefully designed response activities, we can move them into different, divergent, critical, and deeper levels of thinking, feeling, and learning. We can discover with our students what they think they saw and heard and felt, helping them come to grips with their own and others' perceptions. The printed/visual text, the conversation text, and the response text wrap us, as readers, in layers of new meaning.

As students work with a text, they add their voices to the meaning making, bringing their own life stories in conversation with the ideas the text has generated. Through their talk, inquiries, graphic representations, written responses, artistic representations, role playing, and connected readings, students find their language and their thinking respected and valued. They are active and involved agents in making sense of what they are experiencing and learning — the behavior of effective readers is the essence of an informed and critical citizenry.

Organizing the Classroom for Deep Understanding

We want our students to build habits of mind, ways of thinking that will help them carry their learning into their lives in the larger world. Our classrooms need to demonstrate a sense of democracy and responsibility. Having deep and meaningful conversations can help achieve this. So does requiring written and artistic responses to all types of texts: these can both stimulate thinking and promote critical and creative understanding. Eventually as a result, students may engage in considering social action and change.

We can move towards these goals by organizing opportunities for literacy events that go beyond traditional curriculum delivery. We can offer classroom situations where students read and write in order to engage in inquiries that matter to them. What we model and share in whole-class meetings can set the scene for their own explorations as learners. Just as we present significant mentor texts as models for them to draw upon in their own reading and writing, we set up our classrooms as models of learning studios, places for groups of students to work on collaborative projects — reading and dialoguing, researching and sharing; we also create time for independent reading, writing, and responding. We involve them in working with all types of resources, from computers to novel sets, from poems to documentaries, from letters to e-pals to classroom guests. Students need to see this literacy studio as a place of work and excitement. There, they are important members of a community committed to growth through authentic discourse, with a serious and intense belief in cognitive, aesthetic, and social development. Students must feel that belonging to this community is worth it.

Reading and thinking aloud

Throughout the year, we can use our time for reading aloud or viewing films as an opportunity for think-aloud sessions as a community. We can share our own reading strategies as we read aloud and think aloud in classroom demonstrations with a common text. Students can see how we construct meaning in a variety of ways with different types of texts, how we continue to grow as readers. We want our students to notice us as readers, how we function within the culture of literacy, and we want to be aware of our own thinking and strategies with print, how we handle confusion and breakdowns when reading.

When we demonstrate our own thinking "out loud," we make our thinking visible to our students, so that they see how we handle a piece of text, before we read, while we are reading, and after we read. When students have opportunities to see our processes in action, they may be able use these strategies in their own work.

It is helpful to choose a text that is easily accessed, so that students can focus on the reading strategies. Select a short text that will enable you to say aloud what you are thinking as you read it through. You might begin with a passage that you have thought through first or use a sight piece that will give the students an authentic picture of how readers read. You can share the text on an overhead transparency or SMART Board. Choose a selection that will focus on a particular strategy that you feel the students need.

Independent reading

In independent reading, students select books and read them silently, but while both individualized and independent reading increase the time students spend reading in school, independent reading provides explicit instruction and encourages students to monitor their own reading. The teacher's role is to guide the selection and increase reading competence through book talks, conferences, and mini-lessons, and by promoting reading journals. It also includes modelling reading during the reading time as well as offering productive instruction.

Encourage students to read at their own pace, using materials they have chosen. We can give advice and help if asked, but the students should decide what they will read. Offering a range of books in our class and in the school library will promote good choices. We need to represent a wide range of genres, including non-fiction, novels, folklore, poetry, and picture books. While a few should be classics, most should be contemporary. By having the students keep up-to-date records of books read, they can notice their reading patterns and widen the range if necessary.

I like to begin independent reading with a book talk featuring additions to the classroom library: new books by favorite authors, books that I need to "sell" to the students because they are less familiar, books on relevant issues or media connections, or books representing different genres. During a book talk, we can

We have all read of or been part of projects in which a whole school, including the children, the teachers, the principal, the secretary, and the caretaker, reads silently for 20 minutes, but these motivating schemes can be successful only if the participants value the program and if their reading presents to the students a picture of adults engaged with print because they value the process.

Having everyone read the same novel can be beneficial if used occasionally and as a demonstration of how literature groups can function. You need to select a book that most students can read or offer support to some struggling readers, such as having them listen to a recorded version first. I always think of this type of activity as a community-building event, and take time to incorporate a variety of response modes into the work.

present the issues involved in the story and connect the book to other books and issues. We can provide a brief outline of the book, talk a bit about the plot or the people, show the cover or illustrations, and offer personal responses, being careful not to over-inflate our power as teacher.

Organizing literature groups

In our schedule for literacy growth, it is important to create time for students to work in groups with copies of novels they have self-selected from resources that we have provided. As their ability to follow the routine of participating in literature groups progresses, students may make suggestions as to books that could be added to the resources. They may choose to read different novels by the same author or books on a related theme.

Heterogeneous groups are formed on the basis of their book choices. Members of each group meet two or three times a week in order to carry on a conversation about their books. The in-depth discussions will be supported by the notes, comments, and drawings they have prepared in their reading journals while reading the novel.

As teachers, we are responsible for establishing the routines that will make possible the management of literature groups in the classroom, making the expectations clear and repairing any disruptions to the flow of the work through demonstrations and direct instruction. We can contribute to the functioning of literature circles in a variety of ways depending upon group or individual student needs.

- Sometimes, I am a silent participant, observing and gathering information concerning their reading behaviors, their group dynamics, and their comprehension strategies.
- Other times, I can model and demonstrate effective ways to contribute to a discussion. I can serve as a facilitator, making positive comments that support and affirm the contributions of the students, encouraging them to refer to the text to provide evidence for their ideas, and moving them towards analyzing and synthesizing their thoughts as they move along in the conversation.
- And sometimes I need to intervene directly about problems students are having with the text, pointing out information they have missed or clarifying a complex issue. I can restate a point for emphasis, synthesize the ideas they have presented, or extend the direction of their thinking on an issue. But my teaching/learning goal is to guide the group's growing ability to monitor its own progress, so that members can take charge of their learning and move into a deeper and more meaningful discussion.

Participants can share their personal insights, their emotional responses, and the connections they are making to the text and to the comments of others. As they begin to hitchhike on each other's comments, they build background knowledge and incorporate new meanings and different perspectives into their own world picture.

It is important that participants speak up and take turns. Everyone should participate, support one another's comments, move the discussion along, and help to keep the talk focused on the ideas generated by the text. Through these conversations, students learn to support their ideas with references in the texts,

Chapter 3: Deepening Text Understanding through Book Talk outlines innovative ways of organizing literature groups.

to pose questions that have real significance, and to accept or at least consider the opinions of others when they disagree. In this collaborative activity, they interact with others, learning about themselves as they deepen and expand their meaning making.

A few moments for guided reflection, oral or written, at the conclusion of each session will help the students assess their own contributions and the quality of the group's participation. They can share comments, questions, and insights and make decisions about the direction the next meeting should take, such as clarifying their roles to strengthen subsequent discussions.

Sometimes, at the end of a discussion about a book that has had an impact on them, students may want to take part in a response project, individually or cooperatively, where they explore an issue or theme in the text. At times, I will suggest an activity that suits the book or that supports a need the students have revealed.

From Theory into Practice

Teaching for deep understanding is a lifelong professional stance. We need to continue to reflect on our own teaching, observe our colleagues in action, engage in action research inside our classrooms, read research and professional books and articles in print and online, assess our teaching progress with our students, and participate in policy discussions with the school community, the district, and the nation. Good teachers take our profession seriously.

In moving to classroom practice, we can examine the ways in which classroom teachers explore teaching for deep understanding, the strategies and techniques they use with their students to promote thoughtful, critical, and creative engagement with the texts they will meet. As you read the different experiences of the teachers and students in Part B, you will be able to observe and consider the explorations of students from Kindergarten to Grade 8, involved in making sense of different text forms within a variety of classroom literacy events. The many educators contributing to Part B of this resource represent schools throughout urban and rural areas, in different socio-economic areas, and from different school districts and universities. You will find literacy events that connect to your own programs, teachers who are experimenting with ideas you may want to implement, and schools that have resources you dream of acquiring. However, all the teachers want their students to think deeply, to read more than the words, to connect to a wider world frame, and to reflect critically on the texts with which they engage as individuals, as groups, and as a classroom community.

The blackline master "Promoting Deep Understanding through Classroom Literacy Events" can work as a reflective tool for you, as a teacher in a professional community, to consider your classroom practice, to think about your literacy program and events, and to increase your awareness about the issues that build a classroom culture that supports and celebrates teaching and learning for critical and creative understanding.

Promoting Deep Understanding through Classroom Literacy Events

1. **When do you bring the classroom community together? What texts do you use for read-alouds and think-alouds?**
   - Do you include fiction, newspaper columns, letters, and poems?
   - How do you incorporate think-alouds while reading aloud to the students?
   - Do you reveal your own comprehension strategies, and show how they deepen your meaning making with the text?
   - Do you include texts for shared reading, such as choral speaking or Readers theatre?
   - Do students share their own writing and research findings, as well as presenting carefully prepared units for other students?
   - Do students reflect on their progress in using strategies, do they articulate their knowledge of strategic reading, and do they help others to see the impact of strategic reading?

2. **What texts do you use for modelling your own literacy life?**
   - How do you reveal your own text preferences concerning authors, style, and content, both in print and on screen? Do you approach issues critically, explaining your data and research?
   - Do you keep dialogue journals with your students, on paper or online, where you share and model your own views and responses?

3. **Are your demonstrations helpful in showing students how effective readers and writers function?**
   - Do you present "run-throughs" of useful processes for selecting resources, working in small groups, having thoughtful conversations about a shared text, or incorporating a variety of response modes for deepening understanding?
   - Do you demonstrate a variety of instructional strategies for students, providing lessons in how readers and writers use the tools of their crafts?
   - Do you model how to write for different audiences — colleagues, parents, critics, politicians, reporters, and principals?
   - Do you create an environment where literacy texts and events surround the students, where records of their thinking about the literacy strategies are displayed, and where their own inquiry projects and writings are available?

4. **How do you organize the students for literacy activities in groups?**
   - Do you organize literature circles and guided reading groups, especially for focused instruction to meet specific learning needs?
   - What texts do you use for group activities? Who chooses them?
   - What role do you play during group literacy activities? How do you encourage group members to stretch their thinking, to elaborate on each other's ideas, to challenge the text, to alter their opinions, and to think deeply?

5. **What texts do you provide for independent reading?**
   - Do students choose their own texts, or do they negotiate with you?
   - What role do you play during independent reading time? Do you confer with individuals, promoting reflective thinking about their reading strengths and progress, their choice of text, and their insights about their literacy lives?

6. **Which response modes work best for your students? Which new ones could you try?**
   - Do your students make explicit their thinking about the text they have read or viewed? How do you connect the reading and writing processes?

- How does talking with others before, during, and after working on a draft of writing affect student writing?
- How do you incorporate technology in your literacy work? Are a variety of text forms representing the new literacies available in your classroom?
- Are students constructing and creating different types of texts in their responses to model texts?
- What role can the Arts play in helping students to reveal and construct their thinking about a text?

7. **How are you building language muscles with your children, so that they have the word and sentence power necessary for effective reading and writing?**
   - Are they increasing their word banks of recognizable words in fluent reading and in spelling?
   - Are they growing in their use of word analysis strategies, such as words within words, root words, prefixes and suffixes?
   - Are they retaining and building vocabulary from their reading and listening experiences?
   - Are they becoming aware of different variations and patterns of English, from standard to colloquial to argot, and learning when to use them?
   - Are they using increasingly complex sentence and text structures in their writing?

8. **What ways have you found to provide differentiated literacy opportunities?**
   - What kind of record keeping helps you to track the literacy progress of each child as a reader and a writer?
   - How do you mentor struggling readers?
   - Do students keep individual portfolios of their work and their progress, on paper and online?

9. **Is the inquiry process at the heart of your teaching/learning dynamic in other areas of the curriculum?**
   - How do you assist students in working with the texts used in the content areas?
   - How do you promote the reading of a variety of genres?
   - Do students notice and identify their literacy strategies during reading?
   - Are students moving towards a deepened understanding of the texts they encounter?
   - How do you support and encourage intertextuality among the different texts they experience?
   - Are students approaching a variety of texts with a critical lens?
   - How does reading, discussing and responding affect the thinking and social action of the students about a theme or an issue?
   - Do the students read different text types with effective strategies for deepening their understanding? Do they share the results of their inquiries using PowerPoint and SMART Boards?

10. **Do your students have a sense of ownership and satisfaction with their literacy work?**
    - Is there a culture of literacy developing in your classroom, with a predictable and supportive schedule conducive to having students work together as a community, in small groups, and independently? Do you incorporate the school and public libraries into your classroom program?

11. **Do you create opportunities for moving critical learning experiences into greater engagement with the outside community, as in interacting with parents/guardians, working with volunteers, inviting guests into the classroom, going on field trips, interviewing authorities, using technology, and taking part in social action programs?**

12. **Do you share with your colleagues professional books, journal articles, and reports that offer strategies and structures for helping students deepen their literacy experiences?**

3

Deepening Text Understanding through Book Talk

A few years ago, the well-known educator Gordon Wells introduced me to the concept of transcribing the conversations among members of a literature circle. At the time, I was team-teaching graduate education courses with him. Using a transcript, teachers could analyze the process in which students had engaged as they interacted with each other's ideas, hitchhiking on what was said, disagreeing and supporting their views with examples from the text, changing their perceptions as they listened, and deepening their understanding of the experience of the text.

Today, we have both technology to support "freezing the talk" for reflective analysis and the knowledge that students can benefit from reading transcripts captured on chat lines, blogs, and wikis. I have seen students tape-recording their literature discussions, and then at the end of the week, selecting four or five memorable moments from them; they then transcribe these moments for reconsidering and re-examining their thoughts on the text.

In this chapter, you will meet teachers who have moved further into transcripts by using technology to capture student responses to the novel or novels they are reading. Beverly Strachan reports on Rickesh Kotecha's action research project using a wiki site, where students write responses to one another about a shared novel and also periodically meet in face-to-face conversation groups. Amy Mohr's class uses writing journals to capture their ideas so that they can reflect on their progress while reading independent novels on a common theme. Larry Swartz created a transcript of his students as they responded aloud to a poem read together and used it to note the growth in their understanding. Krzysztof Rakuc organized book clubs for boys to help them realize their strong potential as readers. In Konrad Glogowski's classroom, students write blogs and share them with each other, responding to the text as they read it and to the comments of their group members. As you read the words of the students, you can observe them thinking, rethinking, and making connections to the text, to each other, and to their own lives and even global concerns. Deep understanding resonates in their conversations.

Virtual Literature Circles

BY BEVERLY STRACHAN

The last few chapters when Tamara constantly helped Miss Barclay while they drove to Seattle and Vancouver reminds me of Grandpa who recently passed away. When my family and I went to go visit him in his nursing home a couple of times a year in Ottawa, he slept frequently so we could only see him for short periods of time, and sometimes he was in a grumpy mood and he did not want to see any company (just like Miss Barclay in Chapter 15). He had a disease called Alzheimer's (a brain disorder) and the effects on him were: he lost almost ALL of his memory, he sometimes had trouble speaking, he was in a wheelchair, and he basically acted like a kid. My family and I always had to haul him around to wherever he wanted to go, just like Tamara is starting to do in a different way more and more and not as severe. I recall how hard it was sometimes, and I think Tamara has, and will have to help Miss Barclay more and more. She probably is getting used to it, but I know it is hard on her, but it is worth the deal she is getting for it.

Grade 8 student
Posted at 6:16 p.m., March 30, 2008

What a powerful text-to-self connection this student has made in this response to a passage she has read from a Red Maple Award–winning novel, *Skinnybones and the Wrinkle Queen* by Glen Huser. The book is about Tamara, a 15-year-old who has made her way through the foster-care system, and Miss Barclay, a wealthy, cranky, and frail former schoolteacher. As part of a school community project, Tamara is volunteering at a local seniors' home where she meets Miss Barclay. Both Tamara and Miss Barclay have a goal and recognize that they must rely on each other in order to meet their respective goals. These two very different individuals embark on a road trip. Will they be able to make the journey and meet their goals? A reason to keep reading!

The student is sharing her response with a small group of peers who belong to an online literature circle. In this instance, students are engaging with different award-winning novels to build interactive online communities in support of deepening each other's understanding. Here, I share how a team of teachers at a Toronto public school integrated technology with literature circles, offering another venue in which students could converse about the texts they were reading.

The teachers developed a wiki site that included information about the authors, links to various websites related to the book, multi-media reflections that celebrated their learning, and most important, an online discussion forum that allowed students to reflect on and make connections to the novels they were reading. The initiative came about after teacher candidate Rickesh Kotecha shared his action research question with his associate teacher, Alison Hall; their librarian, Gianna Dassios, who was already thinking about creating such an online environment; and their principal, Helen Fisher.

This teachers' initiative recognizes the importance of providing opportunities for students to have meaningful conversations about the texts they read. Teaching reading is a complex process — we are constantly learning about and questioning our practice. We make decisions about how we can help students understand what they are reading and take that understanding to a deeper level. As we learn, we share.

We have moved well beyond merely asking students to read parts of a novel and independently respond to a series of factual recall questions. We recognize the power of having students discuss what they have read in small, peer-led discussion groups much as we may experience in book clubs.

The work of Harvey Daniels has provided us with insight into how to engage students in meaningful conversations about the texts they read. Daniels has shared strategies and presented the structure of "literature circles." Research confirms the validity and relevance of using literature circles in the classroom. These circles are often known under different titles, such as book clubs, cooperative book discussions, and literature discussion groups.

Before technology was integrated with literature circles, the students in this Grade 7/8 classroom had often met in literature circle groups within the classroom. The teacher had provided opportunities for students to make text-to-text, text-to-self, and text-to-world connections as they responded to texts they were reading. She created opportunities for students to build on their previous knowledge of reading strategies, such as inferring, visualizing, predicting, questioning, and synthesizing as discussed and modelled in class. Below is an online example of a student making connections.

Connecting: The first section of Skinnybones and the Wrinkle Queen reminded me of an episode of 'That's so Raven'. In the episode, Raven Baxter had to help an elderly lady at a retirement home with things she needed, and Raven had to spend time with her to get tickets to a show she wanted to go to. The elderly lady Raven had to look after was stubborn, not friendly, and did not want a helper at first. In the book I quote "she can be a bit difficult at times, and she may not be too friendly right to start with." Pg. 20. Both retired women acted the same. And in both the episode and the book, both elderly women ended up appreciating the help, and the company of their selected partners, with time. To add to the connection, Raven helped her partner let her dreams come back to life, and in Skinnybones and the Wrinkle Queen, on the back cover it says that they go on a road trip to try and fulfill their own dreams, and I infer that they will develop a deep and strong relationship together.

> Grade 8 student
> Posted at 7:34 a.m, March 16, 2008

After analyzing various free wiki spaces online, the teachers decided to register at www.wikispaces.com. One reason this site was chosen was because educators are provided with many special services. The site's physical setup is not too technologically challenging as there are easily accessible and detailed procedures for setup and follow-up assistance. Furthermore, specific sites can be made public or private; those that are public can be viewed for ideas and formats for personal sites. The team created a wiki space called "Chine Drive Red Maple" which, for this project, was made accessible to only invited members: the Grade 7/8 students, the teacher candidate, the associate teacher, the resource librarian, the principal, the faculty adviser from OISE (Ontario Institute for Studies in Education), and most important, the authors of the selected novels.

Having an online discussion forum enabled the students to create questions and make comments directly to the authors who were participants. The students were excited about being able to engage in conversation the authors of the texts they were reading. They felt encouraged to take part in ongoing dialogue. An example:

Mr. Huser, why did you write the book in two different points of view switching chapter by chapter? My answer: I think you did it because it provides two different points of

perspective and engages the reader more. I know it made the book more captivating, and I felt like I was in two different characters' shoes. It was amazing to see what they thought of each other. I think you, as the author created good character traits for the characters, and did not just make Tamara and Miss Barclay normal people, but unique.

> Grade 8 student
> Posted at 7:34 a.m., March 16, 2008

Of the six Red Maple Award winners that the students selected, the teacher candidate piloted online literature circles with only two groups of students. The groups that went online were reading *Skinnybones and the Wrinkle Queen* by Glen Huser and *Stolen Away* by Christopher Dinsdale. These two novels were chosen because they had been read by all members of the team, enabling everyone to be active participants and facilitators in the discussions with the students.

As you can see from the following quotations, the interactions between the students and the teacher candidate reflect a progressive discussion thread.

I also really liked these chapters because I could relate to them very well. The majority of these chapters are set while Tamara and Miss Barclay are driving across Canada. I could relate to that very well. I have traveled to Jasper, Banff and Vancouver. I liked how the author described the weather conditions. He was talking about the country side and the mountains. I felt like I was back there again. I think that was the reason I enjoyed these chapters the most. I really cannot wait to read on! I want to see what happens the rest of the trip!

> Grade 8 student
> Posted at 5:16 a.m., April 1, 2008

This is a really good reflection! I remember how much tension there was with my family when we had to go on long trips. Imagine being cramped in a car with everyone! Although it is just the two of them, you can imagine how Tamara is feeling (especially since they are of different ages). I have never driven across Canada but would like to do this one day. Keep on reading and posting!

> Teacher candidate
> Posted at 1:03 p.m., April 1, 2008

One time when I was like 8, my family and one of my dad's friend's family members decided to rent a minivan and go to Quebec. I do remember by the time we got there everyone was sick and tired of each other, and that was when I had people there who were my age. I can imagine how

Tamara is feeling. Driving for hours with a person who is like 5 times your age. I think that just listening to the opera music would have driven me crazy.

Grade 8 student
Posted at 6:54 p.m., April 1, 2008

One of the main reasons many of the students enjoyed this online format was that they could discuss and post their reflections at varying times throughout the day and night. The students in this particular community were fortunate to have access to computers at home. As teachers, we recognize the importance of equity of access. For those students who do not have computers at home, we must find alternative ways to ensure that they learn the skills to become digital citizens and be part of the learning environment we have structured. Ensuring that computer time at school is allocated to students who require access is essential. Encouraging students to become members of their local library also provides more Internet access.

Some students found that this format for sharing enabled them to channel their feelings or thoughts in a deeper, more meaningful way than they could in a face-to-face setting. For some students and adults, expressing feelings in writing can be less threatening or intimidating; however, this advantage does not negate the importance of having face-to-face conversations, a skill that students and adults of any age need to develop. A combination of both formats would be ideal to address the varying needs of many learners.

Providing an online space for students to respond to texts can be inspiring and energizing; however, the space need not be a wiki. If schools have access to First Class or other online conferencing systems, an online conference environment could be created for students to respond to text. As you read more about the students' reactions to wiki spaces, however, it may inspire you to pursue this particular environment.

Students were able to provide meaningful and detailed reflections and responses throughout the process. There was definitely a difference between what they would write on paper and talk about and what they would write in an online dialogue. They were quick to understand how to navigate their way while using the wiki, and they continuously provided feedback and suggestions.

The librarian was both a help and a strong advocate of this initiative. Interested in the program and the entire process, she constantly encouraged the team to implement new things as we created our space. For example, after the site was fully functional, the librarian researched and found a code for an online voting poll where the students could place their votes about the degree to which they enjoyed the book they were reading (on a scale from 1 to 5). The code came from another public wiki site. All she had to do was copy and paste it into a text box on our page. There were, and still are, several surprises and challenges with the process that need to be addressed for future wiki projects.

- It was essential to remind students to check the site frequently (I tried to have them check at least once a day). It was frustrating to post an important message on the general discussion board and not have it read by students until the night before.
- We decided to assess students based on the requirements of posting a minimum of one reflection and two responses to other students' reflections. We recognized that we were assessing students' work based on the participation of others. If group members didn't post their reflections, it was difficult for other students to post responses. We needed to reassess our practice.
- We recognized that some students find it challenging to learn how to write "professionally" or for an audience that is diverse and wider in scope. Spelling errors, instant messaging lingo, and casual e-mail jargon were evident in most discussion posts. Students were encouraged to use a writing program to draft their reflection, to use spell check, and to save their reflections for backup. Judging by the continuous evidence of grammatical errors and spelling mistakes in their posted work, only a few students adopted this strategy. When I implement this process next, I plan to have the students use a writing program and then I will teach them how to post their work into the wiki site. (All it takes is a simple copy and paste.)
- One huge concern with this process is the reliability of the technology. If the Internet or site goes down, what do you do? There was one instance where the site was down and students were unable to read or respond to any of the reflections. This is where the previous point plays a major role: if students had a backup file of their work, they could easily print off a copy and

implement the strategies used in the face-to-face literature circle discussions.

I expect that student involvement will increase over time as students become more familiar with the process. As they continue to receive constructive feedback about their work, they will not only be more engaged at using the technology, but will benefit both academically and socially. Because the idea is a new concept for most students, it would be worthwhile to designate students as explorers of the development of a wiki page, its functions and format, and most important, of ways it can enhance their learning. There are unbelievable tools and unique features that will complement students' creativity and ideas.

The interest and support of everyone on this team provided a risk-free learning environment for all concerned, especially the students involved. This initiative taught the students how to be professional digital citizens and what responsibilities they had as authors of authentic pieces of work that could be viewed on the World Wide Web. Combining the opportunity to experience "virtual" literature circles and face-to-face literature circles would open doors for many students and provide more opportunities for students to talk about and reach a deeper understanding of the texts being read in small peer-led discussion groups.

> Overall, I REALLY enjoyed using Wiki rather than just having a plain discussion about the book. Everyone's voice could be heard instead of in a discussion when people cut people out and talked over people. The only thing that I did not like was the fact that you did not know when some- one responded to everyone's comment. You had to open each discussion and figure out if anyone responded to a comment you had. Otherwise it was a great experience, but also I wish there was a spell check on Wiki so you did not have to cut and paste in Word.

So, to end our foray into the world of virtual literature circles, we will share one last entry, made by a student as she completes reading the novel. She still has questions and is still thinking about the events in the story . . . and that's what we want our readers to be doing — always thinking and trying to understand, trying to make meaning and deepen comprehension.

> I found that the last few chapters were amazing as they were very engaging and I could not put the book down after there was a hunt for Tamara and Miss Barclay, and Miss Barclay had a brutal fall. Many of the things we predicted came true! Overall I think this book was excellent and I think the author ended the book well with a good overall conclusion of Tamara having to never miss another day of school, having to go to group therapy, and helping at the Sierra Sunset Seniors' Lodge. I think that was a good punishment for Tamara to learn a lesson about what she did was wrong. I thought she might have to kid's jail . . . but it was not that bad. Without her punishment though, I think Tamara would get back up on her feet without thinking about it and plan once again the next second. Will Tamara learn her lesson, or will she keep on doing things like that again? Will her punishment really help her, or just go to the back of her mind?
>
> Grade 8 student
> Posted on April 9, 2008

Reading and Responding to a Theme-Based Collection of Novels

BY AMY MOHR

One way to foster the type of deep thinking represented by critical thinking skills and higher order thinking is to teach units thematically. I have developed units thematically within my own teaching in a Grade 8 classroom. In order to develop units that are engaging and that increase student motivation, it is essential to include the students in the planning process. Doing so will help differentiate instruction.

At the beginning of the year, it is important to create a community of learners, where students can work collaboratively and independently. We want students to feel respected and welcomed, and we want them to know we care about their interests. Within a community of learners, students will feel safe and will want to contribute to the group. They will come together to meet the needs of the whole class and to work through problems as a collective. As Regie Routman (2003) says, "Unless we reach into our students' hearts, we have no entry into their minds."

Before teaching thematically, which involves using book talks, it is essential to establish norms for accountable talk. These include listening actively, participating actively, clarifying ideas, expanding on ideas raised, disagreeing constructively, focusing on the conversation, supporting opinions with evidence, and encouraging all group members.

Setting clear expectations and modelling accountable talk is essential to having students work on task and independently. I begin by doing whole-class lessons showing students what accountable talk looks like and sounds like. After modelling this several times, I release responsibility to the students. Similarly, establishing routines is critical to having students work on task and independently. When I teach thematically, I begin by having a clear understanding of what I want to teach based on curriculum standards; however, I do not plan in isolation. I talk with the students about what they want to learn. Although I may have an idea in mind, I offer it to the class for their input and feedback. Meeting students where they are at and tapping into their interests allow for differentiated instruction and increased engagement.

For example, I wanted to do a unit on the theme of war, but depended upon the students' input to determine how to develop it and what to make it look like.

After talking with the students, I put four charts up on the wall: What I Want to Learn; How I Am Going to Learn It; How I Will Show What I Learned; and Resources: Movies I Want to See or Field Trips I Want to Go On. Students wrote their opinions on sticky notes and posted them on the chart paper; when they were done, I collated the responses and used their input to create the unit. I ensured that the unit was mapped back to the curriculum standards and that either an essential question or an inquiry question tied into the theme and provided a focus for the work we would do during the unit. Adolescents need to feel they have a voice in the classroom. By asking for their input and taking their responses into consideration, I was able to provide a space for their voices; by valuing their input, I was better able to engage students in the unit.

There are two possible ways to group students for book talks when teaching thematically: homogeneously and heterogeneously. When grouping homogeneously, select four to six different novels that pertain to the theme. Selecting novels at the varying reading levels of your students is important so that students are able to read and comprehend independently; this way allows for students who are reading the same book to meet during book talk and talk about that book.

In heterogeneous groupings, students select their own novels that tie into the overall theme. There will be several different books in groups that are linked by the same common theme. Students select novels from a variety of places: a class library, suggested authors/titles list, or a school or public library. Asking the school librarian to pull out books related to a theme is a great way to build a list of possible titles, and books not selected by students may be placed in a central location so students can use them and review them as wanted. Titles may be either fiction or non-fiction. Selecting texts this way allows students choice and ownership over their selections; however, they are expected to seek teacher approval. Approval is dependent upon the link to the theme and the appropriateness of the reading/interest level.

Once you have decided how to form your groups and students have novels, determine how you want students to work through the novels and come together to discuss them. The goal is for students to meet and engage in dialogue that is relevant, purposeful, and authentic. Students are to talk about what they're reading and to think critically and deeply about it. To realize this I have them record their thinking while they are reading and to meet regularly with their peers for discussion.

There are a couple of ways to have students come together and talk about their books. If you use a literature circle approach, you would chunk the novel into sections, students would read the assigned pages independently and at the same pace, and then they would complete assigned roles (Daniels 2002). Students come to the literature circle meeting with their roles fulfilled and share their material. Some of the roles Daniels identifies are discussion director, literary luminary, connector, and illustrator. Role cards are a tool for students to use as a scaffold to help guide them to have lively text-focused conversations.

To move students to think more critically and deeply about their texts, set expectations for the discussion to also focus on how the texts connect to the overall theme. For students to successfully engage in more meaningful literacy conversations, you need to explicitly model and teach the actions and statements that would occur. A teacher may also provide guiding questions to facilitate higher level thinking. Possible guiding questions and prompts are as follows:

- What appears to be the author's message in the text?
- Whose positions are being expressed? Whose voices are missing?
- What types of connections can you make with this text: text-to-self; text-to-text; text-to-world?
- This is similar to/different from . . .
- I think this is important because . . .
- What comprehension strategies did you use while reading this selection?
- How does this text connect to the overall theme? What proof supports your answer?

There are several ways to monitor group discussion.

One way to help monitor which members of the group are contributing is to have a container with Popsicle sticks (say, three per student in the group). The person in charge of getting the conversation going would distribute the same number of sticks to each group member. To add something to the conversation, someone places a stick in the container. If you notice that someone still has all provided sticks, then you can determine that the student has not yet contributed to the conversation. I think it's a great way to encourage all group members to participate in the discussion.

Another way to track what students are focusing on in their literature circle conversations is to have a minute taker (perhaps another rotating role). In a notebook that the teacher collects after each meeting, the minute taker records what was discussed and identifies possible next steps. By reading the minutes, the teacher develops a good understanding of how deeply or critically students are thinking about the texts they are reading. The minutes would also inform whole-class instruction (for example, if a common theme or question came up in several groups' minutes, then the teacher could address it with the whole class). A caveat about using the minutes is that just like any new strategy, tool, or approach, students will need explicit instruction and modelling to understand how to use the minutes and what the expectations are.

If you use a book talk format instead of literature circles, you would require students to read a certain number of pages and complete a reading response or reading journal. Students bring their reading journals to weekly book talk meetings and use their responses as the basis for conversation. I use "Book Talk Guideline" (Booth 2001), which is laminated and stays at the book talk table.

When beginning book talks I, as the teacher, am both a contributing member of the group and a facilitator. I model for my students the importance of reading. I choose a book that is geared towards their age group and I read and complete my own (scaled-down version) of the reading journal so I can contribute to the group discussion. As the book talks become part of our classroom routines, I gradually release the responsibility of facilitating the book talk discussion to the students. Each week they take turns being the facilitator and are able to use the laminated guideline for possible ways to begin the conversation. Some of the prompts on "Book Talk Guideline" are these:

Let's discuss why. . . Tell us what you mean by . . . Tell us why you agree . . . Let's talk about . . . So you're saying . . . I'm wondering . . .

Other guiding questions are similar to those that might be provided during literature circles:

- How are your novels connected? What proof can you use to support your answer?

- What connections can you make: text-to-self; text-to-text; text-to-world?
- Which comprehension strategies did you use while you read?
- How do your texts connect to the overall theme?
- What is the common message among all your novels?

Through book talks students are developing a deeper understanding of texts read and are thinking and talking critically. The following is a transcript of a video-taped book talk in my Grade 8 classroom (*T* is the teacher and *S* is student):

T: For the response: What do you think about while you're reading? Don't just summarize in here because that doesn't help me. I want to know, what are your thoughts? We'll go around the table today and because some of us have changed our books and some of us are still finishing up our books — and that's fine — if you could just provide us with a brief synopsis, maybe about one or two sentences about the book, and then maybe you could pull something from your reading journal to share.

S: [shares a quotation from the book and questions he had]

T: Okay, good questions. So what I'm hearing when you're talking is that the book deals with issues of abandonment and fear of the unknown. We call those issues "themes." So when we talk about what are issues in a book, those are the themes. This is an idea that we should be able to use in our language: theme.

S: My book is still talking about his past with Lisa and stuff [from book *Lisa*] and actually with Lisa's brother, Jasper. And he's talking about how he fought with him [read quote]. I write that he must be really upset by that because it was his friend, a person he knew. And he had a lot of anger at that time because he went through a lot in the war. 'Cause it was a really bad time and I guess he saw a lot of stuff and had to kill people and stuff.

T: Can we make any connections at all? *(pause)* Because it sounds to me that the sentiment that was expressed in the quote reminds me of your book *(directed towards another student)* in a way.

S: Yes, it does.

T: Do you know how?

S: Yes.

T: Can you tell us?

S: Well, the connection is that a lot of anger and rage from the people who have invaded their homeland and that's like in this book because the Germans invaded Russia and the Russians have a lot of rage at the Germans and they're killing and raping everybody so that's the connection, like your guy's killing *(pointing back to other student)*.

T: Good. And I like how in the opening [of the shared quote] it's very strong and we can hear this person's voice through the writing. Read the opening again.

This transcript shows two things: first, how important teacher modelling is and second, students who are reading different texts are still able to make deep connections and understand the bigger picture. Students need explicit instruction and prodding to think more deeply and critically. As book talks become more routine, students are able to use higher level thinking more and more independently.

Whether students are meeting in homogeneous groups with the same text or in heterogeneous groups with different texts does not matter. What is truly important is to provide students with the opportunity to talk and interact. Through meaningful and purposeful talk, students are learning from one another and learning how to think more critically.

Students complete reading journal entries once a week and bring them along to book talk as the basis for discussion. Before students use their reading journals independently, I model how to write an entry. Using a whole-class shared reading piece, I create a modelled and shared reading journal entry.

The use of reading journals is a way for students to demonstrate what they are doing while reading. I use a format based on Cris Tovani's ideas (2004). Students are required to record what they are reading (title, author, pages), to summarize, to respond, and to attach sticky notes that show they are using a variety of strategies while reading. I always tell my students that the sticky notes should be a combination of quotations, questions, connections, and comments.

The reading journal is a way for me to see what students are reading and how well they grasp comprehension strategies. Through this written reflection, I am able to provide written feedback, prodding them to think more deeply and critically. The reading journals are also a form of assessment for learning because students are receiving regular and immediate feedback on their entries. Furthermore, the entries inform my instruction as a teacher because I am able to discover what needs to be addressed with the whole class and which students would benefit from small-group guided instruction. Below are some samples of students' reading journal entries from my Grade 8 class: they demonstrate how students are moved to think critically about what they are reading.

Sample 1 [based on *Enemy at the Gates*]: Response: In my book I read up to page 84 and I've already learned so much about the war of Stalingrad. In my studies of Stalingrad, I was shocked to learn how many men died just in this one battle. . . . I'm doing my war unit on the battle of Stalingrad, and out of all the kinds of battles and wars I've ever learned about, I find this battle the most shocking and interesting. In the battle of Stalingrad, the city was completely demolished. I remember seeing a picture of the battle and not one single building was left standing. . . . I would like to say that all these soldiers that died didn't die in vain but I can't. This war was fought for a very weak cause. . . . I don't realize how the German people couldn't see that all the wars that Hitler started are totally useless. I can't believe Hitler actually had supporters.

Sample 2 [based on *Days of Victory*]: Response: As I read this book, I find that I feel very sad about the events that took place in World War II. I really can't believe that the world was so blind to what the Nazis were doing to the Jewish people. That so many millions of people could die because of the belief of the Nazi Nation and one evil leader.

These journal entries show that students were thinking about big issues posed by their texts as well as making connections, asking questions, making inferences, and identifying important information. Students were reflecting on what they were reading. When writing their journal entries, students were also deepening their understanding of the text and of the overall theme. In these two entries students questioned how Hitler came into power and had supporters. It is also obvious that although the entries were based on different novels, a unifying thread connects them to the theme.

When we teach thematically, students are able to make those links between texts and to the overall theme and the connection to the world. Specifically through the war unit, students began to consider their role as a global citizen, reading, reflecting in writing, sharing through book talk, and discussing critical points. When students have to make independent reading journal entries, they have to start thinking about the text and the theme. This thinking moves into discussion — either literature circle or book talk — where students formalize their thinking, expand on their ideas, and possibly learn from others. This process leads to a more meaningful understanding for all students. When we allow students to have a voice in the classroom and provide multiple entry points to the same theme, we increase student engagement and deepen their literacy comprehension.

Transcribing Literature Circle Conversations

BY LARRY SWARTZ

The classrooms I remember as a student were, on the whole, silent places where learning happened independent of those around us. My classmates and I were seldom given opportunities to work, talk, or learn together.

Now, as a teacher, I believe in personal response to literature and in the potential that collaborative situations have for students to reveal their thoughts out loud. Group talk, I believe, can provide a meaningful social dynamic for cooperative learning where interaction, negotiation, and communication can develop effectively. It is concerned with getting things done as students explore, question, and arrive at conclusions that no one student could have reached alone. When students believe that their ideas are respected and valued, the skills promoted through interaction may deepen both social and language growth.

Talk helps to both validate and stretch our initial responses. It takes time and questions and trust to get to a place where we each can clarify our own views or understand new things through conversation. It is not uncommon for us to want to find someone to talk to in order to share our impressions of a movie, play, or television show we've just seen or a book we've just read. Such conversations enable us to sort out what we think and to distance ourselves a little from the immediacy of our involvement in the experience. These conversations involve sharing of enthusiasms, sharing of puzzles, and sharing of connections. When all group members have seen the film or read the book, this sharing allows us to rub our ideas and opinions against those of other group members and can often lead us to insights we might never have otherwise discovered.

I came to learn about the work of Harvey Daniels, who invites teachers to use role sheets in the literature circle. The sheets ensure that students arrive with a responsibility (or a role) to contribute to the group discussion. Assigned roles do help students to inspect a text more carefully but to me, the role sheets did not promote authentic conversation where students listened carefully, responded to each other's ideas, and built on issues and topics that emerged both from the literature being discussed and from the conversation. Recognizing the potential for text talk to encourage, support, and promote literacy growth, I chose to set up

some events that helped me work towards a richer interactive classroom community.

By implementing interactive sessions, where students are invited to discuss literature selections, I sought to have students discuss the meaning of the text in terms of possibilities, not in terms of exact answers to specific questions. I was aware that the group talk supported the participants in their rough draft understanding of literature. By having students with different interests, backgrounds, and experiences collaborating, I built communities where learners work together towards making personal and shared textual meaning. Like any architectural construction, the building of group talk involved a layering upon layering. Each conversation taught the students not only about the uniqueness of every reader, but also about the stuff of good conversations.

Poem Talk: A group discussion with the teacher

For this event, I decided to participate in the discussion of the poem "Lines" by Judith Nicholls. I like this poem, not only for its sense of word play but for its portrayal of a schoolchild whose mind wanders as lessons are being taught. Would the students in my class feel the same way about the poem as I did? Would they be able to know the person in the poem and come to understand what Nicholls was saying about daydreams and daydreamers?

For a discussion of the poem, I offered these three questions to the students:

- What do we know about the daydreamer?
- What do you think Judith Nicholls was saying about school?
- How do you think the poet came to write this poem?

For the first part of the conversation, I participated as a listener and didn't contribute much to the students' analysis. The students had some questions to deal with, and I was conscious about not directing the interpretations of the poem. One might then ask why I would be part of the group at all, if I wasn't going to contribute to the conversation. For one thing, discussions tend to go in many directions and for this discussion, I wanted to gently edge the students back to the text if they strayed too far. More important, however, I was interested in witnessing the nature of the conversation as it unfolded in the presence of the teacher, as opposed to the students being left to their own devices as they had been with the poem "Famous."

The participants began by confessing that they were confused by the poem. They said "the words didn't make any sense," (James) and "the title, 'Lines,' doesn't correspond to the dreams being talked about in the poem" (Liza). As the conversation evolved, the students frequently returned to the page, reading aloud certain lines or words, such as *paydream, timeschool,* and *cryschool.* The students didn't try to determine meanings for these words except for *greydream* which was interpreted as a "bad dream that she must (right) have had when it begin to storm" (Heidi). James thought that maybe the printer scrambled all the lines and decided that there must be some kind of code in the poem.

In their further attempts to make sense of "Lines," it was decided that students would read the poem in various ways. Sunny suggested that they read only the nonsense words alphabetically, and Heidi thought the middle word on each line held some clues to a puzzle. At one point, the whole group read the poem backwards from bottom to top.

I did, however, change the direction of the conversation by asking the students to consider whether they understood "Lines" any better after having a group discussion. Sunny said that at first he thought the poem was "weird" because he didn't understand what lines the poet was talking about. When James suggested that the lines were assigned by a teacher to a girl who must not have been paying attention in class, Georgette said that the poem made a bit more sense to her. Heidi suggested that by talking to others, she came to understand that "it was really clear that this poem was trying to get across that it is okay to daydream."

One comment by Liza implied that the students were coming to see the benefits of making private responses public: "If someone was to go to the poem in a book, she'd probably just look at it, say, 'this doesn't make sense,' turn the page and leave it, but we talked about it and everybody understands it." Liza's words suggest that she was beginning to understand how we can make meaning through collaboration.

I then asked the students how talk helped them to make sense of a poem, and in the following conversation, the students talk about their talk experiences:

J: The first time — if you don't read it properly — it's like all the poet did was bunch up all these words together and make a poem out of it.

H: Like when you first read it, you think, you read it and say, "Oh gee . . . this is a stupid poem."

L: You need a title or . . .

H: Or you don't ever want to see it ever again.

S: (to me) Like you once told us "life between . . . no words between the lines" is living or something like that . . . that the lines between the words and between the lines

H: The first time I read this, I thought there were lines or words or bits of pieces of information.

T: So, how do you understand it better now?

H: Well, like after you talk about it . . . you just think more . . . like everyone's saying what it reminds them of . . . and like then you read it backwards and forwards again and again and then it eventually explains itself.

T: Well then, I'd like to ask since you talked about talking. How does talking help you understand this poem?

J: Well, different people have different ideas and you can combine those ideas and that makes a poem a bit clearer.

G: You let out your problems about the story and then other people try to mix in with you.

L: You start imagining it in your mind while other people are talking and then you understand it.

S: It's like a jigsaw puzzle. Like everyone has different pieces and if you use your own pieces, you can't make a picture, but if you use everyone's pieces you can build a picture together.

H: Well, if you hear what other people think about it, you could stop and think . . . well . . . my answer was kind of like that, but I think this person is right in this way . . . and I think I'm right in this way.

T: How did this happen with the discussion about "Lines"?

H: Well, when we talked about it, like everyone had different ways of reading it, and then everyone was saying what word reminded them of "this" and how "this" word is combined with "this" . . . and then you stop to think about it and you get a better answer.

S: That reminds me of equivalent fractions, because Heidi just said that everyone has the same thought, but they like . . . just like say it in a different way . . . like different numbers, but the same . . .

J: the same value!

From this rich piece of conversation, two main questions arise:

- What did the students learn about discussion?
- What did the teacher learn about students talking together?

From their comments it seems that these students have understood that each of us brings and takes different meanings from a text. Moreover, they have come to understand that by sharing ideas about a poem, they clarify their private understandings. It is evident that they were becoming more adept at building on one another's thoughts and refining their own responses as they listened to the insights of others: "Well, different people have different ideas and you can combine those ideas and that makes a poem a bit clearer." All said that they were confused when they first encountered the poem; all claimed that they understood the poem better by talking about it.

As I later listened to the tape recording of this conversation, I realized that I offered little in the way of personal interpretations, but asked questions to help guide the conversation. (For example: "What do you know about the girl in this poem?" "How do you think the poem came up with these invented words?") Rather than indicate to the group that here was a correct answer, these open-ended questions allowed the students to formulate their own views, inviting them to explore their in-the-head thoughts aroused by this text.

As the transcript indicates, the students came to understand the potential for small-group discussion. Upon reflection, I recognize that I was too careful about revealing my own interpretations for fear that the students would consider my thoughts as "correct." I was there to support the students' ideas by suggesting possibilities rather than stating probabilities.

To conclude their discussion about the poem "Lines," the students considered the appropriateness of the title:

J: I think this poem should be called "Daydreaming" or "Daydreams."
H: I think it should be called "Confusion," or something like that.
L: "Lines" suits this poem because it gives the reader something to figure out while they're reading each line.
J: It should be called . . . it should be called "Figure It Out!"

My research into text talk demanded that I consider a number of significant teaching strategies, and several questions emerged: Should the teacher be a member of the group and work inside the conversation with the students, or can students be allowed to talk among themselves? Do the students need questions or prompts to guide their discussion, or can we trust that they will dig and dig into the text on their own terms? How can I best pay attention to the contributions of each student as well as assess the success of each conversation?

During the course of any week in a classroom, hundreds of conversations take place, and teachers can catch the buzz of talk passing from student to student to student. To enrich their talk, however, we need to take a more fruitful role as a listener in order to tune in to the sea of conversations. When we take the time to "freeze talk" with recorded technology, listen to the conversations over and over, or prepare a written transcription of what each participant said, we can isolate specific exploratory talk which can then serve the purpose of working towards deeper understanding.

Blogging Our Way into a Novel Study Unit

BY KONRAD GLOGOWSKI

Blogs, also known as weblogs, appealed to me as a teacher of language arts because of their potential use as electronic writing journals. They offered the possibility of providing each student with an easy-to-use online writing journal or electronic portfolio. I decided to use them in my Grade 8 Language Arts class to promote engagement and ownership. In addition to having their own iblogs, the students had access to the blogs of all their classmates and could comment on the work of their peers by posting a response to a specific entry on an individual blog. As a teacher and a researcher, I was interested in the impact of blogging on the emergence of competent and literate modes of thinking and communicating in a senior elementary school classroom.

The following series of interactions is one of many that ensued within the class blogging community. Much like many other virtual conversations in the community, it emerged in response to a single entry written about *The Diary of a Young Girl* by Anne Frank, one of three texts we had been discussing in class.

In one of her first entries on Anne Frank's diary, Vanessa shows that, in addition to using her own blog to record her thoughts, she is an active reader who visits other blogs and responds to her classmates:

> Many people often talk about how Anne had a very different personality portrayed on the inside than the outside however I have a point to make. [...] Throughout the beginning of this diary, and actually almost the entire diary, Anne constantly was trying to find her identity. She was always trying to judge herself, and comment on all the remarks shot at her. Was she really selfish? Was she really immature? [...] If you were stuck inside a room, hiding from almost everyone out there, wouldn't you start to wonder why EVERYONE seems to hate you? Then, when your mother and 'friends' constantly criticize you, wouldn't you feel that you needed to change yourself or find out just really who you were? No wonder Anne spent so much time trying to figure out who she should be.

Vanessa begins by stating that she is responding to discussions that had taken place in the online community. She wrote her entry not because she had been asked to write a response, but because she chose to react to entries posted online. As soon as she posted her response and addressed the question of Anne's personality — a question that many of her classmates had been writing about — the community engaged with her entry.

Vanessa's entry on Anne's personality generated 21 comments, some supporting her views and some challenging her opinion and interpretation of Anne Frank's actions and personality. In addition, two of Vanessa's classmates decided not to leave a comment on her blog, but to write more exhaustive responses on their own blogs. Those responses also received comments, including some posted by Vanessa who continued her deep engagement with the text and the work of her classmates by following the growth of her post throughout the class blogosphere.

The responses, posted in the form of comments, focused on specific aspects of Vanessa's entry. Terry, the author of the first comment, zeroed in on Anne's identity:

> I agree when you write that "Throughout the beginning of this diary, and actually almost the entire diary, Anne constantly was trying to find her identity. She was always trying to judge herself, and comment on all the remarks shot at her." I think you're right — she is always trying to find herself. She's always questioning who she is and why people respond to her the way they do. I think she's very insecure, too. I think that's why she doesn't really confront people or tell them her thoughts . . . it's almost like she hides in her diary because like she says at the beginning somewhere (in the second entry). I think that she wants the diary to be her friend. So she feels safe with her diary and it's easier to be herself on paper. Her diary doesn't judge.

In his comment, Terry used a reference to a specific passage in the diary and thus helped to start a conversation. Terry states that he agrees with Vanessa, but he also continues the conversation by expanding on the concept of identity formation. He suggests to Vanessa that the diary is more than just a notebook. It is a significant part of Anne's personality and a kind of coping mechanism.

Before Vanessa had a chance to respond, the conversation was enriched by yet another student. Alexandra's thoughts suggest to both Vanessa and Terry that they should consider another point of view:

I agree that Anne is constantly trying to find herself and I agree that the diary is a kind of friend to her but after reading the sections that she wrote before the hiding I thought that Anne was very confident and actually very full of herself. So we're all feeling sorry for her but look at the incident with her math teacher . . . who in our class today would do that?! She doesn't doubt herself there . . . I wish I had the confidence she does!

Alexandra's comment redirected the flow of the conversation by drawing Terry's and Vanessa's attention to an important discrepancy. Alexandra is referring to Anne's response to an assignment she was given as punishment for talking in class. Anne wrote a response in which she tried to prove in a creative and humorous way that she was genetically predisposed to talking and that nothing could be done about what she calls her "feminine characteristic." Alexandra rightly points out that this incident suggests that Anne is a confident young woman who does not need to hide behind her diary.

As a teacher observing this exchange, I was tempted to post a response, but I refrained. I wanted to explain that both points of view are valid: Anne does use her diary as a coping mechanism and she also displays much confidence before going into hiding. I was also tempted to use the comments as a basis for a class discussion. However, I chose not to respond and began to look for opportunities to assist my students in a more conversational and less formal way.

I was waiting for an opportunity to enter the conversation not only as their teacher, but as yet another reader who wants to share views on Anne's personality. I also wanted to see whether the conversation would lead the students to the conclusion I wanted them to reach on their own — that Anne becomes a very different person once she's hiding in the Secret Annex and that, throughout her diary, we are given insightful glimpses into her growing maturity.

When Vanessa, Terry, and two other students, Ryan and Veronica, responded to Alexandra's comment, it was clear that the students were on their way to a deep engagement with text. Veronica wrote:

Yeah, Alex you're right . . . she was so confident and actually I find her kind of arrogant to think that she can

out-smart the teacher like that and just do her own thing! I wouldn't have the guts to to that that! Look at what she says after the teacher read her poem to the class: "Since then I am allowed to talk, never get extra work, in fact Keptor always jokes about it" So, yeah I think she's a bit too high on herself and her creativity. I mean it's great to be able to write so well and kinda trick the teacher into letting you talk in class but, ok, who would do that today . . . seriously . . . I think she was very confident and I don't agree that she was trying to find herself . . . look at the entry (June 21, 1942) she knows who she is very well! But then she kinda falls apart and is not sure of anything. Why?

Veronica addressed an important change in Anne's personality: the impact of adolescence and going into hiding on her identity. She also referred to a specific passage to provide support. The next entry, posted by Ryan, included a reference to a specific passage in the diary, as well:

I think both Alex and Veronica are right — Anne is really full of herself and I think she also really wants attention: look at that passage where she talks about boyfriends . . . it's June 20th, 1942: She says that boys fall in love with her "immediately"! IMMEDIATELY!!!! Who says that?! Seriously! Immediately?? She says a boy "won't allow me out of his sight." I think she's very arrogant here and very sure of herself.

Veronica responded:

Ok, that's all true and it makes her sound very cocky but look at when this happens . . . it's like we talked in class, she has everything in this part of her life: she has loving parents and they are well-off and she doesn't have a care in the world. She kind of reminds me of us, you know? I don't talk about boyfriends like that but I think we're just as carefree as she was, think about it guys — think about your life and the life of kids in other countries today. We're very fortunate and she was too.

When Vanessa responded to these comments, it was clear that she had thought carefully about the views her classmates had shared with her:

I think I get it . . . the part before they go into hiding she is more like us, just a regular teenager who really doesn't have much to worry about in life so she writes about everyday things, and her writing is not as deep as later on because she just has a regular happy life. But then when they go into the Secret Annex her life is so different and there are more conflicts because they're all in the same place stuck together. I think she is very confident and cocky as Veronica says in the first few entries because she had a happy life and was spoiled by her parents. She was getting all this attention and was very friendly and creative so maybe it all went to her head? So, I think you're right, but I'm talking about after they are in the Secret Annex. What happened to her confidence? It's like she's a different person! Look how unsure of herself she is, and like I said before, she spends all this time questioning her identity. She's a different person.

I never thought about it this way, but it makes perfect sense, Alex! Of course it's maturity! Because later on life gets so tough for her and she has to grow up fast and deal with things that we don't have to deal with and we're her age.

Terry:

Yeah, that's what I meant — she has to deal with all this stuff like parents criticizing her and sibling rivalry and always being told what to do and not being able to just leave and go for a walk and chat with friends or go on MSN. That makes her really different and there's all this pressure that she has to deal with.

Alexandra:

Right, that's what I meant to say: Before she had no pressures and now she does and doesn't know how to deal with it but it gives her "adult" things to write about. That's why her entries are so different after she goes into hiding and that's why she has no confidence in these entries. I think it's all new to her and she's trying to find her self. Like Terry and Vanessa said at the beginning, she uses the diary to cope. I think at first the diary is just like a place to record what happens in her life but then it's a place to think things through and have a friend to talk to.

Veronica:

I just found this loooong entry — January 2, 1944 — where she feels sorry for being so unkind to her mom. I think this really shows her maturity and how she uses the diary to cope and find her identity. I think this could be one of those "Self-portraits"! Take a look at it . . . I think it's a pretty good entry!

Vanessa:

Thanks for posting that entry. Now I remember reading it, but I must've been tired when I read it because the things she says didn't jump out the way they did now. Anne says, "Anne, how could you!" and she also says, "Anne, is it really you who mentioned hate?" But my favourite part is when she says this: "I have been trying to understand the Anne of a year ago and to excuse her, because my conscience isn't clear as long as I leave you with these accusations, without being able to explain, on looking back, how it happened." I think it shows she's matured because she knows she made mistakes.

Terry:

Great quote, Vanessa! I just re-read it too and I think you're right. There is so much here that shows how she has matured. She actually stops to think about her behaviour when they first moved into the Secret Annex. She says that she's trying to understand Anne which I think shows that she has a good idea of who she is now and how she treated people wrongly before. This shows maturity. I know I often find it hard to admit I was wrong.

Alexandra:

Guys, you're forgetting that she also explains here why she thinks she acted the way she did when interacting with adults. Thanks for posting this, BTW! I also had to re-read this and I don't remember this entry being so important when I first read this. I had to look up "subjectively" and I also asked my parents because she says:

"I suffer now — and suffered then — from moods which kept my head under water (so to speak) and only allowed me to see the things subjectively without enabling me to consider quietly the words of the other side."

Subjectively means: (1): peculiar to a particular individual: personal (2): modified or affected by personal views, experience, or background.

So, I think she's saying here that she's been too self-obsessed and looked at all those conflicts only from her own point of view.

Ryan:

I think it takes a lot of maturity to say that she's been too subjective. Thanks for the definition, Alex! I think that she finally understands that she's been too harsh with her family. I'm not sure though, what she means by "moods." Do you think she means her way of dealing with things or does she mean personality traits?

Alexandra:

I think she means personality traits. I think she says here that she was too stubborn and thought only about herself. So, I think she blames herself for being like that, because she was too focused on herself, too much like a spoiled kid expecting everyone else to make her life easy. She says: "I hid myself within myself. I only considered myself."

Vanessa:

Guys!!! Keep reading! I found this after she says that part about acting subjectively: "I was rude and aggravating to Mummy, which, in turn, made her unhappy." I think it's a great sign of maturity because she says that the reason her mom wasn't always nice to her was because she wasn't nice to her mom.

Terry:

You're right. She says, "it was really a matter of unpleasantness and misery rebounding all the time." So, she blames the Secret Anne, kind of, right? I mean, this sounds like she's also saying that life was difficult for everyone so they all found it hard and there was a lot of conflicts and frustration.

Alexandra:

Yeah, but also look at what she says about her personality. Maybe she blames the situation but she also knows that she was wrong. If you keep reading you will see this: "I just didn't want to see all this, and pitied myself very much; but that too was unavoidable. These violent outbursts on paper were only giving vent to anger which in a normal life could have been worked off by stamping my feet a couple of times in a locked room." I think this shows that she was too selfish and never thought about anyone else in the Secret Annex.

Terry:

Hold on, so she does blame both, right, herself and the Secret Annex? She blames her personality but she also says that if they were at home, she would have reacted differently and there these feelings wouldn't get bottled up and then written down in the diary.

Vanessa:

The important thing is that she also has matured because she can look back and be cool and not still angry. She writes about being too hot-headed and too self-obsessed. She also says that being in the Annex caused many of these conflicts: I think she's right. I don't think there's anything wrong with saying that being locked up in a small space for years caused everyone to be different and that it caused many conflicts. I think this would happen to all of us . . . but just because she says that the Annex caused many conflicts doesn't mean that she had not matured or that she doesn't recognize her own mistakes. She has much more maturity here. She looks at her mistakes and then has a plan, she actually writes about what she will do next to stop these conflicts that she's been having with her mom and some other people in the Annex. I think this shows that she is very mature . . .

"The period when I caused Mummy to shed tears is over. I have grown wiser . . . I usually keep my mouth shut if I get annoyed, and so does she, so we appear to get on much better together."

I think in this entry Anne is very honest with herself. She knows she had made some mistakes and she also has a plan — she doesn't want to cause pain anymore and will keep her mouth shut if she ever has anything negative to say. This is just like what we talked about in class when Mr. G mentioned self-knowledge. I think Anne has self-knowledge now and before she was too blinded by being spoiled and her childlike personality.

So, if I think there are three stages in Anne's diary. There is the first part that we talked about [link to the discussion] when she had everything and was spoiled. . . . She was really just a kid then. Then there is the part at the beginning of hiding in the Annex where she is unpleasant to her mom and expects everyone to treat her like a princess and gets upset when they don't. And then finally there is the third stage where she recognizes that she had done some selfish and self obsessed things and thinks calmly about who she is. Here she has a plan for the future. She knows that everyone is stressed and frustrated in the Annex and she decides to just keep her thoughts to herself and not hurt people like she did before.

I think all this shows that she now has self-knowledge and maturity because she can point to her own mistakes and also decides not to be mean to people around her. So, this shows me that she knows how not to be subjective.

Throughout this discussion, the students encouraged one another to keep reading, challenged points of view, and collectively achieved a strong grasp of the studied text. The conversation encouraged them to engage with the text: many of them returned to entries they had already read to re-examine them in the light of new comments posted by their peers.

Vanessa's final entry shows that the online discussion had a strong impact on her understanding of Anne's personality. Her initial post was filled with questions and, while it demonstrated a good level of engagement with the text, it lacked the critical insight that she developed later through interactions with her classmates and the text itself. The conversational tone of the interactions that emerged from her initial entry helped Vanessa engage with the text on a deeper level.

Student interactions about Anne Frank suggest that students in a blogging community see their blogs not as a series of unrelated personal writing spaces, but as a network of writers and thinkers. Their reactions and interactions give rise to sustained commentary. Readership and meaningful interactions that emerged from students' attempts to deconstruct the text created a sense of community and participation which, in turn, contributed to a deeper understanding of the text.

The Boys Club: Moving Deeply into Text Forms

BY KRZYSZTOF RAKUC

From my classroom experiences, I know that many boys are disengaged from the language arts program and struggle with basic reading and writing skills. This situation reflects an intersection of issues that contribute to a general lack of academic self-esteem among them.

This disengagement not only stifles the development of literacy skills, as is evidenced by data collected provincially, nationally, and internationally, but also precludes the development of higher level thinking. In our information-driven society, superficial information is commonly accessed by hyperlinks; many students find it difficult to achieve the kind of deep, analytical understanding generated by a close reading of text and thoughtful contemplation. Rather than resisting popular culture and new technology, we can use it to provide an entry point for boys who may be reluctant readers.

The boys I have worked with all demonstrated a different form of literacy — one often ignored in many classrooms and curricula. In response to research and experiences with many young boys who were directly and indirectly expressing, "It's hard for boys to show they are smart," I began developing a boys' book club. Its purpose was to improve boys' literacy skills and academic self-esteem. This initiative also included the development of an Internet-based literature circle that allowed participants to write responses to the reading material online. By incorporating technology in the endeavor, I enabled my students to draw upon their existing literacies — and many reluctant readers could find an entry point.

Based on suggestions from the students, I selected a graphic novel for the students to read. The novel allowed for an in-depth analysis of social justice issues, more specifically discrimination and oppression, as well as issues of masculinity. During our weekly lunchtime meetings, the boys could talk about the book in an open-ended, natural conversation setting before working online to complete digital elements on the literature circle structure. The graphic novel selected, the use of a literature circle format, and the engagement of technology together provided an entry point for many of the participants, especially reluctant readers, English language learners, and students with behavioral exceptionalities. By allowing students to read material that appealed to them and to share their ideas with one another in small groups and online, those students who struggled with the classroom language arts program were able to contribute most to the club.

The students began by reading *Satchel Paige, Striking Out Jim Crowe*, a short graphic novel about segregated baseball leagues in the 1930s, both independently and as a group. Each student had access to a copy of the text and was encouraged to read daily at his own pace. At our first meeting we began a shared reading of the text and continued until we had finished the novel as a group. Despite many of the students having finished reading independently, all of the participants were eager to read aloud during our group meetings. Having read the text on their own, the students had greater confidence so actively participated in reading aloud to the group. While reading in our group, I asked knowledge and comprehension questions, but focused more on higher order thinking questions that were largely guided by the students and allowed them to make connections while urging them to delve deeper. My role in our group meetings was largely that of a facilitator, guiding the students' questions, scaffolding them towards a deeper level of understanding.

After we completed reading the novel as a group, we began meeting in the computer lab. There, students responded to online questions on a website that incorporated elements of a literature circle. As students posted their responses online, other participants read and commented on their peers' work, asking further questions and building upon an exchange of ideas. While working together as a group in the computer lab facilitated a shared writing activity, students were also encouraged to make contributions to the site and post responses independently throughout the week.

During this time I continued in my role as facilitator and asked questions that further promoted their thinking. An electronic conversation ensued with all of the students sharing their responses to the text.

"Ain't no man can avoid being born average, but there ain't no man got to be common."
— Satchel Paige

What do you think Satchel Paige meant when he said this? Why do you think he said it?

Student A: I think what Satchel Paige meant was you can't control if you're born black or white. You also can't control your fate. We can control racism in society. It really doesn't matter if you're black or white. What matters are the person's behavior, characteristics and the inside.

Student B: That every person is special. Everyone is unique.

Student C: What Satchel Paige is trying to say is it doesn't matter what colour you are you have a right for everything. If everybody was born average anyone can make a difference. Any person black or white can make a difference in this world, just like Satchel Paige.

Teacher: I agree with you, C.

Student D: I think that I agree with A, but A, you should also think on what and how they act, as well.

Student D: Oh, and my answer to this question is that no one can stop from how they look on the outside, but then again no person looks the same.

Student A: Thank you, D, for your opinion. I really appreciate it.

Student D: You're welcome, A. But your point really was good.

Teacher: If we are all born average, then it is indeed our actions that can make us great. How does this theme play out in the book? How does it apply to Satchel Paige? to Emmett? Both men are in different positions. How do their actions make them great?

Student D: Well, the people in the book are mostly all different in colour, gender, action, and other visual appearances. Only the Jenkins twins are similar in their appearance. Satchel Paige is tall, tries to be humorous, and he is an excellent pitcher of the black people. Emmet is another excellent baseball player. He is a bit aggressive in the games and he can't play ball anymore because he was hit by the ball in one game. He is also black. They are both different and are good at baseball and other things in their own way. Both of them are great because they played baseball in their best position and they tried their best to be the best. They put all their effort in baseball and try to do things that others don't do like Emmet going for Paige's speed ball. They are both strong headed and determined. That's why they are great and others aren't as great as them.

At this point the students had responded to the original text by sharing their initial reactions and interpretations, but more significantly, were also beginning to identify and engage with some of the themes raised in the novel. They began making connections to their own prior knowledge and background experiences.

Teacher: Do both characters respond to racism in society in the same way?

Student A: No, I don't think so. This is because Satchel Paige responds to it by being humorous or not caring about it much. Emmet on the other hand responds defensively and takes it as a huge insult. I think that what Emmet does is giving satisfaction to some of the whites because he gets angry. But Satchel Paige's actions make them frustrated because he doesn't seem to care. But I think in their minds they each are hurt by the racism. So no, they both don't respond to racism in society in the same way.

Student E: Not exactly. Both Emmet and Satchel Paige respond to racism differently. For example, Emmet bursts out in anger at racism and easily becomes upset and frustrated. On the other hand, Satchel Paige ignores the insults that people give him and does not respond making the insulter quite angry like A said.

After students responded to the novel and began asking one another deeper questions, I began basing my questions upon the themes they were exploring. The students quickly made connections of their own and continued to expand their ideas, facilitating a dialogue about the intersections of race and gender.

Teacher: Lets also think about how our culture or society expects men to behave. What is considered "male" behavior? How do Emmet and/or Satchel Paige challenge what it means to "act like a man" (especially when confronting their enemies)? What connections can you make to situations in your life when boys are expected to behave a certain way (especially in school)?

Student D: I think that Emmet responds like that because he is afraid that the Jennings twins might beat up another person in his family or himself. So he wants safety for his family as well as his son. So he tries his best to restrain his anger. So the Jennings twins are again using fear to control people. I think that "male" behavior is something like everyone does things for the benefit of themselves more than others. Or that you act manly and take every deserved blow and problem that is in your way. I think that the main reason Emmet and Satchel Paige challenge what it means to act like a man because of their colour. So they get an abnormal amount of situations they don't take up. They just either make their enemies angry or make themselves in danger. Well kind of. Well, at school we have the Jump Rope for Heart contest coming up. Most people don't expect boys to be any good at skipping. But some boys are good at it. But the boys are expected to like hockey, soccer etc. Not that I'm dissing those sports, but sometimes I find it hard to do sports that are unusual for a boy. So yes, I can connect to situations that happen in real life with this situation.

Student A: Why do you think that people give each other roles and expectations such as "acting like a man"?

Teacher: Who gives people roles and expectations? Where do ideas like "acting like a man" come from? Are the categories "man/woman," "male/female" natural, or do society and culture create them?

Student A: I think people who give roles and expectations in the story were usually the white people. This is because they usually formed the Us group and held the thought that men were stronger and therefore more useful than women. So men were given more respect and reverence than woman. I think that the idea "acting like a man" comes from the way people are viewed. Women were viewed with less respect than men because they always did the household chores while men went out hunting or trading, et cetera. So most people think that that is what men should do, not women. That's how all this "acting like a man" role started. I think that the categories "man/woman," "male/female" are kind of half natural and half created. This is because it seems only right to separate humans into 2 groups, one feminine and the other masculine than just one group of humans. But I also think that the separations also by society and culture to show that males/females are different. I also just found some strange connection. It also seems to be created by religion. This is because most of the white people, the Us group, seem to be Christian. I'm also Christian and in the bible it says that women were created from a rib of a man. It is strange to see that the word "male" and "man" is the root word of "female" and "woman." So just like man helped to create woman, the word for man helps create the word for woman. Therefore it's natural, and society and religion create the categories.

After reading and reflecting on the comments the students were making both in our group meetings and online, I decided to take the endeavor a step further: to encourage the students to explore the interconnected nature of oppression, discrimination, and power. While the first novel focused on racial discrimination, the students' responses prompted me to introduce an appropriate excerpt from another graphic novel by the same author, *James Sturm's America: God, Gold and Golems.* This excerpt was about a Jewish baseball team during the Depression in the United States. Once the students responded to it, I introduced a newspaper article about the racially motivated riots during a 1939 baseball game at Christie Pitts Park in Toronto. After reading this short piece both on their own and as a group, following the same structure used initially, students were encouraged to make further connections on a more immediate, localized level. By comparing the three texts they had read, students could begin to evaluate thematic elements as well as their own ideas.

Online conversation continued.

Student D: Firstly, the obvious is that each story has a baseball game in it. Secondly, each of the stories talks about fear used to control people. Like for example in the Satchel Paige book, the Jennings twins used fear of being lynched as a way to control people. In the Zion Lion booklet piece it shows that the Jews are being scared and bullied so that they won't win the match. The Jews were attacked by the Torontonian hypocrites. They were made to fear the Torontonians and the Torontonians could have had power over them to make them leave. And lastly as A mentioned, there is deep racism going on, as well. But in Satchel Paige it was between blacks and whites. In the other two it is between Jews and Gentiles. So these are the connections I found.

Student A: Here's a question. How would you feel if you were part of the Jewish people in the article? Why or why not? Would you be ashamed of being a Jew? (This was especially built for you, C.)

Teacher: Now I'd like you to consider the three pieces that we read: *Satchel Paige,* the Zion Lion piece, and the article about the Christie Pitts riots. Think about all of the insightful ideas that you have shared about discrimination, power, and the process of creating an "Us" and "Them" way of thinking. How are different types of discrimination connected? Why is it important to keep this (the interconnectedness of discrimination) in mind? If we know this, what can we do to deal with problems of racism, gender-based discrimination, classism, et cetera?

Student A: I would feel angry because just because you are a different religion doesn't mean you are another type of creature. No matter how many different religions there are, we're all the same. That's why I wouldn't be ashamed if I was a Jew in the Christie Pitts riots.

Student D: Whoa, A! I agree with you no doubt on the religion part. I also agree with the unashamed part of what you wrote. I think that discriminations connect by the abusive way they are used. The time it is used can also connect them. This is because they are all linked with their similarities. Like what each discrimination is pointing particularly at. But then again, that is a difference between the discriminations. So they could be connected by their differences. And I think that it is important to keep the connections in mind because these connections can help us understand each discrimination that is said. I can't explain more than that. It's a bit complex in my head. We can deal with the problem by raising awareness of the full meaning of the discriminations. We can also encourage the class or families et cetera to not discriminate.

Teacher: Why do you think I chose these stories or articles on discrimination rather than another type of story?

Student D: I think that you chose those stories/articles on discrimination because of 2 reasons. One, it was black history month and two, there were some conflicts you saw that made you choose these reading passages. In studying these stories I learned that discrimination comes in many forms. But it mostly comes from forms inside (thought and feelings, et cetera) than physical forms. Another reason for question 1 has come to me. I also think that you chose these stories/articles on discrimination because of things happening around the world and what we studied in class. It is important to think about the issues of discrimination and unequal distributions of power in our society so that I may help them or spread the news for others to hear or remember more suffering people around the world to help me in hardships that I encounter in my life.

Through the course of our collaborative weekly meetings, twice weekly in the last four weeks of the project, the students came to demonstrate a deep understanding of the nature of oppression and discrimination. While the subject matter was indeed complex, they were able to articulate connections between the texts we studied, current events, and most significantly, their own lives.

The initial theme of racial discrimination was familiar to them and easily identifiable, but other forms of discrimination were not. When we first talked about other forms, particularly issues of gender-based discrimination, many of the students were unable to draw parallels. In my first conversations with this group of students, many were unable to recognize the interconnectedness of oppression and discrimination (many adults are also unable to make such connections).

During our final group meeting, students took their deep understanding further. We engaged in a discussion about some of the major issues that arose during the project. Students revealed an awareness of the process of "othering" that perpetuates oppression and likened it to the power dynamics between students at their own school when rumors are started: "Discrimination happens because the people who are part of the 'Us' group have more power and decide what is 'wrong' and create a group of 'Them.'"

4

Deepening Understanding through Graphic Texts

The last few years have seen the rise in texts that are visually based, and the art of the graphic book has dominated the publishing industry for young people. The concept of the graphic novel is conveyed through two separate terms: *novel* and *graphic*. The *Oxford English Dictionary*, for example, defines a novel as "a fictitious prose narrative or tale of considerable length . . . in which characters and actions representative of the real life of past or present time are portrayed in a plot of more or less complexity." The graphic novel is a branch of this literary form, with the addition of the graphic concept — the use of pictures, diagrams, symbols, and so forth to support and enhance text. In other words, it is a stand-alone narrative presented through text and pictures. Like a literary novel, it may deal with a complex plot, varied characters and settings, and multifarious subject matters — serious or light, appropriate for adults or young people. And like text-only novels, graphic novels come in various genres, superhero, romance, historical fiction, fantasy, science fiction, manga (Japanese graphic novels), and more. Graphic novels are closely related to comics, another form of printed work in which thematic and cohesive stories are told with the fusion of sequential picture-frames and written text. Because of this apparent similarity, the two genres are often confused with one another; however, they are distinct.

Students can learn about how graphic novels work through reading a variety of texts and through composing frames of visuals and words. They can do the latter as responses to what they have read or as original compositions.

The selections in this chapter are taken from classroom experiences by teachers who work with graphic texts alongside print-only texts to support students in meaning making with narrative, both fiction and non-fiction. Terry Thompson outlines his reasons for his using these text forms with his students and presents a mini-description of the components that make up this new form of text. Stephanie Tan found computer programs that enabled her students to construct their own graphic texts, supporting her curriculum initiatives on character development. Brian Okamoto, working with Larry Swartz, incorporated role playing as a response to a shared community novel, which acted as stimulus for graphic retelling. The students in Ernest Agbuya's class researched Greek mythic heroes, retold their exploits on chart paper, and then created graphic texts. These narratives involved reading, retelling, representing, and designing images and texts — students dug deeply into story to visualize their understanding.

Graphic Texts: More Than Meets the Eye

BY TERRY THOMPSON

Comic books and graphic novels have taken the field of children's literature by storm and, while doing so, have established themselves as a medium that is not just alluring, but educationally valuable. Clearly no longer the literary ogre that naysayers of yesteryear would have had us believe, these graphic texts present a wide range of opportunities to support comprehension instruction.

Any challengers of comics and graphic novels would be hard pressed to debate the research that shows the educational value of the medium; they would be even harder pressed to argue that there are no appropriate titles for our younger readers.

Despite this — and the fact that our students take to graphic texts with incredible fervor — many teachers are left wondering what to do with this popular format. You see, knowing that graphic texts are popular is one thing, but savvy teachers also want to know how they can take advantage of their influence to support comprehension instruction. In essence, this question concerns mining the potential lurking within a text form that speaks to readers the way graphic texts do. Luckily, the answers are plentiful.

As the pictures and the words work interdependently, they convey the gist of graphic texts. Here, the pictures share power with the text in that they help support and hold the meaning. Readers can't just look at the pictures or read the words for graphic texts to make sense. They *have* to do both. With this relationship strongly in place, the illustrative nature of the medium acts as a visual representation of comprehension strategies in a way that traditional texts cannot. In a nutshell, graphic texts make the unseen, in-the-head components of comprehension visible. They thereby offer new ways to fortify comprehension strategy instruction.

We notice this when readers get past difficult vocabulary words in graphic texts because the words are illustrated in panels right in front of them. A few years ago, I was working with a group of fourth graders, and we were reading a graphic novel about westward expansion in the United States. When we reached the part where some Native Americans were preparing to attack a settlement, I was surprised to find that none of the group members knew what a fort was. While we were discussing this, one reader noticed a clue — a drawing of a fort in the background of the panel — and within seconds, the entire group had a symbolic representation of what we mean by the word "fort." In this way, the picture offered the group the support needed to learn a new word. I used this experience to lead the group in a small discussion about using context clues in traditional texts. The illustration of fort made the concept easier to teach and gave the group a scaffold for understanding what it means to search for clues to understand new words.

Consider the importance that understanding dialogue plays in comprehending texts. Struggling readers often get confused while navigating dialogue in traditional texts and quickly lose the meaning. But graphic novels and comic books offer a visual model of this often difficult-to-understand component of reading comprehension. Who is speaking and what the character is saying are represented with speech bubbles, so there's little confusion for struggling readers. Additionally, the artful nature of graphic texts shows readers

- how the character is feeling when speaking (through actions and facial expressions)
- what words he or she emphasizes when speaking (shown through italicized and bolded words within the speech bubble)
- how the character says what he or she says (through the shape and size of the speech bubble and lettering)

Beyond such clear depictions of character discourse, this visible format can free up readers to attend to and practise working with the often invisible nuances of dialogue, thereby giving them space and support enough to gain some confidence in navigating the ins and outs of the ways characters communicate within texts.

But graphic texts can do more than represent words for learning new vocabulary and visibly support readers in understanding dialogue. Deeper comprehension components, such as visualizing, determining importance, and monitoring meaning, are visibly represented as well. For instance, many of our readers continually struggle to create mental pictures as they are reading. In such cases, we can use graphic texts to model effective visualization strategies. As we direct their attention to the way comics and graphic novels depict images from text, student readers can be encouraged to mimic these processes in their minds. In this way, graphic texts can represent a concrete example of what good readers do in their heads when visualizing.

Consider the components of a strong mental image. Effective readers add as much detail as possible to their mental images to help deepen their understanding of texts. They use sensory representations (sight, sound, and so forth) as well as depictions of action and mood. By design, the artwork in comics and graphic novels offers visible examples of these same representations:

- sight: displayed through well-illustrated, detailed scenes, and focused panels
- sound: heard through onomatopoeic words and explosive word art
- touch: depicted through shaded and textured, almost life-like drawings that make you feel like you can reach out and touch them
- action: illustrated through artful drawings as well as character responses, activities, and movement
- mood: represented through coloring, shading, facial expressions, layout of the panel, direction of the reader's viewpoint, and zooming in or out on particular aspects of the characters or scene

Once students have learned to attend to the various ways graphic texts exemplify how images coordinate with texts, encourage them to do something similar in their mind's eye as they are reading. During a conference with a reader working on creating stronger mental images, consider asking questions such as these:

- How would that paragraph you just read look if it were in a panel in a comic book?
- What characters would need to be included?
- What sound words and word art would you need?
- What type of shading and colors would best represent the mood of the paragraph?
- Who would be talking and what would their faces look like?
- What type of movement would be happening?
- What would be the most important part of the panel? What should stand out?
- What from the text makes you include all of these elements?

Since mental images should constantly change in order to represent the forward movement of the text, you could then discuss several text-based imaginative panels that spring forward from consecutive paragraphs. By allowing use of the visual format of the medium as a support for building stronger mental images, you can capitalize on the illustrations in graphic texts.

One major strategy effective readers use in order to deepen their comprehension is determining importance, and comics and graphic novels can offer instructional support in this area. Just as they do in traditional texts, readers must wade through a great deal of extra information in graphic texts while focusing their attention on the most important pieces. The difference here, again, is the visual representation of the meaning afforded through the illustrations in graphic texts.

Even though much is happening in each panel, most of it is pictorial, making the wading more manageable — especially for readers who get "lost in the words" of traditional texts. Often, artists use skill and style to depict a panel in such a way that it forces the reader to sit up and take notice of its important components. It's almost as if that component is saying: "Hey! Look over here! I'm important!"

I often ask small groups to look at a panel in a selection and come to a consensus about the one thing — picture or text — that is the most important. I lead with questions such as these:

- What's the most important thing happening in this panel? What from the text makes you think that?
- What do you think the illustrator wanted you to really notice? What makes you say that?
- Are there some things in this panel that are less important than others?
- What's interesting to you in this panel? Is it important too or just interesting? How can you tell or decide?

The conversations this activity stimulates are always interesting.

From there, we quickly move on to looking at an entire page of panels while choosing the three most important occurrences on the page. Here, the discussion is what's important as students learn to fine-tune their focus to glean the most intricate aspects of the meaning. This freedom to move about the pictures while sharpening their ability to determine importance is valuable: it can serve as a set of training wheels as students move to do the same thing in traditional text. Readers eventually transfer this skill. They allow previous graphic text–based discussions to act as scaffolds as they think through the most important occurrence in a single paragraph (or the three most important happenings on a page).

When it comes to determining importance in graphic texts, readers have an extra level of help. Appearing within the panels, narrative boxes are rectangular text boxes that serve to narrate graphic texts, and through this role, act as another indicator of importance. Narrative boxes alert readers when something in the text's meaning is being introduced, is changing, or needs to be adjusted. They can signify

- changes in the setting
- transitions within the story line
- important details to the development of the meaning

- the main idea of the panel (or series of panels)
- the introduction of new characters
- a summarization of a panel (or series of panels)These are just a few ways that graphic texts utilize narrative boxes to support readers in understanding what's most important.

As readers gain confidence in the way narrative boxes focus their attention, follow-up activities might include reading a paragraph in a traditional text and asking, "If you had to write a narrative box for that paragraph, what would it need to say?"

Use of speech bubbles: From *The First Emperor* (Timeline series, Rubicon Publishers, pages 8–9)

Exploring Character Development through Graphic Novels

BY STEPHANIE TAN

During my senior years in high school, I witnessed the introduction of character education to schools. While communities have always believed in the nurturing of good character, the new Character Matters! program seemed to really put character education on the map. Despite this new push, however, my sole experience with it was in a number of street signs posted in the school hallways. Whether it was Empathy Avenue or Respect Boulevard, it did not result in the development of character in students in any novel way.

My return to elementary school as a beginning teacher presented me with the opportunity to expand on my experience with character education. During a month-long internship, I was fortunate to be in a school equipped with an excellent library that included an extensive computer lab. A well-frequented hub in the school, the library and computer lab provided several opportunities for students to broaden their learning. Among the cutting edge resources, interactive SMART Boards and iMac computers were gradually being integrated into the classrooms.

Faced with abundant resources, I considered ways to explore character education while making use of the new computer technology. A positive experience in teaching and creating graphic texts by hand with a Grade 3 class inspired me to add graphic texts to the mix with computers and character education. The students — particularly the boys in the class — had received the opportunity to read and create graphic texts with great enthusiasm. This experience confirmed for me the growing popularity of graphic texts among students. I was astonished by the degree of analysis that students shared when interpreting the graphic texts.

With these three components in mind — computers, character, and comics — I placed a morning announcement calling all junior students interested in one, two, or all three of the Cs to attend the first meeting of the Triple C Club during recess. The club would operate as an extra-curricular activity where participating students would transform children's storybooks about character into the form of comics.

The turnout was interesting and became more so when the students were asked to introduce themselves, as well as state which of the three Cs had caught their attention and inspired them to join the club. Of the seven girls present, the majority asserted that they were interested in the character component of the club. A few girls also said that they wanted to explore the computers component. *All* 12 boys claimed that both the comics and the computers had sparked their interest. This was especially apparent during a later analysis of graphic texts, where the boys were eager to share their knowledge of graphic text features with the rest of the group.

During this first meeting, the Triple C Club discussed what character education was and why it was important. Students learned that the objective of the club would be to use computers to create comic versions of storybooks about character. They discovered that they would be using the new iMac computers and Comic Life software to comicify themselves as characters in their storybooks. After I read a storybook about courage to the students, we discussed the appearance (or initial lack) of courage in the story. I modelled to the students how to pick out the critical events in a book to create a storyboard. The students spent the remainder of the first meeting browsing through a selection of books that dealt with at least one of the 12 character traits from Character Matters! Once students had identified a book they enjoyed, they formed groups of three and reread the book to pick out the character traits and discuss how they appeared within the story. I provided a storyboard template for each group to use, and, with assistance, they proceeded to storyboard the events in their respective stories.

While storyboarding, students were encouraged to think about how to break down the narration and dialogue in their stories to present both in a comic format. In doing so, students considered how they might use thought and speech bubbles, captions, as well as symbols for sound effects, to convey characters' thoughts, words, and actions. Over the course of one week, groups of students met in the library during their lunch recesses to work on their pencil-and-paper storyboards.

To kick off the Triple C Club's second week and introduce students to the computer technology they would be using, I designed a lesson for the SMART Board using SMART Notebook software. The students actively took part in a series of activities that required them to learn about and apply their knowledge of graphic text features on the interactive SMART Board. I then demonstrated to the students how to use the Comic Life software on the iMac computer.

A mini-lesson on drama resulted in students portraying a variety of emotions and facial expressions. They were encouraged to consider how they might convey the character traits and feelings when taking pictures for their comics. After seeing the variety of features available on the iMac computer, as well as their comicified selves, the groups were eager to book the computers and digital cameras so that they could create their storyboards on the computer.

Three of the six groups began working on the iMac computers right away, while the three groups still working on their storyboards became eager to finish so that they could start working on the computers. It became clear that the requirement for groups to complete their pencil-and-paper storyboards *before* proceeding to the computer was a necessary step. Having a completed storyboard where they had taken time to visualize how their story might be laid out as a comic helped the groups to guide the development of their comic on the computer. I strongly suspect that had the storyboards been omitted from the process or partially completed, students may have lost sight of the literacy and character elements in the excitement of the new iMac computer and Comic Life software.

Groups began their comics by taking photographs and comicifying them using various filters available on Comic Life. In addition to digital cameras, students could use Photobooth software and an iCapture feature within Comic Life to take pictures. Students varied the means with which they took photographs to capture different perspectives within their stories. To complement the pictures, they added speech balloons, thought bubbles, captions, and sound effects to their comics.

Although most groups were excited to get started by taking photographs, one group of boys came to me with the concern that the time and effort spent on finishing their storyboard had all been for naught. The boys had created their storyboard for a picture book titled *Leonardo's Dream* (by Hans de Beer). A number of the books I had included in the character books that students chose from were based on animal main characters. These were purposefully selected to encourage students to focus on the character trait within a story and consider how to portray the story and character trait among humans. The protagonist of *Leonardo's Dream* was a penguin. I asked the boys to retell the story to me in their own words, as well as tell me what character traits they thought were important in the story.

I then asked the boys to think about how a similar pattern of events might occur in the schoolyard. Building on their recess football games, the boys decided to modify the story so that it would focus on a boy who was made fun of by his peers because he was unable to throw a spiral. In addition to creating a comic about perseverance, the group tackled issues of bullying.

Groups underwent an editing process with me and another teacher once they had turned their stories into comics on Comic Life. In addition to editing spelling and grammar, conferences focused on improving the graphic text features and highlighting character traits in the story. The groups also completed a page at the end of their comic where they reflected on the character traits present in the story. Some students commented on the actions of characters, while others reflected on why certain character traits were important.

At the end of the one-month internship, the Triple C Club showcased the finished comics at a Triple C Celebration. With fellow Triple C Club members, teachers, and the principal and vice-principal as their audience, groups drew on their presentation skills and provided an excellent dramatization of their comics. The students also provided a thorough commentary on the character traits appearing in their stories, as well as their importance. The celebration was the perfect summation to the one month of hard work that these students had put into creating their comics about character traits.

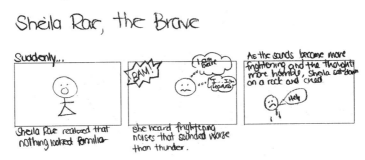

Sharing a Community Novel

BY BRIAN OKAMOTO

The novel *Home of the Brave*, written by Katherine Applegate, tells the story of Kek, an African refugee who arrives in Minnesota to live with his aunt and cousin. A fifth-grade student, Kek is suddenly confronted by many strange things in school and in the farmland community. Kek longs to be reunited with his mother and awaits her arrival in the United States. Until then, he is comforted by new friendships and finds strength in his memories. A sense of responsibility is developed as Kek takes care of a cow which he names "Gol," meaning family in his African language. This novel is written in free verse style, with chapters no longer than four pages. Working with Larry Swartz as a consultant, we gave each student in my Grade 4/5 class a copy of the book to read.

We worked together to help the students look closer and closer at the text through activities that focused them on the poetic language used by the author, the character relationships, and the complexity of being a stranger in a new land.

Phase One: Introducing the novel

To begin, we invited the students to examine the cover of the book and through discussion, we prompted them to consider the illustration and offer speculations about why Kek would put his head against a cow. Students also offered thoughts about the story setting, and some made connections by sharing their experiences of having lived in or visited a similar farmyard and field.

We next drew attention to a chapter, "Old Words, New Words," where Kek is met by the "helping man" from the Refugee Resettlement Centre. To identify main ideas and to help examine Applegate's style and language, we asked the students to share information learned about Kek from reading the chapter's two pages.

Each student was then asked to randomly select one chapter of the book and read it independently. The students were used to the talk-and-turn activity and knew how to share their initial responses. They chatted with one or two friends seated nearby, reporting what they had learned about Kek by reading a single chapter. In this way, students identified key pieces of information and at this stage were mostly offering literal interpretations.

To move them further in their understanding of the main character, the strategy Role on the Wall was then introduced to the students. For this drama technique, a character's role is represented in picture form or diagram and displayed on a chart "on the wall." We asked students to offer any words that they would use to describe this young African refugee and to find evidence from the text that would support their choices (e.g., curious, confused, worried). Each contribution was recorded inside the Role on the Wall diagram.

This activity provided students with a distanced, reflective way of building a deep understanding of a character or role. Students could add new words to the diagram or revise their original descriptions as they learned more about a character's behavior or actions from reading the novel. As a final activity, we asked students to brainstorm any questions they had about Kek. These were recorded outside the diagram (e.g., What is going to be the hardest thing for Kek to adjust to in Minnesota? How can a cow make Kek feel better?).

Phase Two: Dramatizing the novel

In a second session, the students explored the book through drama. We arranged the students in groups to create an improvisation that would show an important scene in Kek's life. To plan for the activity, students needed to recall and retell important story events. Students worked together to negotiate ideas and plan their work. After practice time, they shared their improvisations.

Each student revisited the chapter that he or she had read and was invited to consider one short passage that best seemed to tell something about Kek from his point of view. After rehearsing ways to read their lines out loud, each student in turn read a one- or two-sentence excerpt: "I try some English but my mouth just wants to chew the words and spit them on the ground." "I pause, as a memory pokes at me like a knife in my back." Since the novel is written in the first person, the out loud snippets that the students shared provided a collective voice of the young African boy. We proceeded through the novel chronologically.

Phase Three: Transforming the novel into a graphic text

We worked together to help the students identify the text features of a graphic page from the graphic novel *Bone*, by Jeff Smith, which was familiar to many students. This page served as a model for considering how verbal and visual text work together to tell a story and provide information.

We explained to the students that they were going to collaboratively create a graphic novel of *Home of the Brave*. They couldn't do the whole novel, we agreed, but choosing scenes from throughout the book would allow them to highlight a range of important events and scenes that would depict Kek's life in the United States. Each student would be responsible for contributing one page of comic layout, using the words, conversations, and descriptions featured in one chapter of the book. Students were given the choice of a four-panel or six-panel template to create their comic strip page.

The students prepared drafts of their work. As we observed them, we recognized the careful attention they were paying to the dialogue as written by the author. The activity also prompted a meaningful way not only to promote visualization, but to summarize and synthesize information: students were restricted to four or six frames.

Each student prepared a final copy of graphic text. These pages were arranged in chronological order and collected into a class publication: *Home of the Brave: The Graphic Novel*. On the final day of school, the students were each given a photocopy of the publication.

Tales from Mount Olympus

ERNEST AGBUYA

The idea to have my Grade 5 students create their own graphic novels came from a need for an interesting way to introduce a third term unit on comparative mythology. I knew we would be starting with the 12 Olympians, the main gods and goddesses in Greek mythology. The question was, how could I bring them to life for the class?

Luckily, my student teacher, Marissa Cheskey, had introduced a short unit on inferring through graphic novels in her last week. She had also been teaching the word "characteristics," which she used in different subject areas. (Examples: What are some characteristics of liquids, solids, and gases? What are some characteristics of graphic novels?) I decided to build on the momentum she had created by doing a mini-unit in which students would show the characteristics of one of the 12 Olympians in graphic novel form.

As part of the introduction to Greek mythology, I encouraged my students to find books and use the classroom computer to learn something about the 12 Olympians. When it came time to choose one, they could then make an informed choice. There would be two students for each god or goddess; some groups were made up of two or three ELLs (English Language Learners) as well as struggling readers. Using stories from *D'Aulaire's Book of Greek Myths* by Ingri D'Aulaire, I listed each god or goddess on a piece of chart paper and let the class know that the stories about them appeared in order of length and difficulty. Students chose their texts accordingly and received copies of them.

Students read their texts and then created wordless retellings on chart paper. This activity forced them to think of the stories in terms of visual events. At this point they did not know they would be doing graphic novels. With my open-ended instructions they took a variety of approaches, including flow charts, pictograms, and maps.

I prepared transparencies of various graphic novels, ranging from traditional *Archie* ones to more modern Japanese manga. Looking at them one at a time over a couple of weeks, we made a list of graphic novel elements (e.g., speech bubbles, thought clouds, frames, and sound effects), while also discovering what made each one unique in style. These were ideas they would bring to their own graphic novels.

While learning about the characteristics of graphic novels, students created storyboards of their stories, again without words. Working in pairs, they used their inference skills to try to tell their partner's story based on the pictures. In this workshop, students would ask for clarification and offer advice to sharpen the visual impact. By this point, students could identify parts in which pictures alone could not tell the whole story. This discovery led to a series of workshops and discussions in which we decided that, with graphic novels, the narrative was told first through pictures, next with dialogue (or thoughts), and finally with narration (but only as a last resort).

With this order in mind, they created a draft that combined visual and text. Again, mini-lessons were given on writing effective dialogue (to move the story forward and to provide back story) and recognizing narrative redundancies. There was a lot of peer sharing, with students enjoying the task of spotting unnecessary narration or asking questions to draw out missing information.

During the whole process, students read about and discussed the gods and goddesses that their classmates were exploring. Circulating around the class, I was able to gauge from their informal discussions who was developing a large store of Greek mythology knowledge and who needed a good book or website recommendation. Overall, they learned much about the 12 Olympians. One ELL/LD student who loved to learn through drawing was able to tell the story of Hephaestus and explain the detailed pictures she made. Another student, a reluctant reader, became so engrossed in mythology that he began to visit the public library to feed his new appetite for these ancient Greek stories.

In the last two weeks of the month-long project, students completed their work independently. I had given them many lessons on the visual aspects of graphic novels. They worked armed with pencils, fine markers, a poster-sized paper, and a detailed checklist. By this point, assessments covering reading, writing, art, and social studies were mostly done.

As the final products came in, I realized what an enriched unit the students had had. Some who struggled with reading for detail were now explaining mythology to teachers and peers admiring their work on the hallway bulletin boards. Still others who typically rushed through their work were asking for extensions because they were losing themselves in the construction of subtle layers of meaning so inherent in graphic novels.

In the end, most had produced their best work of the year. One Grade 2 teacher took her class to our bulletin board and completed an art lesson in the hallway. Students from other classes would stop to read the stories on their way to lunch. Four of the graphic novels were elected by the class to be framed for permanent display in the school collection.

5

Deepening Understanding through Text Sets

A *text set* is a collection of types of texts that have some connection to one another. There can be any number of them in the set. *Text* can be defined as a book, an article, a poem, a movie, a video, a chapter, a piece of music, a sermon, a sign — something that communicates and holds meaning.

Texts become connected through themes, topics, issues, genres, author or illustrator, story structure, historical time frame, receipt of a certain award, or status as curriculum resources. Texts can also be connected by their raising the same question or answering a question, providing different versions of the same tale, or presenting similar characters or similar settings. Different individuals will see different connections.

Multiple texts inform each other, and we grow from the interconnections as one idea builds on another to develop a wider and wiser world picture. The texts treat similar themes with varied perspectives, with different styles and points of view; they can offer new facts and details.

A text set will mean something unique to every reader during each reading or rereading. Time, place, and experience are some of the things that alter our perspective taking and meaning making. If a group of people responds to a text or a text set, the richness of the construction of meaning is enhanced exponentially.

Think of all the diverse and language-rich resources we could find to fill our classrooms: some we can use as read-aloud material; some will work well for demonstrating a particular point; some will be part of the language play that brightens our community time; some will be effective as the shared text for our small group time; some will support independent reading; some will act as models for the students' own writing; and some will be there to strengthen our resolve as literacy teachers.

Two articles discuss aspects of text sets here. Linda Cameron explores the texts that have been constructed around the iconic portrayal of the wolf in literature and reveals how the intertextuality of these texts would deepen and challenge any class's experience with this theme. Corey Follett begins his unit with a shared novel and then extends the students' backgrounds with downloaded articles from a variety of websites about women in Afghanistan. His inquiry moves into an examination of social justice. These educators have taken their students far beyond the limits of a single text for all.

Exploring a Theme: When Different Wolves Enter Our Literacy Forest

BY LINDA CAMERON

Once upon a time there were three little pigs, and in another part of the world, a little girl with a red cape was going to visit her grandmother. . . . There was, in both instances, a wolf.

In each of these stories — and hundreds of others around the world — we recognize the wolf as the serious and dangerous antagonist. Wolf's proper name is Canis Lupus and he (or she) belongs to a formerly large group — a culture, you might say, a race perhaps — which has met its demise as the result of the power of literature and a few stolen lunches.

Once in a Grade 5 classroom, a student named Hamid shared with the class some questions about wolves. His inquiry was stirred by the novel he was reading about a wolf that was "neither big nor bad" but "powerful in a positive way." Classmates were eager to hear about this wolf hero and began to wonder together why they were convinced that wolves were dark characters with an evil persona. We decided to follow this up by exploring a text set of books, websites, movies, selected interviews with experts, as well as searches of newspapers and magazines, to see whether Canis Lupus deserved this wicked, sinister reputation.

Quite possibly, B.B. Wolf is a good example of what can happen if we don't critically examine literature. Is there power and potential to develop, disrupt, distort, and destroy identity through literature? Ed Young dedicated *Lon Po Po* to all the wolves of the world, saying:

> To all the wolves of the world
> for lending their good name
> as a tangible symbol
> for our darkness

We began our investigation by working in small groups, discussing and recording on large chart paper everything we think of when we say "wolf" or "wolfness." There was an enthusiastic hum as the ideas blurted out, sometimes with stories, sometimes with giggles, ofttimes with excitement. We noted that Canis Lupus (the kids loved this fancy name) has relatives in as many countries as the children in the class. "There are wolves everywhere!" None of us had really encountered one except in a zoo. "There are dogs that are in the same family!" "Are coyotes the same as wolves? We have

heard them at the cottage." "Are wolves bigger than foxes?" "I have heard that boys who flirt with girls are called wolves . . . yes, there are wolf whistles!"

After about five minutes, the groups left their charts and each moved to another group's graffiti chart paper, read their notations, and added their ideas, some triggered by the suggestions on the page. After another five minutes, they moved to the next table and repeated the process. When they finished, they went back to the paper they had started, and with markers, classified the information in order to report their findings and the questions for further investigation.

Facts, fiction, fears, and foolishness, characteristics, fairy tales, food, enemies and friends, famous sayings . . . , the categories and questions were many.

How would you define "wolfness"?

"Big, bad wolf" wins without contest when kids begin to brainstorm their responses. Fairy tales, folk tales, and folklore are the predominant informants. Once the big teeth, big eyes, and big mouth are presented, the list goes on to describe with uncertainty the characteristics of the wolf. Few facts are known. Confusions exist between the wolf and the fox. Is there more than one kind of wolf? Where do wolves live other than in the forest near Red Riding Hood's grandmother or in the three little pigs' neighborhood in North America and Europe? Do they live in Africa and if so, where? The wolves there seem to be just as questionable citizens.

As brainstorming continues, questions quickly follow suggestions with an "I think" or "I've heard," and wondering begins when we stop to interrogate our assumptions — going deeper. Adjectives, when analyzed, are long on the derogatory and short on positive attributes. Wicked, big and bad, sly, mean, manipulative, cunning, deceitful, treacherous, hungry — all wolves are hungry, aren't they? — child molesting, sneaky, unstoppable, villainous, howling . . . are but a few of the most common.

Is wolf deserving of such scandalous international and historical incrimination? Power seems to shift and be exercised among characters from domination to agency with the wolf generally acting as the aggressor, but ending up as the duped and victimized. The reputation of big and bad remains, however.

Jack Zipes (1983) suggests that "the essence of our lives has been prescribed and circumscribed by common cultural discourses and filled with artifacts that we can never really bypass." It is striking how indelible the impressions on our imaginations and our psyche, our behaviors and our attitudes that fairy tales and folk tales make. Fairy tales were used in the 17th century to civilize children and their "discourse on manners and norms has contributed more to the creation of social norms than we realize" (Zipes 1983, xi). It seems that the power and potential of story has gone far beyond making children mind their manners and into the realm of forming fundamental beliefs and attitudes, prejudices and opinions, knowledge base, and philosophy. What first came into your mind when you thought "wolf"?

If we consider one tale that has survived for over 300 years, being retold around the world, being fractured by modern storytellers, and even hitting the silver screen in 2006 (*Hoodwinked*), we must acknowledge that power. Red Riding Hood is but one of hundreds of stories that have starred Canis Lupus and cast him in a role that is evil personified. Why is the wolf in fairy tales always a male — an alpha male at that? What has that done to the male identity?

The children are fascinated and want to dig deeper. One girl read that there are more than 500 versions of Red Riding Hood published around the world and she bustled off with friend in tow to find how many they had in their library. Another started checking this out on the Web. When they came back to report, a young boy declared that the Red Riding Hood story was as old as Adam and Eve — warned, disobeyed, and paid the price! This old and effective structure has built many a story for telling and writing. But back to Canis Lupus.

Maligned, persecuted, and destroyed, Canis Lupus's worst enemy is misunderstanding and misappropriation caused by story and creating the stereotype. Wolves are portrayed as the "bad guys" of fable, myth, and folklore originating in the experiences and stories of medieval Europe. Early Puritan storytelling denounced the wilderness as a heathen sanctuary and accused Canis Lupus of being all things pagan and treacherous to the soul. In the 17th century, Canis Lupus became the devil, depicted as a vile, demented, and immoral beast and therefore necessarily destroyed because, at that time, religious belief was equated with law. Images of the devil had the likeness of Canis Lupus.

The boys got busy at this point and created wild images of the beast, all the while discussing what makes an image look evil — blood dripping here and there won for the most popular trait. This was visual literacy. They were going deeper into how message can be portrayed through the visual media. The talk that emerged as they added features to their monstrous wolves focused on the wicked acts that had happened as a result of these features. Poor Canis Lupus!

The power and persuasion of these pernicious portrayals have persisted through time, perpetuated by stories, the various media, word of mouth, and the lap. The identity of Canis Lupus has been created and perpetuated through illustration and text in folklore, fantasy, and falsities. If only wolves were literate! They might have been able to take appropriate action and counter the accusations. Maybe Jon Scieszka, the author of *The True Story of the Three Little Pigs*, is really a wolf as he claims. If wolves had been exposed to the hundreds of stories about them, how would their sense of identity have been affected?

In 1630, the colony at Massachusetts Bay offered sizable bounties for destroying the wolf, and in the mid-17th century, people were hired to kill wolves, with the highest rates given for the head of a female. Although true that Canis Lupus was guilty of enjoying the delicacy of the odd cow or sheep, nary a human was on their menu. The fear frenzy was perpetuated through gossip, storytelling, preaching, and the press.

The stereotype had shifted along the continuum to prejudice and resulted in the racist slaughtering of Canis Lupus. What are the results of stereotyping? In the case of the wolf, the results are fear, aggression, and destruction. Prejudice with judgment results. With prejudice (a preformed opinion or attitude based on insufficient knowledge, irrational feelings, or inaccurate stereotypes), there emerges racist, bigoted behavior: discrimination.

It is clear that the wolf is a victim.

Drama was the perfect tool to go deeper into this dilemma. Why not put Canis Lupus on trial and see who might testify against him and who might give support? The class was divided in half for the great debate. They were given freedom to use any resource to search for the evidence to support or destroy Canis Lupus. They worked feverishly as they engaged in developing their cases, whispering, plotting, calling in experts, checking out facts, developing more questions. Learning, wondering, problem-solving . . . going deeper and deeper with purpose and power.

Many sources of information, including fine examples of children's literature, present a positive image of the wolf and give Canis Lupus an identity to be proud of. Stories about the admirable family life, the social responsibility of the wolf, the important place the wolf holds in the fragile ecosystem, the high level of intelligence (often maligned in literature), the fact that healthy wolves are not a threat to humans and so on do not refute "big and bad." Incidentally, in the over 30 children interviewed, no one knew for sure how big the wolf really is!

In our exploration of the text set, which included both expository text and fiction, we noted that many of the positive portrayals of Canis Lupus came from aboriginal tales. It would seem that a more fine-grained textured view of the wolf comes as a result of many varied experiences with and knowledge of the wolf who is a citizen sharing their wilderness. In aboriginal tales the authors and illustrators portray wolves as powerful, strong, wild, good as parents, worthy of respect, and able as hunters — creatures to be revered. Much of the world has a more simple stereotype of the wolf and has generalized to the whole genus because of a few terrorists — big and bad wolves, real and fictionalized.

What will it take to disrupt, disprove, dislodge, rebut, or counter this false identity?

Children's literature has the power and potential of working in any of the following ways although, as Rosenblatt (1978) suggests, it "goes on largely below the threshold of awareness."

- **Construction:** It can help the child to construct, create, or build a sense of self — to construct meaning. Through vicarious experiences and feeling or growing with characters through their lived experiences, the child can learn about new feelings, new attitudes, new knowledge. For example, while doing a drama around *The Kapok Tree*, one child sobbed out: "I never thought about these things. Why do humans destroy their world? I am going to help stop this. It is horrible and scary. I can do this!"
- **Connections:** Not until literature connects with us emotionally, intellectually, spiritually, or even physically does any real impact occur. If we see its relevance to our lives and if it is real and meaningful, joining, linking, coherent, and related to us, then deep meaning making occurs. If we can see ourselves somehow deeply in the text, there is power. Marcus, a watcher and good listener, chose *Soda Jerk* by Cynthia Rylant as a powerful text. He found himself on every page struggling with late

maturation, a poor self-image, worries about love and life, and a community that makes no sense to him.
- **Confluence:** Literature can bring the reader's life story and the text together, and at the point of juncture where they flow together, there is energy and potential for understanding of self to happen. The text might collide with an ideology, a fear, a tension, a curiosity or question, a memory, an idiosyncrasy, a relationship, and at that point be a significant *aha* for you, reverberating with meaning. "'The Poem' seen as an event in the life of a reader, as embodied in a process resulting from the confluence of reader and text, should be central to a systematic theory of literature" (Rosenblatt 1978, 16).
- **Compenetration:** This is the coming together of reader and text towards coherence, something that Rosenblatt (1978) talks about poignantly. In her preface she calls the reader's reaction while reading a literary work "the reader's contribution in the two-way, 'transactional' relationship with the text." While it contextualizes text, I would argue that it contextualizes the self towards further self-understanding, as well.

> The poem [...] must be thought of as an event in time. It is not an object or an ideal entity. It happens during a coming-together, a compenetration, of a reader and a text. The reader brings to the text his past experience and present personality. Under the magnetism of the ordered symbols of the text, he marshals his resources and crystallizes out from the stuff of memory, thought, and feeling a new order, a new experience, which he sees as the poem. This becomes part of the ongoing stream of his life experience, to be reflected on from any angle important to him as a human being (Rosenblatt 1978, 12).

- **Comparisons and contrasts:** The reader is active here, tossing the meaning back and forth between the text and his/her own life. The reader asks, "How is this the same or different in my experience or feelings?" The text here can be a mirror into which one looks and asks, "Who am I?" and determines likenesses or differences; it also gives criteria, a model, ideas, and questions.
- **Contextualizations:** For significant connections and reflections to develop, the reader needs to find himself or herself contextualized in the text. That

does not mean that the setting or time has to be congruent with the reader's own experience, but rather that the reader can fit the shoes, be there and alerted to memories, with reservoirs of experiences, understanding, feelings merging and reverberating with implication. Does the context feel familiar? Does the situation fit? Does the time feel like now? Do the characters seem familiar?

• **Confusions and condemnations:** There is always danger that what children read may have a negative impact on their sense of identity and healthy self-concept, self-efficacy, or emotional stability. This is one of the fears about young adult realistic fiction and definitely of pornographic materials. Texts — visual, auditory, or written — can impact the healthy, well-adjusted self into all sorts of difficult and dysfunctional behaviors. This caveat cannot be denied.

• **No connotations:** There are the benign texts that just don't reach the reader. If there are no suggestive or associative implications beyond the literal, it is not the reader's fault. Some texts do not connect, construct, compenetrate or contextualize and culminate in any response that matters at that moment. Like all learning, the experience of reading some materials may be empty of significance at one time, but in the future, hold deep meaning.

Building a Unit on Afghanistan with Multitexts

BY COREY FOLLETT

I developed a multi-disciplinary unit using the novel *The Breadwinner*, by Deborah Ellis, as the central text connecting my students with the enduring understandings of the unit. I wanted students to better understand themselves through exploring the lives of children in Afghanistan. When students connect with the texts they are reading and experiencing, then real learning occurs.

One enduring understanding of the unit explores the concept of power: Who has power? How is power used? What are the impacts of power falling into the wrong hands? What power do I have and how can I use it? Through a critical analysis of *The Breadwinner*, and a multitude of other texts, students can understand the concept of power, connect to the experiences of characters , and learn they have the power within them to have an impact on the world. In *Pedagogy of Freedom*, Paulo Freire states: "Washing one's hands of the conflict between the powerful and the powerless means to side with the powerful, not to be neutral." Although we are not in the business of creating social activists, we have a duty to teach students to critically engage in the struggles and act accordingly. Exposing students to a wide selection of texts helps them to begin this journey of critical comprehension. A unit on power and empowerment, filtered through the stories and struggles of Afghani women and children, would be the vessel to carry us on that journey.

A hook I provided for the unit was an essay, "My Body Is My Own Business" by Sultana Yusufali (*Sightlines 10 Anthology*, Prentice Hall). In the essay, a Toronto high school student and Muslim female presents readers with an alternative view of the hijab. She describes herself as a "rebel" who feels empowered when she wears the traditional clothing because she doesn't feel pressured to conform to the latest body image. Where many people see her as repressed, she sees herself as liberated.

Many great lessons derived from exposing students to this essay. First, it was a great example of opinion piece writing and they were asked to identify the three parts of the essay: introduction, body, and conclusion. Second, it allowed the students to develop anchor charts for effective opinion piece writing, which they could use when writing their own opinion pieces later in the unit. Third, it provided the students with an opportunity to reflect on their own understanding of the role of women in society and in advertising.

I asked students to find examples of advertising from electronic and print media where body images, male or female, are used to sell things. I wanted them to view the advertisements in terms of power, that is, who has the power in the advertisement? The discussions that ensued from their findings were rich with information about my students and their collective experiences. All students agreed that the media uses body image to sell; however, not all students felt that this impacted their lives in any way. Although some students did express concern about the negative effects of media exploitation, many students still felt that advertising was harmless and entertaining. After all, didn't all things "cool" come from muscular guys and Barbie-type girls?

Later that week, I discovered in the *Owen Sound Sun Times* two opposing letters to the editor written about a controversial Dairy Queen commercial. In the commercial a girl, not much younger than my Grade 7 students, flirts with a boy in order to get a Waffle Bowl Sundae. Once she succeeds, she claims that it was as easy as "shooting fish in a barrel." I presented these articles to my students. We read them together and I noticed a few more students beginning to connect with and understand the impact of media exploitation of body image. The more these students read and engaged in the topic, the deeper they dove into their own understanding of the struggle for power.

As always, I tried to bring them back to the enduring understandings of the unit. Our first writing project was an opinion piece letter to DQ headquarters about the impact of their commercial. Here is one Grade 7 student's letter.

To Whom It May Concern:

Your TV commercial for the Fudge Brownie Temptation Waffle Bowl Sundae depicts a girl "selling" herself for a sundae which is extremely inappropriate and dangerous. The TV advertisement sends a message which says that girls are objects for sale and that boys are nothing more than dumb consumers and predators. According to statistics, 54.5% of girls under the age of 16 have experienced unwanted sexual attention. TV advertisements like yours contribute to this problem.

If the commercial stays on the air, it will teach girls that this is appropriate behavior and that they can sell themselves for things. You should make a commercial that does not use sex appeal to sell ice cream or anything else for that matter. There is NO age that what the girl in the commercial did would be appropriate.

This commercial is also telling boys that you can get girls by buying them something. It is also saying that boys are so dumb and gullible that they are like "shooting fish in a barrel". Is it a coincidence that the boy who buys the ice cream is wearing a "donkey" shirt? Which means he is a jackass? In my opinion, the advertisement can only do more harm than good to boys and girls. So you should take off the TV commercial and make a new one that does not use a girl's sex appeal to sell ice cream. This is really the only TV commercial I have ever hated in my life, so please take it off.

Sincerely,
Concerned Student, Class 73

The Breadwinner raises questions about power and who has it. What power do the women and girls of Afghanistan have? What power do children have? Who has power and how are they using it? These were all critical questions I wanted the students to explore. As my students loved it when I read to them, I used this novel as an opportunity to do some read-aloud activities with the class. Each day I would read a chapter or so and while we would have wonderful discussions about plot, character, setting, and theme, we would dive even deeper into the text. We would make predictions about what would happen next and later confirm our predictions with evidence from the text. We would visualize the novel and put that image into words or on paper as art. We would paraphrase what we had already read and then summarize the main ideas in a comic strip. We would then find other texts we could connect to the novel; life experiences we were reminded of while reading; and traits of the novel's characters that reflected our own selves — all great critical comprehension strategies.

Before long, I saw that my students felt passionately about a girl in Afghanistan. They had made a connection to Parvana and wanted to know more about how she lived, where she lived, and why her living conditions were so extremely different from ours. Their thirst for knowledge led them naturally into other texts. Sometimes, these texts were found by the students; others were brought to their attention by me.

In an attempt to give them a sense of the setting of the novel, I asked students to compare human and physical characteristics of Canada to those of Afghanistan. The World Wide Web is an endless source of information and there are many valuable websites available for student access. Working with the World Fact Book website, students read the information and then completed a specially designed web-quest consisting of a list of questions pertaining to the human and physical geography of both countries. After they had collected the data on both countries, in small groups they had to use a graphic organizer to present their data to the class. They also had to share what the data revealed about life in Afghanistan compared to life in Canada.

Once students recognized the differences between literacy rates, birth rates, and unemployment rates, they began to better understand Parvana's situation. Parvana, the main character in *The Breadwinner*, is a girl close in age to these students and not unlike them in many other ways. But what, exactly, could Parvana's story teach students about their own lives and the power they hold? What power did Parvana hold? These questions would lead us to explore in greater detail the reality of life for girls and women in Afghanistan.

While researching on the Internet for stories about the conditions of life for women and girls in Afghanistan, I happened upon a list of restrictions that the Taliban had placed on the lives of females. (It appears at http://www.rawa.org/rules.htm.) The list, several pages long, was quite shocking. I printed it and shared the restrictions with my students. Here are the first four:

1. Complete ban on women's work outside the home, which also applies to female teachers, engineers and most professionals. Only a few female doctors and nurses are allowed to work in some hospitals in Kabul.
2. Complete ban on women's activity outside the home unless accompanied by a *mahram* (close male relative such as a father, brother or husband).
3. Ban on women dealing with male shopkeepers.
4. Ban on women being treated by male doctors.

As I walked around the room I could hear the students reacting to the list in many different ways. They were angry, saddened, confused, ready to take action, and some were just silent. I asked them if they could tell me how and why something like this could happen. How is it that women and girls in Ontario, Canada, can live freely while girls like Parvana are so heavily restricted?

I also asked whether this situation reminded them of anything else we had read or studied that year. Within minutes students were raising their hands to tell me that the restrictions on the lives of the people in Afghanistan reminded them of the rules that governed the lives of the characters in Lois Lowry's *The Giver*. They told me, too, that these restrictions reminded them of those placed on Anne Frank and her family during the Second World War. The situation also reminded the class of the high school student in the article "My Body Is My Own Business," who viewed the covering of her body with the hijab as something positive. One student shared personal information about his African-American ancestors who had fled to Owen Sound on the Underground Railroad.

After realizing that most women in Afghanistan did not have access to doctors (almost all doctors were male, and females were forbidden to be seen by a male doctor), another student wrote in her reflection journal:

> When I was born my mom had to have a c-section because her diabetes was causing problems with my birth. So, if she had been in Afghanistan there probably would not have been a doctor to help out . . . that means I probably would have died.

This is what another student wrote:

> After learning about the lives of other kids who are less fortunate than I, I realized that I am lucky to be a Canadian. During the course of this unit we have read many texts about kids our age who have hope and make a difference despite the challenges they face every day. Through these texts I've learned a lot about myself. I've learned that if children my age can make a difference, who have even greater setbacks than I, I know that I can make a difference too. No matter what race or religion, everyone can make a difference. You just need hope!

I realized after reading the student responses that they had made the connections I was hoping they would — they were critically reading and comprehending. I could have spent all year trying to teach them the definition of theme and how to connect to the big ideas of the story, but instead I allowed them to discover those elements on their own through engaging them in a variety of texts. Not only was this method much easier, but it was much more effective. And still, there were so many other texts to explore: films, song lyrics, poetry, multi-media presentations.

The list is endless. One student discovered a video on YouTube that introduced the class to a group called Little Women for Little Women in Afghanistan. We hooked up the LCD projector to the laptop in the classroom and watched a *CBC National News* story about a 10-year-old girl, Alaina Podmorrow, from British Columbia. Podmorrow felt compelled to start up Little Women for Little Women in Afghanistan after hearing journalist Sally Armstrong speak about the situation in Afghanistan for women and children. I remember one child then asking, "She's only ten?" I said, "Yes, and look how she is making a difference. You are all 12 or 13. Imagine what you could do!"

The student's YouTube discovery led into *Daughters of Afghanistan*, a film I had already planned to show. In the film the same journalist who made an impact on Alaina Podmorrow, Sally Armstrong, exposes the ongoing struggles of women in modern Afghanistan. She follows the lives of five courageous women from diverse backgrounds, asks some really tough questions, and gets some really startling answers. Through viewing the film, students had yet another opportunity to delve deeper into the enduring understanding of the unit. They saw some strong women taking back the power and forging a new future for their country. After viewing the film, one student remarked:

> I think the women in Afghanistan are doing a good thing exercising their rights . . . Hopefully the Taliban will someday be defeated. I don't believe that guns solve problems, people do!

I had planned to end the unit by having students prepare PowerPoint presentations, but we ran out of time. In role as either a male or a female Afghani child, students would have provided viewers with a glimpse of how they live. Students would have each chosen a town and researched it. They would have created personal narratives for their characters that reflected the reality of life as we had discovered. They would then have created PowerPoint presentations incorporating music and art into the slide shows. Finally, they would have presented their slide shows to the class in role.

I look forward to journeying into these texts again and discovering new texts to add to my library. I also look forward to having students do the culminating task and share their critical understanding with me through PowerPoint. In the meantime, I am confident that these students finished the unit with a good understanding of the concept of power. I am also certain that they all left feeling empowered and hopeful that they, too, can make a positive impact on the world.

6

Deepening Understanding through Storytelling

Putting a story in your own words is one of the most effective ways to achieve a reflective and revealing response to a text. So often reading and the activities around reading are "hurry up, hurry up" — we are getting through the text, the story, the book, or the course. Students miss so much if they don't have a chance to linger with a story. By encouraging students to retell a story, we can enable them to go back to that story and find out more and more.

We have always recognized retelling as a standard response for revealing comprehension, but now we see the powerful storying constructs that can occur when students explore a story as a retelling experience. As they read the selection, explore it, and try retelling it in different styles, we have been able to get students thinking about point of view. They retell stories in the first person or third person, or mix up a first-person narration with a third-person narration, two first-person speakers, and all of these in combination. Together they produce interesting storytelling, and the more they do it, the more they project themselves imaginatively into the text. We go back and examine other questions. How did the author tell this story? How did we tell this story? At this point we are so inside the story that we're getting into everything from character development to dialogue to structure, without ever using any of those words.

Students can choose stories from their own backgrounds or narratives from other cultures that present issues of interpretation, of recognizing cultural values, differing viewpoints, power roles, past time frames, and misappropriation of cultural references.

Three articles share insights on ways to use storytelling. Stephen Hurley builds a unit around his Grade 7 students' life stories, having them explore incidents from their own backgrounds, developing them into polished retellings that involve contexts and bigger themes, and then sharing them with their families. Judy Caulfield, a teacher and a storyteller, offers a lunch hour storytelling club to volunteers in her school, where the students explore the techniques of storytelling. By reworking and retelling shared stories, they find other voices, other ways of interpretation, choosing different words and original sequencing of ideas. The well-known storyteller, Bob Barton, takes us through a unit based on a little-known nursery rhyme, mining this condensed narrative for significant learning moments. Students role-play and tell stories in role. All three teachers recognize storytelling as a means of extending students' comprehension of personal and literary stories into lived-through experiences of narrative making.

Life Stories as Texts

BY STEPHEN HURLEY

The words of Canadian writer and teacher Thomas King were posted on the wall of Room 25 when my 34 Grade 7 students entered on the first day of classes last September:

> The truth about stories is that that's all we are.
> —Thomas King

Throughout the year, these same words reminded us of our theme for the year: Stories of Home. Finally, on a Thursday evening in May, they were proclaimed again as we presented our very first Storytellers Festival, "In Celebration of the Story."

A year earlier, I had been given permission by our school district to explore what it might look like if we set out to use the Arts to help us create an alternative learning space for Grades 7 and 8 students. As I began imagining, formulating, consulting, and writing around the journey on which I was about to embark, the importance of having an overall theme became extremely important. What theme could inform our planning, maintain a sense of connectedness throughout the year, and provide inspiration for our efforts?

In reflecting on the role of literacy in my own life, it dawned on me that my most memorable moments were almost always enriched by a strong tradition of story-telling. Conversations around the family dinner table, awkward moments at a funeral home, the unexpected meeting of an old high school friend, and even the introductions to formal talks I've been asked to give — all of these moments have been energized and brought to life through the telling of a story.

In turning to my own students, I began to under-stand that the literacies they brought to the classroom — the movies they watched, the video games they played, and the life memories they shared — were all grounded in a sense of story.

What an awesome program we could build if we could learn to read, write, and tell the stories of our lives with a sense of proficiency and power! We are a storied people. What better place to explore that dimension of our personal and cultural selves than in an arts-based classroom?

As the planning process continued, a more specific theme, Stories of Home, emerged. Home, after all, is where we begin our lives. It's the place we leave when we set out on our own, and it's the place to which we return at the end of our journey.

Growing up with stories

During our first two terms, we took time to examine the way that strong, memorable stories are written. I asked students to bring in stories that they remembered hearing from their early childhood. Students flooded the classroom with picture books that their parents and grandparents had read aloud to put them to sleep at night. Some brought in the very first books they were able to read on their own.

We took time to share these stories with one another, read them aloud, and savor the language used and the pictures that the words created in our minds. Last, but certainly not least, we listened to the personal *stories behind the stories* — students' memories of experiencing these stories for the first time. "I remember that story too," Micheal announced as Anika began reading *Who Is My Mother?* by Dr. Seuss. That, of course, would lead to a discussion of how many others remembered where they were when they first heard that story.

There were students, however, who had no memo-ries of some of the stories presented. Some had begun their lives in different parts of the world, and this reality allowed us to explore other storytelling traditions.

We also looked at stories within students' current lit-eracy lives. We looked at the storytelling culture present in the video games that they play, in the movies and television programs that they watch, and even in the advertisements to which they are exposed.

The Hero's Journey

In searching for a literacy structure that might help organize our thinking around the stories we were exploring, I found myself returning to the work of Joseph Campbell. In *The Hero Has a Thousand Faces*, Campbell outlines a multi-stage "journey" that charac-ters in the world's greatest stories go through. From the *call to adventure* that causes the hero to leave home, through to the final stages where the hero returns home with new skills, powers, and insights, the Hero's

Journey structure provided us a way to help look at some of the stories in our lives.

We began to use the structure to interrogate stories with which many students were already familiar. In December, we looked at a favorite holiday story, *Rudolph the Red-Nosed Reindeer*, through the eyes of the Hero's Journey. Students analyzed the story using the basic structure of the journey, discussed and debated evidence from the story, and used their insights to explore formal essay writing.

In January, we examined a classic story of home: *The Wizard of Oz*. We gained more experience at reading stories from the perspective of the Hero's Journey structure, and the ensuing discussions launched us into the writing of our own Hero's Journey stories.

Students used the structure to help plan their writing, but it also helped us talk about our stories in new and powerful ways. It formed a common framework.

Towards a celebration of story

When we began our year together, I gave students a choice. They could plan to participate in the annual public speaking contest held every January, or they could choose to sign up as a storyteller in our class Storytellers Festival planned for May. I was surprised when only one student volunteered for the more traditional public speaking contest.

When we began planning for the festival, I told students that they would be required to choose a story with which they were already familiar, learn it, make it their own, and present it to friends and family on the evening of our festival. Soon after introducing the idea, the questions began to emerge:

- "Can we write our own stories and tell those?"
- "Are we allowed to tell the Hero's Journey story that we wrote?"
- "Can we do a video story and present that?"

Good questions, I thought. In fact, the students, through their questions and ideas, were forcing me to return to Thomas King's words. In essence, many were saying: "Our stories are important. These are the stories that we would like to tell." I set about to adjust my plan!

The task

Following our discussions, students settled to work on listing "events" from their own lives that they consid-ered memorable. They had taken part in a similar activity at the beginning of the school year so, for many, this was a matter of revising and adding to that original list.

I asked students to consider the stories we had encountered throughout the year, to think about the events in these stories that were powerful, meaningful, and memorable for them. I gave them time to look at their lists and highlight the events that could be transformed into an engaging story — one with which others might connect and remember.

Once students had each identified at least five "events with possibility," they were asked to share their lists with other students who, through discussion and questions, helped them make a final decision on the event that would form the basis of their story.

This part of the process took a little more time than I expected. The group conversations were lively, full of laughter and connections!

I asked students to imagine that the event they had chosen was the beginning, middle, or end of a story. They were given two days to write a first draft.

Walking around the story

In my career, I've had limited to moderate success in finding a peer editing format that is both engaging and effective. In one of those "unplanned" moments, I decided to take a risk, and it worked! I randomly assigned students partners and asked them to grab their stories and their jackets. Students gathered with their editing partners in the field outside the school; from there I sent them out two by two with the following instructions:

"I want you to find a place in the field, away from other students, and I simply want you to tell each other your stories. You may use what you've written as a guide, but I really want you to tell the story — just like you would if you were sitting around with friends after school."

This activity provided a good foundation for the development of their stories as pieces of oral text. Students offered suggestions to each other about how their stories might be more engaging: what parts of the story could be emphasized more, what parts could stand to be eliminated, and what questions were left unanswered once the story was told.

Towards a theme

During the next week, students massaged their stories, working closely with their editing partners.

In the next part of the process, I asked students to imagine that someone else was reading or hearing their story for the first time. What message might the person get from the story? What would the reader or listener identify as the theme? We had been working a fair bit on identifying the main idea of stories, news articles, and novels that we had been reading, but translating this concept to their own writing was difficult. Many students wanted to tell the specific details of the story, but I pressed them to think beyond the "facts" to consider why someone would care about their story.

I had been listening to an interview with Doug Atchison, the screenwriter responsible for the film *Akeelah and the Bee*. He said, "Most experts will tell you to write what you know, but I say, 'Write what you feel.'" The light went on for me. When I walked into class the next day, we talked about the feelings that the characters in our stories experienced. The connections slowly emerged as we began to list the themes of our various pieces: there were stories that spoke of the fear of abandonment; others that resounded with the sadness of loss, the joy of being free to play, embarrassment, adventure, and discovery. These were all emotions and feelings that everyone in the class recognized and related to. These were the stories of our lives, and these were the stories I wanted to hear them tell!

Over the next few days, we worked on introductions and conclusions that would draw attention to their newly emergent themes. We took time to tell the stories to each other. We videotaped their work and did our final editing in preparation for our storytellers' evening. Then, after students took one last "walk" with their editing partners, the evening of our first Storytellers Festival arrived.

Parents listened with a combination of anticipation, recognition, and surprise as Marcus told an entertaining story about the time when, at age three, he ate a worm — or two.

Jenna's story, "I Want My Mommy," began:

"I was about 5 years old, when I had one of the worst experiences of my young life. I got lost in a mall. I had gone to the mall with my mom and she was doing what I hated the most: browsing."

Lawrence continued with "Santa Paws," the story of a special Christmas visitor:

"For some reason animals seem to be attracted our family. They like to climb down our chimney, crawl all over our roof; fall off our roof and run around inside our house. Raccoons, skunks, birds, cats, dogs . . . and squirrels . . . but I better start from the beginning . . ."

Grace got out of her sickbed to come and share a delightful memory that reminded us of imagination, curiosity, and the power of story:

"Things have a habit of flying in and out of my life — mostly animals . . . some flew in on their own; others take flight with the help of me.

"When I was four years old, my brother had a black and white bunny and that night my mom read me a story, Dumbo . . . you know the elephant with big ears that flies. Well, what I didn't know about that story is that it was make-believe and while that story was being read all I could think about was that bunny with big ears. So after the story was finished, I went into my brother's room, picked up the bunny, and threw it out the window with anticipation to see it fly. That bunny did not fly; it hit the floor, and that bunny was gone . . . my brother loved that bunny. . . ."

Jonathan worked hard on creating a context for his story. He had recently broken his ankle, but our process allowed him to think about the deeper emotions attached to the theme of brokenness in his life:

"Humpty Dumpty sat on a wall. Humpty Dumpty had a great fall. . . .

"One day I took my PSP to school without asking. When I got home, my mom grounded me for a week. . . .

"My mom was upset when she found out. I was sorry for what I had done, and it broke my heart to see my mom upset. I cried with my mom. . . .

"When I liked Power Ranger, my friend brought over a Megazore for me and my brother. When I was playing with it, I got too excited and I broke its arm. It couldn't be fixed. I cried because it was a gift. . . .

"A few years ago I liked drinking milk from coffee cups. One day I tried to grab a coffee cup. It slipped from my hand then shattered onto the tile floor. It was my mom's favorite cup and that made me cry."

Our Storytellers Festival was a chance to recognize the importance and power of story in our lives. It was a chance to explore our own storied existence and discover the connections, the joy, and the power that living in the story can bring. We may forget the details that were recalled during those weeks of preparation; we may even forget some of the names of the storytellers, but one thing is certain: we will *never* forget the stories. They have become part of who we are!

The Storytelling Club

BY JUDY CAULFIELD

Lunch time in my small suburban school: A group of students aged 8 to 11 and a few teachers gathered in the Kindergarten room, a space in which to hear and tell stories. First, we would eat our lunches scrunched down at the Kindergarten tables, students chattering companionably. A few minutes later, students would sit on the carpet, eyes focused on a storyteller. They might laugh, lean forward, or even begin to chant along with a repeated phrase. Later, they might share responses and connections to the story or work in small groups to retell it. Students and teachers met together once a week to listen to and tell stories. We were The Storytelling Club.

The stories we chose to share were usually traditional folk and fairy tales. The teachers' sources were other storytellers or the folk and fairy tale section of the library. These folk and fairy tales, with their universal themes, were chosen as our texts because they have been honed by generations of telling. The language patterns are clear and their strong structure supports retelling. The language may also be playful, which invites students to explore their own language use and patterns.

When a story is told, the gift lies in the personal connections between the teller and the listeners and the teller and the tale. The teller's voice warms the words and brings to life the plot as well as the affective elements of excitement, suspense, or surprise. As the teller makes eye contact with the listeners, it affirms to them that this story is told for them and to them.

As I worked with the students in The Storytelling Club, I saw how engaged they were in listening and exploring the stories more deeply. In our weekly meetings, we retold and reconsidered stories. Revisiting and connecting current stories to past stories during discussions gave the students time to linger and delve deeper into the narratives and the meanings they held for them. After many opportunities to hear and discuss stories, students often worked with partners, preparing to tell a story in their own words. (The students whose stories I share here chose their own pseudonyms.)

Lorraine and Shantel were working together on a version of an Anansi story, one of those stories brought to the West Indies by the West Africans captured as slaves. The Anansi character is a man who can elude trouble by changing into a spider and scurrying away. (As a trickster, Anansi often needs a quick escape!) Lorraine used visualization to move more deeply into the context and place of her story. When I asked her what she saw when she visualized the setting of the story, she said:

"And sometimes I picture it in my own mind. I picture the Caribbean — homeland. Sun. Well, I see it as Jamaica because I have the feeling of the heat. And I mostly see Jamaica because . . . you might see St. Vincent and some people might see the Cuba, but in my mind, I see Jamaica. . . . Like sort of in a way, palm trees, bumpy road, um, coconut trees — yah."

Here, Lorraine reveals how she used her own personal context to illuminate more clearly for herself the setting and context of the story. She also reveals an understanding and acceptance that others may bring a different perspective to the same story. There is great value in students hearing and acknowledging other perspectives since their understanding of the range of possibilities is broadened.

Lorraine and Shantel retold the story several times while preparing to tell it to an audience. Each time they discussed how effective their telling was. They planned to include further details to convey Tiger's fury at being called an "old riding horse," and Anansi's sly manipulation that ended in Tiger carrying him on his back to Miss Selina — the lady they were both courting — so that Anansi could "clear up the misunderstanding." In the first telling of the story, when Miss Selina informed Tiger that Anansi had told her that Tiger was just an old riding horse, the girls' telling of the storyline was bare: "And she did [tell Tiger what Anansi had said] and Tiger was very angry."

Later, when I suggested that the girls try retelling the story in the first person as the characters, their perspective deepened markedly. Lorraine further developed the characters by lingering on the moment when Tiger heard Anansi's lie about him:

"So the next day Miss Selina walked by and found Tiger, and she was just ignoring him, completely ignoring him! And Tiger wondered why 'cause she always came along and said, 'Come over here let me talk to you' or 'What would you like to talk about?' But she . . . that day she completely ignored him. So Tiger went up to her and said, 'Why aren't you talking to me? Why are you ignoring me as if I don't exist?' 'Anansi told me that you're a riding horse . . .'"

Shantel expressed the full anger that Tiger was experiencing as she told his part: "Oh, wait 'till I get my hands on that Anansi. I'm going to rip him from limb to limb. But first I'm going to bring him here and let him tell you [Miss Selina]."

In seeking to convey the story fully to their audience, the girls explored more deeply the emotions of the various characters in the story. Lorraine explained for me the difference in telling the story as the narrator or as the character: "It's like you are telling the story, but the character has more experience." I asked if it felt as though she was experiencing the story, and she clarified: "Well, it feels as though I am experiencing the person, as well."

Some of the stories shared had been told to the students by grandparents. In some instances, students first heard them in another language and then retold them in English to the group. For example, Marium joined The Storytelling Club mid-year as a recent immigrant to Canada. As her friend (the only other Arabic-speaking student in the school) was a member of The Storytelling Club, Marium came along and then stayed as a member. Gradually, she gained confidence in contributing ideas to the group, and the next year she began to share stories that her grandmother had told her. It was some while before I learned that she had not seen her grandmother in a couple of years, yet the stories and the memory of their telling had lingered.

One day Marium asked us what the moral of a story was. "My grandmother's stories always had morals in them," she stated. We then began to consider the intent of the various texts we were sharing. In the weeks that followed, we often discussed the morals of stories. The following is a segment of a conversation in response to my telling of the folk tale "Too Much Noise":

(Miss) Marion: There is a truism in that story — something of value in the story.
Biff: Live with what you get.
(Miss) Marion: Like riding my bike in the rain and then having a bath — the bath feels so much better! It's a relative experience.
Marium: It's like fasting. The food tastes so much better after you have fasted.
Sharon: Like the Skohottentot story — a cumulative story.
Sara: The wise man is like the cat in "The Cat That Walked by Himself."

Once when I visited a colleague's classroom, I was delighted to see a community of students immersed in story. During read-aloud, my colleague initiated "Say Something." She would pause and give students the space and time to respond without input or reaction from her. It gave them the freedom to express their ideas without wondering whether they were pleasing her and giving "the right answer." What has evolved is that the students respond in a variety of ways from asking each other questions about the text, to making predictions about and connections to the text. My colleague says, "My favorite is when they question the action of a character and the other students respond positively or critically, using evidence from the story — a teacher's dream!" Like the students in The Storytelling Club, her students have affirmed for me that students who share, celebrate, and explore stories as a community are drawn into a closer and more intense understanding of the text.

Mining the Nursery Rhyme for Treasure

BY BOB BARTON

There are men in the village of Erith
Whom nobody seeth or heareth.
And there looms on the marge
Of the river, a barge
That nobody roweth or steereth.

"Erith" is a little known text that has appeared from time to time in collections of nursery verse. I can't prove that it is a genuine piece of the oral tradition. It is possible that it is the work of an anonymous writer. When I visited the Erith history museum, upstairs over the Erith Public Library in 2006, staff there had no knowledge of the verse.

My attention has always been arrested by details which are not supplied. The verse has foreboding, mystery, darkly anonymous figures tending to some secretive business, and so on. It is ripe for speculation, so how better to explore ideas than through drama? I like to think of the drama work as mining the text. We begin on the surface, working with the lines; dig into the spaces between the lines where inference lives; and finally burrow beyond the lines to explore and create multiple interpretations.

Once you have read the text aloud, encourage student speculation about it. Ask students whether the piece is modern or old fashioned and how they know. I also encourage students to guess what they can about the people, the barges, and the place called Erith.

Present the lines so that they can be read easily by all the students, using chart paper or electronic devices. I have the students read in unison, then in call and response, with solos and whole-group acts as chorus, quickly, slowly, loudly, and softly. In some cases, we even sing. Prolonging the time we spend with our eyes on the text further builds on the earlier speculations the students have made.

Now that the text is quite familiar, the class can begin to explore the spaces between the lines. For this activity the students should form groups of four. The challenge posed to each group is, can you read the text in such a way that we, the listeners, will know just by your voices who is speaking the words to whom and why?

At this point the groups brainstorm the possibilities for speakers. Some examples that students have worked with include scolding parents using the verse to scare their children from playing near the water; sirens who lure passersby into danger; children playing a street game; supernatural voices of dead returning warriors; a play rehearsal; a password used as entry to a secret meeting; and just gossip leading to panic.

Encourage the students to focus on using their voices. They don't have to rely on unison; the choral speaking they did earlier gives them possibilities for using the voice. They may also repeat lines, but at this point it's best if they don't add new material. When all the groups have developed a plan and rehearsed their interpretations, bring the students together to share. I liken the sharing to a riddle contest: each group performs its piece and the listeners use the clues provided by the vocal interpretation to guess who is speaking to whom and why. By now the students should have many ideas about the text and can move more deeply into developing multiple interpretations. The work can now take several directions as they work in small groups.

1. The students could enact scenes from the verse.
   - Identify three key moments in the verse.
   - Determine whether you want them to introduce new characters, a new fact or two, and dialogue.
   - Students in their small groups can create three tableaux to depict their ideas. (Tableaux are "frozen pictures.")
   - When the tableaux are ready, have the students link the tableaux in a sequence along with the spoken words of the text.
   - Prompt the students to go back over their work and examine details of gestures and facial expressions. They might also consider the mood and atmosphere that they are trying to portray.

2. The students could create a missing scene.
   - Mysterious activity is a feature of the verse. Have students create a flashback scene to insert into the tableaux created in the last activity. The scene should explain why there is such need for silence and secrecy.
   - Discuss ways to create flashbacks on film and in the theatre.
   - Consider how a flashback scene could be signalled in the classroom.

3. The students could explore roles, motives, and intentions.
   - Mysterious activity occurs from dusk to dawn along the waterfront of Erith. Nobody wants to talk about it. The teacher in role as a law enforcement officer could meet with the students in role as villagers and try to make a deal for information. What could this law officer offer that the villagers would find attractive?

4. Students could invent alternative scenes, such as one about how harmless gossip took on greater importance than it deserved and upset everyone in the village.
   - Have them consider these questions: When was this story told for the first time? What was its purpose? Who was involved? How did it end up frightening the residents of Erith?
   - Students could create short improvisations, two to three minutes long, which explain this.

7

Deepening Understanding through Writing

We need to connect reading, writing, and media opportunities in every area of the curriculum. Writing achieves so many goals: students see their thoughts in front of them, and they can revise, rethink, relook at, and rework their original responses. They become more self-aware, self-critical in a helpful way as they focus on what they have constructed, strengthened by peer discussion and by reflective experiences. They learn to innovate on the ideas, patterns, and shapes of the texts they have heard, viewed, or read. We can use the writing of other authors and of fellow students as models for exploring how writers work and how writing functions. We can present demonstrations of interactive and collaborative shared writing experiences, where we compose together a piece of writing, clarifying aloud how we work as writers, what we need to revise, and how we can strengthen our work. We need to let the students in on the secrets of writing.

Students need more time to write, time to compose, rethink, critically examine, and reorganize their ideas. For them, talking about and planning what they will write is a prerequisite for writing, so that they are prepared and confident when they begin to compose their thoughts. Websites, brainstorming sessions, and graphic organizers can help them to move immediately into drafting. As they research, make inquiries about, format, and even transform their texts from one mode to another, they face their own thinking processes, and they can come to understand their own learning.

Three articles provide facets of how students have deepened their understanding through writing. Working with a science text, Shelley Peterson has the students examine informational text for content and vocabulary, and then rework the text into a different form. The students in Crystal May's class took the novel they read and used the poetic forms explored previously to frame personal critical responses to the issues in *Nightjohn*. Rich Roach invited a guest into his classroom, and a series of literacy events grew from the experience, resulting in the writing of mindful and compassionate letters. The students in these classrooms rethought their responses to the texts they had met through a variety of writing events, deepening their initial impressions of the literacy experience.

Refining, Clarifying, and Tinkering with Science: Transforming Text

BY SHELLEY STAGG PETERSON

I know many students who write or type notes when studying for science exams. They say that the act of writing helps them to think about and remember the concepts. Writing in science does not have to be restricted to note taking and studying, however. Students can be writing poetry, narrative, and any number of non-fiction genres. These types of writing help students deepen their learning and clarify their thinking.

When students write, they slow down their thinking in order to capture ideas and express them in a visual form. Their thoughts are given a shape and concreteness. Once written down, ideas can be examined again and again. Students can tinker with the ideas, making new connections with other ideas, bringing in new perspectives to reinterpret them, or refining the ideas to make them clearer. Taking another look at the ideas, rearranging the words on the page, and seeing how new words fit with what has already been written all foster deeper thinking of the concepts. The words and visual images on the page give students something concrete to focus on. The sustained attention to the ideas often sparks new ideas that would not otherwise be imagined (Moffett 1988).

Poetry is an ideal form for deepening students' thinking about science concepts because it "allows students to distill experience using a few words" (Peterson 2006, 67). Poetry writing in science encourages students' creativity and their close attention to science concepts. While playing with the ideas and re-creating them in a new form, students are learning the concepts and making the ideas their own.

I usually start this activity by making an overhead transparency of a paragraph from a text on a science topic under study. The text could come from a book, a reliable source on the Internet, or a magazine or newspaper. A SMART Board works well because students can manipulate the paragraph along with me. I voice my thoughts about what I might do to create a poem from the paragraph: a poem that communicates in as few words as possible the ideas that I think are most important in the paragraph. I want to pare down the paragraph to its essential meanings.

Here is an example of a paragraph taken from Canadian Jan Thornhill's award-winning book, *I Found a Dead Bird: The Kids' Guide to the Cycle of Life and Death* (2006, 41), followed by two poems created by a group of Grade 7 students:

Plant Decomposition: Fungi
Fungi are major decomposers of wood and other plant matter. The various mushrooms and shelf fungi that you see growing on wood or on the ground are actually just the spore-producing parts of the organism, like the fruit of a plant. The main 'body' of any fungus is the mycelium mat made up of threadlike hyphae that grow hidden beneath bark or underground. These parts excrete enzymes that 'digest' even the hardest wood, softening it for other organisms to eat.

Fungi Soften Up Wood for Other Decomposers
Fungi, funky fungi
Friend of wood and plant decomposers.
Your fruit
Are what we see — Mushrooms and shelf fungi.
They produce spores to make more fungi.

Fungi, funky fungi
Your body is a Mycelium mat
Made of hidden threadlike hyphae
That make enzymes
To digest wood and plants.
                                    Shelby, Grade 7

Earth Beings
Mushroom warriors!
I watch you sitting there,
So soft, so innocent.
And all the while you devour
The wood and plants.
Like some space-age creature,
You excrete your enzymes,
Sending the threads of hyphae
To live beneath the bark,
Softening the stems, the stalks, the branches,
For your alien friends —The Organisms,
Whose whole being depends on eating, eating.
                                    Jacob, Grade 8

The students' poems contain many examples of their deep thinking about the science concepts. The key idea of the paragraph from Jan Thornhill's book — that fungi play an important role as decomposers because they excrete enzymes that soften up the wood for other organisms to decompose further — is expressed up front in the first title. The student infers that this capability makes fungi "friend of wood and plant decomposers." The Thornhill text also describes mushrooms and shelf fungi as spore-producing fruit and the student connects this point to the reproductive parts of the fungi. The student makes the ideas her own by using alliteration in the repeated phrase "Fungi, funky fungi" and by taking the perspective of someone addressing the fungi. In "Earth Beings," the writer personifies mushrooms as warriors and compares them to aliens, working all the data contained in the description into his scenario.

When I assess students' writing in content areas, I look for evidence of inferring and interpreting the ideas in their own way using the language of science and their everyday words and expressions. These poems tell me more about students' depth of conceptual learning than answers to test questions ever could.

Transforming ideas from one form to another is one of many ways to deepen students' thinking through writing. The following list provides a starting point for using writing to extend students' content-area learning.

- *Ongoing peer and teacher feedback.* When talking to students about their science writing, I ask questions, make observations, and voice my impressions and feelings. I encourage students to provide similar types of feedback when they respond to each other's writing. Students mull over the new information and weigh the merits of the new perspectives that this feedback provides. They make decisions about whether the feedback helps to clarify their thinking and extend and enhance what they want to achieve with their writing.
- *Writing a pithy statement after reading a passage about a content-area topic.* Students create a headline using as few words as possible to summarize a paragraph or series of paragraphs they have read about a content-area topic. The tone of the headline, as in newspaper headlines, could range from cheeky to profound. The goal is

for them to explain their personal understandings of the content.
- *Writing about the content from various perspectives in a blog.* Students identify the various stakeholders involved in a content-area issue or topic. They write a blog entry or series of entries on the topic in the voice of one stakeholder; they also include comments that other stakeholders might write on the blogger's site.
- *Comparing and contrasting information from various sources.* Students read two to four different texts on the same topic and use a Venn diagram to compare and contrast the information and perspective in each text. They then make decisions about which information and perspective they believe to be accurate and create a brochure or multi-media presentation outlining what they have learned about the topic.
- *Creating picture books for younger audiences.* Students gather information about a content-area topic and communicate what they have learned in a picture book that they will read to younger students. Students must think deeply about the content to make the information understandable for their young readers. The images may come from photographs or from Internet images — students' artistic abilities should not present an obstacle to creating the picture book.
- *Revising a provocative statement in a wiki or small-group setting.* The teacher writes a provocative statement about the content-area topic under study, either on pieces of chart paper given to groups of four or five students, or on a class wiki. Students read to gather information that either confirms or calls into question the tenets of the teacher's statement. They add to the teacher's statement or reword it to reflect their growing understandings of the topic. On chart paper, students would take turns crossing out the parts they feel need to be changed and adding to the statement. The piece of paper would need to be large enough to accommodate a number of revisions. On the wiki, they would simply rewrite or add to the statement as it is changed by classmates.

Transforming Texts: From Novels to Poems

BY CRYSTAL MAY

I teach Grade 7 students in a small community in Ontario, where I try to interconnect the different forms of texts that we engage with in our class so that different levels of meaning are constructed, as, for example, when the students attempt to transform a novel we had shared as a community text into poetic responses. We had explored a variety of forms of poetry during the year, so when we completed the reading of *Nightjohn* by Gary Paulsen I asked them if they would reflect on the issues in the novel through the affective power of the poem. They were free to try different forms of poetry and to write as many responses as they liked.

Nightjohn by Gary Paulsen is set in the southern United States during the time of slavery. Based on an actual incident, it tells about a young slave girl, Sarny, who is taught to read by another slave, Nightjohn, who has escaped to the North where he was taught to read. However, Nightjohn keeps coming back to the South to educate the slaves of the plantations. Each night after the others are asleep, Nightjohn teaches Sarny one letter and makes her promise that she will never say or write the letters that he is teaching her. He tells Sarny: "To know things, for us to know things, is bad for them. We get to wanting and when we get to wanting it's bad for them. They thinks we want what they got ... That's why they don't want us reading."

This book offers the students some powerful insights on slavery and opens up discussion about the fear that some in power have of making everyone literate. As well as writing poems, the students wrote in their journals. The power of the novel resulted in their making deeply emotional responses.

Student thoughts about *Nightjohn*

I think that *Nightjohn* was a very disturbing book. I think that people should not have to go through the things that those people went through. This book really shocked me because I thought when I looked at the cover of this book, I thought that it was about something that actually was not real, but it was about something really important and something that actually happened in real life.

I liked that it taught me the history about life back then, instead of reading out of an old history textbook. The book was exciting . . . but some of the scenes are disturbing.

I thought that the book *Nightjohn* helped me understand what happened, as in what we did to Blacks in the past and how unfair it was. *Nightjohn* was a very good book for our age group. Even though it was sometimes very disturbing in the things that it was talking about, it still helped me grow and learn a lot.

A collection of student poems

Nightjohn Returns
Days had passed when he finally spoke
He told me he would teach me to read
He said I was different from all the other folk
And that letters were all I would need.
Day after day, John teaches me the letters in the dirt.
Today, I learnt the letter 'C'— it is a strange letter weirdly shaped too,
I think what's the next letter but, that's not all I think about
I think what's going to happen the next day
Will Waller be defeated,
These are the questions that haunt me.
Every night I think will I die,
Will I ever escape this horrible nightmare
John says yes John says that he is going to escape and come back
Come back with force and make Waller pay for what he did to us
He will be treated like the animal, not us!
            Allysha

He sits there watching us, hurting us.
He doesn't care about anyone but himself.
He's so selfish, he thinks that he owns us.
He thinks that just because we are black that we don't have rights,
that we don't matter but that's not true.
We should be treated with the amount of respect that white people are treated with.

Sarny disobeyed Night John tried to help her
Got his toes chopped off
Sara

the hell we go through
every day
is unbearable
the tears
sweat and blood all go unnoticed
the life we live
is awful
horrible
we try to stick together
but it's hard
no one helps no one hears
 the tears that we cry
although we try hard
not to we all ware a disguise
the disguise of scars.
Scars and more scars
the scars we wear are long
bumpy and rough
some of them still bleed with our pain
we all try
to stay strong
but it's tough
the evil
the demons in his smile

he has no heart
no soul or conscience
we try to
please him
even though we hate him
with every inch of our souls
I've never met
anyone this hated
or this cold.
Desarae

Day after day,
I'm used to eating out of the cold trough.
Waller treats us like animals

I still wonder if I'll ever be free.
Mammy says I'll be okay but I never listen.
She treats me like her child, I really like it.
I had better be going to bed now, before he sees the light.
Hayley

Name poetry
Want me to chop off your fingers John?
Animals like you are no good for nothing but to be my
    slaves
Like the breeding? Well too bad, Get in there now.
Love to hurt those animals
Enjoy this while it lasts.
Reading? My boy you're going to get whipped.
Hayley

Phrase poetry
Beating those Animals
gotta do it quick
Fore they run away
Up to that Canada, they will never make it though.
Me and my dogs are too quick
Hayley

Nightjohn
always helps friends,
confident, brave, and strong,
not scared of Waller and his whip
Nightjohn
Michaela

Waller is his name,
he was the one to blame,
mistreating Blacks was his game,
they all hoped,
one day, he would pay

Waller
Owner of slaves,
mistreated all
punished Blacks for no good reason
Nasty
Katie

BY RICH ROACH

Clyde is a real hero to Grimsby school kids

Man's trek along Bruce Trail while battling cancer inspires students.

Sometimes, a teacher encounters a story that travels immediately from the brain to the heart; it reaches deep within, striking an inner chord that somehow seems to shout, "Share this with your class!" It becomes a compulsion. Such it was with a short article in the local Niagara newspaper about a retired 55-year-old principal from Niagara Falls. Clyde Carruthers had decided to hike all of Ontario's 800 km Bruce Trail from Queenston to Tobermory. The hike represented a personal challenge and also symbolized his retirement. The article described how just months before he started his hike, Carruthers learned he had lymphoid cancer. He decided to do it anyway while undergoing chemotherapy treatments.

We had just celebrated Terry Fox Day at Smith School in Grimsby, Ontario, and my Grade 7/8 students had opened up their hearts by writing about heroes and how they affected their lives. I read the article about Clyde Carruthers to the students. Immediately, they dubbed him a hero. We discussed why they thought he was a hero. They decided that his decision to do the walk despite the odds made him a hero. It was the spark within that they noticed.

It was decided that each student would write a letter to Clyde Carruthers, telling him how proud they were of his decision to hike the trail and what his journey meant to them. When I collected the letters and began to read them, I was moved to tears and felt the sudden urge to share them. I made copies of them and gave them to my principal, Hilary Abbey. We marvelled not only at their heartfelt messages, but at what their writings revealed about them. It was like peering into their young souls. It was encouraging, to say the least.

Clyde Carruthers received the letters in a large envelope at home (I was able to get his address from his former school, which also supplied my class with any other articles about the hike), and read each of them through with his wife, Rose. He said it took him a while to go through them because of the tears. He was very moved — moved enough to write an individual letter in response to each student.

Beyond receiving letters back, students had an added surprise: that Clyde Carruthers said he would like to visit the school. In November, he had made it as far as Wiarton, on the Bruce Peninsula, where he had to undergo more chemotherapy and decide whether to continue his trek (after 20 treatments!). He decided to halt the hike and start again in April.

The students created a 6 m mural that stretched across the room, carefully labelling the major cities along the Bruce Trail (information they got from various websites). They gave Clyde a hero's welcome. I invited the Grade 7 class to come to the talk as well. All the students were sitting on chairs in our classroom around the chalkboard.

Clyde came into our room with his wife, Rose, who had driven along below the escarpment, trying to keep in touch with Clyde as he moved along the Bruce Trail, and provided support. More of the amazing puzzle of what makes a hero dovetailed into the minds of the students as they learned about Rose's supportive role and asked her questions. Clyde wore the gear he used on his trek and described each item, as well as what he kept in his backpack. It was so *real* and the students were easily able to imagine themselves on the trail with him. Together they showed us an incredible slide show that revealed Clyde's deeply spiritual relationship with nature and his love for the outdoors, as well as a particular penchant for veering off set pathways. There was a lot of emotion in that room. Some students noticed that the rocks Clyde was stepping over were mainly sedimentary. Clyde's declaration that he was "going to finish the hike" was greeted with a triumphant cheer by the students.

As the year progressed I kept in touch with Clyde and the class chose to write to him again. Later, Clyde said that their words of encouragement helped him continue the trek. When he wrote to us on e-mail saying that he and Rose had made it, the roof of the school almost came off with the cheer that burst forth.

There was a special reserved seat at the graduation ceremonies in June. Clyde came on his motorcycle and looked great. His chemotherapy sessions had paid off, and things were looking good for him. He gave a moving speech during the ceremony and received thunderous applause, this time not just from the students, but from the community. Somehow, this man's courageous journey had touched a nerve and inspired a generation of students.

Authentic teaching promotes the most inspired writing, and those letters symbolize something more than any exercise could inspire. Our connections with the outside world can make a difference and the students *did* make a difference. The time they spent writing their letters and describing their complex feelings was well spent and connected them personally with a great man whom they will never forget.

Dear Mr. Carruthers,

I was inspired by your story of tenacity and courage. My favourite pastime in life is running — and, in a way, it's yours too. Maybe you don't actually run, but you are going a distance, without giving up. I am filled with hope after reading your story, hope that it is never really the end. I recently wrote a piece of literature for my teacher, Mr. Richard Roach, and I added in this quote that I have been using since I was very little:

"It's only the end of the world if you want it to be!"

Although you received some terrible news, just a month before your retirement, you didn't give up. It makes me smile to know that you didn't think of it as the end; you saw it as a new beginning. I'm sorry to hear about your diagnosis, but it's like that old saying, "Everything happens for a reason," and maybe this is a blessing in disguise! Your diagnosis has opened your eyes to a new kind of beauty you may have never noticed. It's really amazing what you see when you're not even looking for anything.

Just a few weeks ago, I had to take a break in my training, like I said earlier, I am a runner. I recently got a running injury in my hip. Before my injury occurred, I used to run at least five times a week, and now I can only get out maybe two times. Anymore running causes me too much pain and my chiropractor told me to take a break. Although I still get pain, I still run because I know that it's not very disciplined of me to just give up because of a little pain. I fully understand the concern of my chiropractor, and I am only running twice a week now, but that is another thing we have in common. There might be people in your life that want to "take a break" or "take it easy." But I am here to tell you, don't listen to them. Unless your health is beyond terrible, keep on going, please. As long as you can walk, you have to keep going.

Some people may tell you that one person cannot change the world. I strongly disagree with that statement for numerous reasons. A single person has the power to change the whole world; all they need is the will. Of course, it is easier to better our world with more people helping, but you as one person can in fact change the world. One person can make an impact so enormous that all we have to do is share the story. Take Terry Fox for example: he never gave up until it was absolutely, no doubt about it, mandatory that he stopped. Millions of people have heard that story and are inspired to help out in their own way. I truly believe that your story could do that for other people.

I know there may be times when you feel it is the end, and there *are* going to be times when all you want to do is give up, and that is what a lot of people do. But stand out; don't give up no matter how tired you are. I can say confidently that you can do it! I know that every person has a strength inside of them, just waiting to be released. Are you going to release that strength?

I thank you for your inspiring story again; it has greatly impacted my life. I have decided to tell other people about your story in hope that they will help change the world.

Sincerely,
Olivia

Dear Mr. Carruthers,

My name is Brittany and I am a Grade 8 student at Smith School. I would like to tell you that I am truly inspired by what you are doing. I think that you must be very brave to walk across the entire Bruce Trail, and I know it won't be easy. I do not know you, Mr. Carruthers, but what I do know is that you are on a journey that will touch people's hearts forever. When you finish walking the Bruce Trail, you will feel successful and have achieved a great accomplishment.

Can you believe that you have already finished travelling 75% of the Trail? This also means that you have 213 kilometres to go. I have never been to the Bruce Trail before, but I am sure that it must be very beautiful — you are very lucky to experience such peace in such a dreadful time.

At least two of my family members have been affected by cancer, so I know what you are going through. You must be very scared right now, but walking this trail is the best thing that you could have done. Fearless, dauntless, and courageous are words that describe you and what you are doing for other people. I know that you can fight this because you have given hope to people who needed it the most.

Good luck, Mr. Carruthers. I know this experience will change your life — just hearing about it changed mine.

Sincerely,
Brittany

8

Deepening Understanding through Inquiry

When students are deeply engaged with an issue or topic — and if the inquiry is significant, the exploration authentic, and the students connected to the issue being considered — the learning will be woven together seamlessly.

As processes, reading and writing go unnoticed if the need to discover is strong; researching allows students to meet a variety of text forms and to organize, revise, format, and present their results to an authentic audience of peers or listeners outside the classroom. It may be helpful for the students to incorporate visual diagrams, tapes, PowerPoint, and videos as preparation or as support for their research. Using a simple example of one kind of information resource, we could demonstrate how it functions, how it is organized, and what cues characterize that type of text; we could also draw students' attention to the table of contents, to maps and diagrams, or to illustrations.

Students can write their own researched information using the mentor texts they have found in their inquiries, working with the style, the structure, or the format of the research resources, and incorporating them into their own work. In this way, they construct and comprehend a particular genre at the same time, gradually accumulating the strategies necessary for working with a variety of forms of information. We hope our students will move towards a critical perspective on the work they develop.

This chapter features six contributions. Barb Smith organizes a research club in which students from Grades 3 through 6 are mentored by volunteer teachers. Their topics of inquiry are drawn from a wide selection of interest, augmented by student e-mail contact with authorities. Smith also ran a research inquiry with students, teachers, and parents examining the effect of the project. Ken Pettigrew reports on a unit he explored with Grade 3 students: they made a critical examination of magazines. Eddie Ing participated in a problem-solving competition with volunteers from Grades 4, 5, and 6: students invented a LEGO robot and developed an environmental improvement plan for his school. After observing a traffic accident, Gary Rusland presented his class with a schematic, and they explored the possibilities of who caused the accident. In her mathematics teaching, Kathy Marks Krpan advocates that students discuss their problem solving, hitchhiking on each other's ideas in order to explore all of the issues surrounding the problem. John Myers analyzes a Grade 7 class's exploration of a period in history through a strategy that promotes listening to the views of others.

An Independent Inquiry Program for Students in Grade 3, 4, and 5

BY BARB SMITH

What is inquiry? The question echoes with resounding thunder. I find it a challenge to respond with a simple word or phrase. At The Sterling Hall School, it's not just about engaging students to frame better questions; about inviting students to make thoughtful predictions on where their research plans might take them; about seeking information or research from text sources that others have found, that prompts interest and claims to the truth; about making contacts with experts in the field; about checking out perceptions of non-experts; about displaying findings; about forming conclusions that prompt students to theorize and recommend further actions and questions; about reflecting on change as our boys move from the role of novice to apprentice researcher. It's about *all* these qualities gleaned from a synthesis of best practices from a variety of approaches to inquiry.

The Inquiry program served to consolidate the services of many support professionals in the school. In Grades 3, 4, or 5, five or six boys worked on one research topic with one adviser once a week for one hour; this supervisor could be a homeroom teacher, the teacher-librarian, the technology coordinator, a special needs teacher, or a vice principal.

- Boys in Grade 3 worked on individual research topics around the theme of the environment. During their final phase of the project, they pulled together their findings in small groups to present a dramatic representation of their work.
- Boys in Grade 4 researched the "four elements" in pairs and produced a video documentary to defend their findings.
- Boys in Grade 5 worked with partners to inquire into a specific global issue which they defended in the form of a five-minute PowerPoint presentation. All students engaged in lively conversations about the inquiries.

In the first year of the project, I found most of the experts by browsing commercial and educational sites. I looked to see who was researching in a topic area of student interest.

The students generated questions and letters, and put them in a Word file; I then pulled them all — 72 letters — and e-mailed them from my e-mail address (for safety purposes). Before we sent their letters, I had asked each expert this question: Would you be willing to take 10 minutes to respond to this "authentic inquiry" search? I was surprised at the number who said for sure. (It was about 85 percent.) After the students sent a "snail mail" thank-you note to each expert, we saw that we had fewer folks to find the following year; most were willing to participate again.

The boys thought it was "cool" talking to real people — especially when they found some "secret agents" from Interpol and the CIA.

This inquiry is significant because it has helped us shape the development of our language for inquiry over the course of a two-year exploration of student, teacher, and parent response. The inquiry was guided by five key sub-questions:

- What is inquiry?
- Why do students need to experience being apprentice researchers?
- How do the students in the program know and value inquiry?
- How do the teachers in the program know and value inquiry?
- How do the parents in the program know and value inquiry?

The survey

We gathered data from three sources: students, teachers, and parents. We compared students' understanding of inquiry at the beginning and at the end of the program. All Grades 3, 4, and 5 inquiry students responded to a survey given in March. All 12 teachers responded to a survey in April. Finally, many parents of students in Grades 3, 4, and 5 responded to a survey in May.

A selection of responses to the program appears below.

Student feedback: Grade 3

Student responses to the question "What did you like about inquiry?" included the following: computer work, plays, research at the beginning, survey questions, no homework, props from home for play, marking of own work, writing script, science experiment, inquiry reports, working together, researching different things, fair and no extra credit projects, getting extra credit/ help from teachers, listening to other people's ideas, "nice" teachers, having fun, brainstorming and Inspiration Map, experts helping with topic, second chances to improve, reflections, and choosing topic.

Teacher perceptions of inquiry program

Teachers offered critical comments on how to improve the program, for example:

- simplify number of inquiry actions
- improve scheduling (not at end of day)
- improve technology use
- increase talk time

They identified needs, such as "to make better connections between experts and kids," to ensure that there is "consistent inquiry language all the way through SHS schooling," and "to promote connections in Science, Social Studies, and/or Language Arts."

Parent feedback

Parents provided much positive feedback, as the comment extracts below reflect.

A wonderful beginning for future projects!

Teaches children to think critically on a particular topic; develops researching skills; applies what is being taught in a practical basis.

They did great research and asked good questions.

Well thought out survey questions and information from expert source was very enlightening. Good conclusions.

They picked topics they cared about.

I think it is great that they learned to use so many sources of information, as opposed to just one book or one article. It is also good that they learned to document their sources.

I think the boys learned a lot about the gathering and presenting of information, which will be useful skills in the future.

It is great to get children thinking about global topics and teaching them how to research.

I like the organized approach; if students follow the Inquiry Action plan, they can write a research report on many topics.

Very impressive! Happy to see the boys are encouraged to read newspapers, caring about bigger issues, thinking out of the box!

Findings

- Most students in each grade appropriated the language of inquiry. Many demonstrated a solid ability to articulate many aspects of inquiry, and most were able to put the inquiry actions in a meaningful sequence.
- Many teachers had suggestions for improvements; many teachers wanted to build on the strengths of the program; most teachers wanted to see the students immersed in inquiry time to increase ongoing exposure to the topics.
- Most parents did not know much about inquiry until the project came home at the end of the year. They were asked to talk to their son about the experience before filling in a survey. Most surveys were returned with many supportive comments about the program.
- Based on this examination of student, teacher, and parent perspectives, we were able to move forward in our ongoing deliberations about how our school would define inquiry and what programming best promotes deeper understanding of the process.
- We recognized that 10 inquiry actions were too difficult to use as defining features of the model of inquiry. Evidence of student transformation contributes to the ongoing support for the continued development and enhancement of this program.
- Grade 5 students answered the question "What is Inquiry?" in September; they answered it once again in May. After a year-long program of action research, most of them were able to articulate solid descriptions of inquiry, and some were able to elaborate their descriptions of inquiry like experts.

Sample topics

For each topic, two or three authorities from around the world were identified, and they became e-mentors for the students as they worked on their inquiries.

- Question-based topics: How are we ruining the wolf's land? How does pollution threaten the otter? Does poverty cause terrorism?
- Natural disaster topics: Earthquakes, tsunamis, water in Africa
- Pollution-related topics: Oil leaks, noise pollution
- Energy-related topics: Gasoline, wind power, nuclear power
- Rights-related topics: Racism, child labor in Pakistan
- Current political topics: 9-11, Al-Qaeda, the Taliban in Afghanistan

Advertisements as Texts

BY KEN PETTIGREW

In an east-end Toronto school, the buzz in Room 107 is electric. Twenty eight- and nine-year-olds giggle excitedly while they talk about their favorite back-to-school television commercials. Their teacher, Mrs. McKay, has invited her lively bunch of Grade 3 students to reflect on what it is about these commercials that make them so memorable and to list characteristics of good commercials. Of course, her students are not short on opinions. "Good commercials are funny," proclaims Daniel, with his infectious laughter. "And the best commercials get you to remember them somehow — like, they tell a story or surprise you," Mahdi chimes in. An animated Mishanee adds, "Most of all, good commercials make you think, hey, I want that." Although many students are familiar with commercials, it is abundantly clear that this is not the first time that these students have analyzed commercials as *texts*.

From the first day of school, Mrs. McKay has made it quite clear to her students that reading is about engaging with texts, and to do so, readers must be prepared to ask questions and challenge ideas in texts they read — texts of all types. For Mrs. McKay, it is important that her students understand that the critical literacy skills they have been developing over the school year using printed texts can, just as easily, be transferred to media texts, such as visual and moving images. Just as printed texts rely on the power of language, perspectives, and patterns to communicate their messages, so, too, do media texts, which include the layers of sound and image.

Having invited her students to share the highlights of their partner conversations, Mrs. McKay records their ideas on a whiteboard. In preparation for viewing a commercial, she then models thinking for her students. She explains: "Before *view*ing a text, just like when *reading* a text, I like to stop to think about what I already know about the text or genre. I know that this is a commercial we are about to watch. So, I expect there to be persuasive language used, and I expect the product to be connected to real life somehow. By knowing what to expect from a text, I can then create my own criteria for evaluating how good the text is for me. After all, as a good reader, I know that reading is really about feeling connected to the text."

She then focuses her students' viewing by adding, "So, while you are watching this commercial, I want you to be aware of the questions or thoughts that pop into your head."

As is evident from the escalating murmurs, the students are quite familiar with the commercial shown to them. Mrs. McKay instructs her students to turn to an elbow partner to share their thinking. The following conversation ensues:

Alana: Okay, why would everyone want to be wearing the same thing anyway?

Dhruvil: I know. But the commercial makes it like the girl dressed differently is the one who should feel embarrassed or something.

Alana: Yeah, and the mom looked upset that her daughter would be the only one who looked different. Why wouldn't she want her to be herself?

Dhruvil: I'd like to be the one who dresses differently. Who wants to be the same as everyone else?

Alana: I know. But the company wants to sell lots of hoodies and backpacks, so that's why they show everyone wearing them.

Dhruvil: Right, and then they want us to feel like we HAVE to have them; like we're losers for not wearing them. That way, they sell more, and make more money.

Alana: Right. But commercials are *supposed* to sell things, so it is a pretty good commercial, when you think about it.

Dhruvil: Yeah, but I still don't agree that we should all dress the same. I think it's better to be who you are.

Having made critical literacy a key component of her program this year, Mrs. McKay, to her delight, is no longer surprised by the depth of dialogue in her classroom. A look around the room quickly reveals the preparation that has gone into developing her students' critical literacy skills. A bulletin board, entitled "5 Critical Questions to Ask When You Read," is posted prominently above the area where students congregate on the carpet:

1. How has the creator made this text like, or not like, real life?
2. What might the creator want you to think, feel, or do after reading this text?
3. How has the creator grabbed your interest?
4. Who made this, and why?
5. How does this text follow a pattern or formula?

Along the wall, beside the meeting area, there is also a five-stanza poem that helps to illustrate these key concepts of critical literacy: (1) Texts are constructions; (2) Reading is interaction; (3) Messages contain values; (4) Genres have unique techniques; and (5) Texts are created for a purpose.

Reading is more than calling out at balls and sticks and dots;
It's understanding ideas that began as someone's thoughts;

It's talking with the author, though just inside your head,
To get the answers to your questions on everything you've read.

It's asking what the author wants me to think or do?
And knowing that there could be another point of view.

Texts often follow patterns, so you know what to expect.
Is it fair? Is that my world? I'll just have to reflect.

Texts are filled with messages, though I don't have to agree.
It's fine to wonder *why*, and *how*, and *are you kidding me?*

The classroom environment and the ease with which her students challenge the ideas in texts indicate that Mrs. McKay has succeeded in preparing her students to think critically.

Mrs. McKay invites her students to share their thinking with the whole class. Her students have reacted strongly to the commercial. Moses states: "This commercial was not like real life at all. Our school doesn't look like that, and I've never seen everybody wearing the same thing at the same time." Sahar adds, "Those kids must be rich, because they all got new clothes for school, and they all had cool things to play with."

Mrs. McKay takes this opportunity to invite her students to consider the target audience of the commercial. The students reach a consensus that while the commercial was targeted for their age group, it did not represent the culture of their school.

Back at their desks, working in groups, students sort through a variety of back-to-school print advertisements. They are asked to select one for the group to analyze. Placing the advertisement in the centre of a piece of chart paper, one student acts as the scribe, while the group begins reacting to what they observe. Mrs. McKay has instructed the groups to pay particular attention to the techniques used to appeal to the target audience.

One group notices that all of the characters in the advertisement they chose are dressed as if they are in university. "They look just like the people on that TV show," explains David. "They're trying to sell a laptop." "University kids need a laptop to learn," Colin interjects. "Well, at least that's what the company wants us to think, right?" suggests Abbas. The group agrees that the advertisement implies that every student needs a laptop in order to be successful at school.

In another group, Aimee states, "This ad is definitely for boys." "Why do the boys look like they have so much attitude?" wonders Cheyenne. "I think they are supposed to look tough and cool," says Liam. "Look at their dark clothes, their long hair, and the skater stuff in their lockers." The group concludes that the advertiser hopes that boys will want to buy the jeans, hoodies, shoes, and bags to look just as cool as the boys in the advertisements.

As groups share their thinking with the whole class, one student comments, "Why aren't there any people who look like me in these flyers?" The students in this multicultural classroom express that they do not feel represented in the media texts they are exposed to (e.g., print advertisements, commercials, films, and television programs). The message they perceive is that, as far as advertisers are concerned, they do not matter. This perception prompts Mrs. McKay to invite her students to assume the roles of advertisers and to create commercials for back-to-school clothing, for which students in their own school community are the target audience.

Such is the power of critical literacy. When we invite students to challenge the ideas presented in texts, we usher in the shift in power from the author and text to the reader. It is incumbent upon educators to help students recognize that reading is an interactive — not passive — process, which demands critical thinking.

In Mrs. McKay's classroom, critical literacy is a lens through which all texts are analyzed. By asking critical questions of text, students deepen their understanding about how texts are constructed, extend their learning, and confront representations of the world that may not align with their own. Mrs. McKay has established a solid foundation from which further critical thinking will develop. Dhruvil summarized critical thinking best when he said: "I always thought that asking questions meant that you didn't understand something. Now, I know that asking questions is the *only* way to understand something."

Problem Solving in Groups with Invented Robots

BY EDDIE GEORGE ING

The FIRST LEGO League was founded by Dean Kamen and Kjeld Kirk Kristiansen. A volunteer-driven organization, FLL is built on partnerships with individuals as well as businesses, educational institutions, and government. As a team coach, one joins over 45 000 committed and effective volunteers who are key to introducing 93 000 youths to the joy of problem solving through engineering.

Each September, school-based teams apply for status from around the world. Our school applied for the status of two teams in 2007's challenge. The challenge is based on a set of real-world problems facing scientists and engineers today. It has two parts: a robot game and a project.

- In the robot game, teams design, build, test, and program autonomous robots to perform a series of tasks, or missions.
- In the project, teams conduct research and create a technological or engineering solution to an aspect of the challenge and present that solution.

For roughly eight fast-paced weeks, each team is guided by at least one adult coach and works as a group to overcome obstacles and meet challenges while learning from and interacting with their peers and adult mentors. Teams work to provide creative solutions to the problems presented to them in the Challenge. They then compete in local and regional tournaments where they celebrate their accomplishments with other teams, family, and friends.

After the hard work and a lot of fun, kids come away with a greater appreciation of science and technology and how they might use it to have a positive impact on the world around them. They also cultivate deeper life skills, such as planning, organizing, brainstorming, collaborating, and engaging in teamwork. They learn how to take ownership of their learning and responsibility for their actions, both positive and negative. They come to realize how their action or inaction affects people as individuals or on a global scale. All these deeper life skills can change their outlook on life.

The Power Puzzle Challenge for 2007 was about understanding the elements of energy use in a world that uses more energy every day. As our world grows and changes so do our energy needs. The Power Puzzle missions get teams to consider some of the energy choices available and how those choices affect the world. With the 2007 Power Puzzle project, the students analyzed the possibilities and worked to improve energy use.

As we worked to make the pieces of our puzzle fit together, we had to consider all the parts of energy use, including how energy is made, how it is stored, how we use it, how much we consume, and how we dispose of the waste. We came up with a plan to reduce the energy used daily in our school and much of it is now in effect.

The teams at work

There was a sign-up sheet for all students in Grades 4, 5, and 6 interested in learning about the world of robotics through the manipulation and building of LEGO parts. In total, 24 children signed up for this challenge.

Many things had to be completed before learning how to program a robot and make it work to manipulate its way across a field and place items on that field for specific purposes related to the environment. Within the first three weeks of the school year, tasks to fulfill included the following:

- taking an inventory of all the LEGO pieces that arrived from headquarters, including our two new NXT robots, all the spare parts, and their kits
- building a practice field, using a 4 by 8 piece of plywood and mounting the "Official Power Puzzle Challenge" on it
- building our models from the LEGO pieces and permanently positioning them on the constructed Official Practice Field. (Among the 10 structures to build were Coal Mining, Corn Harvest and Platform, Grid Connection, House, Hydro Dam, Oil Drilling Platform, Power Plant, Railroad and Rail Car, Solar Powered Satellite, Tree Planting, Truck, Uranium Mining, Wave Turbine and Wind Turbine.)
- viewing a video illustrating each of the Power Puzzle missions, including how to place a solar panel, trade your car, extract and use coal, extract and use oil, place a wind turbine, connect a

locality to Power Grid, deploy a Solar Power Satellite, extract and use corn, place an ocean turbine, and extract and use nuclear material
- reading all pertinent materials: Core Values, Coaches' promise, Surface and Borders, Optional Table, Field Setup Instructions, Missions, Rules, Common Questions and Answers, Project Introduction, Project Resources, Web Resources, Glossary of Terms, and a Sample Energy Audit

The children met during morning and afternoon recesses and half of their lunch periods. They made their own time commitments, understanding that if someone missed a meeting, the team would lose time having to explain what had happened. The children held one another accountable for their actions and inactions. Those who missed meetings often stayed after school in Coach Ing's homeroom to catch up on items or in the case of some of the younger children gain clarification for some misunderstanding. A bonding of like minds began to be formed. This bonding would continue until our final moments at the provincial championships.

Close to the end of September, students had largely fulfilled the tasks above. The inventory of parts was completed by all of our members; the Official Field was built by four students and a parent to one of those children; all models were built by mini groups of LEGO members; the viewing of related videos took place during all lunch-hour seminars in Coach Ing's room; and all relevant materials were read in small groups during morning and afternoon recess times.

The children had separated themselves into two equal teams. Each team was encouraged to choose a leader, a recorder, and a speaker to be used during group discussions. These students would best represent the voice of the team and be able to bring forth a common voice, not necessarily their own individual voice or opinion.

Richard Yasui, the teacher and coach in charge of the Robotics team at the high school we worked with, agreed to find some high-school mentors and meet with our junior aged children on a regular basis.

Starting September 24, Coach Yasui, his seven mentors, our 24 children, and our tutelage of two coaches and five regular parent volunteers had our first official meeting. It was the first of many fun-filled deep learning, deep teaching, and deep character bonding opportunities that would carry us throughout our scheduled meeting times and well into our provincial championships in early December.

The children met every Monday and Thursday from 3:40–5:40 p.m. from September 24 until November 9, 2007. From November 12 to November 23, they met every night to prepare themselves and hone their skills before the regional tournament on November 24. After winning an award at the regional tournament, the children met every night after school from November 26 to December 7 to further prepare and hone their skills prior to the provincial tournament on December 8.

Children engaged in problem solving

At a "meeting of the minds," as the children on our team often called our discussions, we all thought about ideas in a general sense. We would then break out into smaller groups (three groups of four members per team; two teams). All of our Runnymede CI mentors agreed to sign the FLL Coaches' Promise. Most important, we all agreed to let the children do the work. The children's responsibility was to teach one another how to program, research, problem-solve, and build with each part of the LEGO system.

We, the coaches, were mere facilitators, often enquiring of the students how they planned to solve each problem encountered. The many prompts we used included these: Did you try . . . ? What would happen if this were to take place? How do you know that works or doesn't work? Show me what you mean. How do your other team members feel about the decision or solution that you came up with? Why is it important to test this theory out? For what purpose does this theory matter in the greater scheme of things? Is that a proficient way to solve that problem? Could you program the computer to solve two or three missions at once? Would this method save you time in the end, seeing as you have only two minutes to complete as many missions as you can on the Official Field?

When children are faced with a problem to solve on their own, following a simple set of rules, the deep learning that takes place is astounding. Children learn from one another's mistakes, challenge one another's thinking, set up arguments to arrive at common understandings, and draw upon one another's expertise and experiences. If they continue to argue and disagree to the extent of hurting someone's feelings, an adult will step in and hold the "arguers" accountable.

The children were always excited to find out new ways to program the robot through the use of the software on the computer. Thanks to our mentors, there was a second laptop for our use during the entire season.

Members of both A and B teams decided to look at the energy costs and changes that needed to take place from a global perspective.

Several students rallied together to research and invite various members of our school community to talk about their fields over several nights in our library. Speakers included a member of Bullfrog Power, a green power initiative; a member of Hewlett Packard's Environmental Impact Team; a member and spokesperson from Zero Footprint, a group of individuals who help us track our carbon footprint and impact on our environment at a global level; a teacher and consultant of our Toronto District School Board's Eco Schools Team; and a parent and project coordinator of our Howard P.S. Rejuvenation/Garden Project, a body of volunteers trying to reshape the future of our playgrounds with an environmental flair to add to the beauty and sustainability of a green playground. All of these contacts were made via the students from Grades 4, 5, and 6. They were in charge of the initial calls, the coordination of

speakers, the time frames in which we had to meet as well as the recording of the new information for their research expectations of the project. Notes of gratitude on behalf of the team for a speaker were also addressed by the children.

As we neared our first competition date, the children thought of a plan to reduce our waste even further. Both teams voted on using PowerPoint presentations so that we would only have to provide separate CDs, thus reducing our carbon footprint.

Cooperation within competition

Then we took part in our first competition, one at the regional level, on November 22. Many events went in our favor: our robots were well put together; the children guarded their robots with their lives; and Team A supported Team B and vice versa through all the robotic competitions and during each judged Power-Point presentation.

December 22, we arrived at St. Mildred's School in Oakville. The team that was chosen from the two entries from our school was based on clear criteria: equal representation of Grades 4, 5, and 6 students; equal representation of boys and girls; the person who had the most consistent attendance.

We did not advance further because there were several glitches with both our robots. One was dropped; the other malfunctioned. Our combined PowerPoint presentation was very successful. A team with perfect points on the robotics portion of the competition advanced to the finals in the United States, to take place in March.

The children involved in this project found their engagement most worthwhile. They committed themselves full-heartedly while completing and staying on top of their classroom work, sports teams, and choir engagements throughout our meetings and competitions. They learned the value of gracious professionalism, character development, integrity, honesty, and respect. They now understand how their actions or inactions, both great and small, affect those around them in positive and negative ways that can be profound or miniscule. Many learned to be assertive, to be considerate, to be able to detach, to be patient, to be thankful, to cooperate, to persevere, to be truthful, to be courageous, to be understanding of others' views, to be confident, to be unified, to take ownership of their learning and responsibility for their own actions.

A Witness Report: Did I See What I Thought I Saw?

BY GARY RUSLAND

I was on the bus on my way home from the St. Lawrence Market when I witnessed the events that prompted this lesson. It was sunny and bright and by all appearances, it was going to be a great day. As I watched, not intentionally paying attention, two children ran from the east side of the street directly into traffic. The bus driver blew the horn and hit the brakes, but was unable to stop the kids from running across. As they crossed the yellow lane markers, they were struck by a southbound car.

There were two children, about 7 and 11 years of age. I saw the older child get thrown clear of the car while the younger child's legs were crushed by the tires as they rolled over him.

It was a traumatic experience to watch. As I stood at the side of the street, I was amazed at how fast people had acted to help the injured children. In the background, as at least three-quarters of the people were on their cell phones, I could hear the word "witness" peppered throughout many conversations. At one point I could hear an account that I didn't think was even close to accurate, but which was given with such sincerity that no one hearing it would have doubted that the accident happened that way.

I turned and headed up the street towards home, struggling to deal with what I had just seen and to get control of my emotions. I made it home and it was all I could do to sit in my living room and stare as the images kept flashing in my mind. Questions about what had happened kept popping into my head, especially the one about whose account was the closest to being accurate. I decided to build a lesson from the experience and deal with my feelings that way.

In fact, teachers deal with this type of situation every day. Without seeing events, we are somehow judging every playground and hallway skirmish. We hear accounts from both sides and know instinctively that the truth lies somewhere in the middle between the two or more versions heard. It seemed then that this type of situation might have some resonance with my students.

I began the lesson by asking whether any of my students had ever been a witness to an event at school. Then, I asked if students had ever been questioned by the principal or vice-principal and if everyone's stories were the same for the same event. Of course, they replied that everyone had a different version.

I wrote an eyewitness account of the accident and read it to them. I also provided copies of my text and encouraged the students to ask about any words they didn't know. I read my account as a guided reading where I stopped and talked about what I was reading as I read it. I provided them with a graphic organizer so that they could keep track of details they heard if they chose to. In the organizer there was also a column to write questions that they wanted answered.

After the first reading, I gave out the picture of the accident scene that I had mocked up in PowerPoint. We looked at it together and identified everything in the picture so that everyone knew what they were looking at. I even identified the street and the north and south directions, which gave them a good geographical context.

I read the story again while they had the picture in front of them and referred to the picture as I read. In terms of asking questions, the students then felt more comfortable as they had a visual representation, which seemed to clarify their thoughts. They asked questions about timing, directions, and even about the direction that the sun was shining from. In turn, I asked some questions, for example: "If I saw what I said I saw, where was I on the bus? Was I sitting or standing?"

Once satisfied that each student had a grasp of what had happened, I asked a few big questions. The first one was, "Whose fault was it?" Many answers were thrown at me at once. My next question was, "Can we tell?" Then the next tough question was, "How do we know my account was right?" In fact, the account I wrote was wrong and I wanted them to discover this during the lesson.

We took a look at the story again and picked out what we thought were important details. After much discussion, the students began to question why the bus driver had hit the brakes because clearly the bus was on the other side of the road. They also figured out that the bus driver couldn't have seen the kids before the driver of the car even though the bus driver had blown the horn to prevent the accident.

Once we determined that something was wrong in my account, I mentioned the fact that a tutoring centre was on the other side of the street. This fact caused the students to wonder if the injured children had come from the other side of the street instead of the direction I said they came from.

We returned to the big question "Who fault was it?" This issue caused quite a bit of stir and I assured the students that their opinions would be respected. One student was convinced that it was absolutely the driver's fault. In response, I asked, "If the children ran into the street, how was he supposed to stop in time?" The student looked puzzled and to help clarify, I rephrased my question: "What would the driver's ability to stop depend on?" This question sparked a discussion about cell phones, the driver's overall skill level, and his sobriety.

To pull the discussion back on track, I asked, "Does it matter how fast the driver was going?" Then the light bulbs went on. But we had no way to assess this without more supporting information. Luckily, I had found an equation on the Internet which related the distance required to stop a vehicle as a function of speed. I graphed this information in Microsoft Excel and presented it to the students. They were working on graphing in Math class so it wasn't foreign to them.

Once we had discussed how to read the graph, I asked, "How fast do people drive on Sherbourne Street on a Saturday morning?" This question prompted many different answers from this group of non-drivers so I said: "For argument's sake, let's say he was driving at about 30 km per hour. What does the graph say about how much space he needs to stop?" As it turns out, if he was going that speed and the children ran directly into the street, he probably could not have stopped.

Of course, my next question was, "Does that mean the accident wasn't his fault?" The first response to this question was silence. The students had used this argument many times in their own lives already. "If it was an accident, it wasn't my fault" is a familiar phrase at school and at home.

The question then became "Even if it is not his fault, does he have a responsibility?" I used the example of a student who ruins another student's shirt by accident. We discussed whether the student was responsible for replacing the shirt or not.

Their attention then turned to the children and their mother. "Was it their fault for running into the street?" The consensus seemed to be that they had reduced culpability due to their age. The students did agree that the children were guilty of not looking both ways as they had been taught since Kindergarten. Once we deter-

mined that the children had little responsibility, the students turned their sights on the children's mother. Their point of view was that, if the children were running across the street to their mother, she should have been more in control of them or should have been on the other side of the street.

One student even thought that perhaps the bus driver had been at fault for honking the horn and distracting everyone. The feeling was that the driver would have been distracted by the bus and perhaps the children could not hear their mother yelling, "No!" over the traffic and the bus horn. Only one student thought this and we explored it a bit.

My final question for the activity was this: "If you were a judge and you had to convict someone of injuring these children, who would it be?" In the end, I was pleased that the students had trouble with this question.

We had been engaged all period so I decided to use the debriefing to discuss some safety issues as well as some moral issues. I pointed out that the nurse who assisted the child who had been run over had done at least one thing wrong. We discussed the idea that if someone has been hit by a car, the person should be moved only by the trained emergency workers, due to the risk of neck and spinal damage. In this case, the nurse should not have put the coat underneath but on top and not moved the child.

Finally, we talked about the moral implications of saying that you saw everything when in reality you haven't. The students were in agreement that a person's brain can fill in blanks and create events that did not happen in order to make sense of a given situation. They were also able to see that there often is more than one side to a story and that these questions are not easy. They saw reasons to assign blame to several of the individuals involved, but felt that no one person was 100 percent at fault.

Even eyewitness accounts are not foolproof.

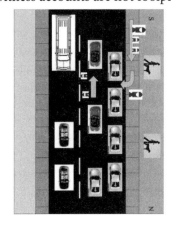

Critical Talk That Matters in Mathematics

BY CATHY MARKS KRPAN

The room was silent. Blank faces stared back at me. Finally, a student spoke up: "Miss, we do not have anything to say. This is mathematics, not language arts." Before I could respond, another student called out: "Yah, we have the answer in our notebook. You just need to tell us if it is correct or not. You give us the rules and then we write them down. That's the way it works."

My Grade 8 students had just finished working through a word problem. Wanting them to share and discuss their approaches, I invited them to talk to each other about their mathematical thinking.

In another teaching context, I asked a Grade 1 student to explain the strategy he used in answering the question $3 + 2 = 5$. He thought a moment and then explained matter of factly: "I don't talk math. You see my answer. That is all we need."

These brief exchanges have been pivot points in my mathematics teaching as I strive to become a better educator. They have taught me that students often view mathematics as an impersonal subject with sets of rules that were created by someone else for them to memorize and follow. They see it as a subject with lots of numbers and little language. They do not understand mathematics as a rich language consisting of words, numbers, and images that need to be explored and taught as an integral part of the mathematics program. Mathematical ideas go well beyond the right answer.

Have we have inadvertently "trained" our students not to think in mathematics? Whether through education or the way mathematics has been presented in social contexts, students have learned that mathematics is a simplistic subject in which the correct answer is all that matters. They understand that if they wait long enough, someone will eventually tell them how to get the answer and what to think.

How do children come to understand that mathematics is not a place for talk and sharing? As a student, I found mathematics to be a distant and cold subject. There were no opportunities for me to make personal connections and I rarely felt confident in my work. However, with the help of some extraordinary teachers and university professors, I became comfortable with mathematics and developed a solid understanding of the concepts I was learning. As I reflect back, I realize that the common strength of these educators was that they invited me to make personal connections in my mathematical thinking. Not only did they create opportunities for mathematical discourse and ask questions that challenged my understanding of mathematical concepts, they also valued my mathematical ideas. I was encouraged to talk about *my* thinking and not just what was written in the textbook. What I thought mattered.

In language arts we often engage our students in interesting discussions about the texts they read. We encourage them to see themselves as authors and appreciate the elements of a good story. We want our students to understand that they can write pieces that matter.

In mathematics, our students need to see themselves as mathematicians and celebrate the beauty of mathematics in their lives. They need to know that they, too, can have mathematical ideas of significance and make discoveries.

Mathematical discourse is key to the development of deep understanding of mathematical concepts and critical thinking skills. It provides opportunities for learners to explore mathematical ideas and connect them together in new ways. When students describe their mathematical thinking, they are consolidating and carefully reflecting on their understanding. Talk makes learning in mathematics personal.

How can educators effectively invite students to engage in mathematical conversations in order to articulate their thinking and deepen their understanding of mathematics?

When I reflect on my social conversations with friends and colleagues, I realize that specific elements make them rich and engaging. We feel comfortable and trust the people to whom we are talking. No matter what opinion, thought, or idea we share, we know that what we say will be valued. If the group does not understand what someone means, they will ask questions. If someone presents a topic with which we are unfamiliar, we ask questions and press further to learn more. One person does not direct discussion or tell others what to say or think. The flow of the conversation is influenced by our own ideas and what matters to us personally. Conversations are an ongoing part of our time together. They are essential to our understanding of each other and the ideas we discuss. Sometimes our discussions break off into smaller ones and other times they become part of a larger group.

There are also social skills we employ to make our conversations work. We know how to wait our turn. We know how to respectfully disagree with someone's idea, and we recognize that everyone has something valuable to share.

Perhaps we can use the attributes and skills I just described to guide our teaching as we support our students in their mathematical conversations in our classrooms. Unlike in language arts, where many students may have read stories, heard stories, and told stories before entering school, in mathematics, students often have limited experiences of sharing and discussing their mathematical thinking (Marks Krpan 2001).

We need to think carefully about how we structure our mathematics programs. Do our children have opportunities to share ideas with each other? Do we create space for talk in our mathematics classrooms that goes beyond our students sharing their answers? Do we provide opportunities for our students to investigate the beauty and patterns of the mathematical concepts they are learning? Through these kinds of experiences, development of critical thinking and student ownership of mathematical ideas begin (Stein 2007).

Creating opportunities in which we explicitly explore the social skills our students require for talk in mathematics is critical. Our students need to know how to disagree with someone in a supportive, respectful way. What does this look like, sound like, and feel like? What does talking about mathematics look like and sound like? How can we communicate our thinking clearly so that others can understand? Creating a class chart that lists the characteristics of these skills can render them more concrete and guide our students as they engage in discussions in mathematics.

Continually modelling rich math talk in our lessons can provide meaningful examples for our students. Modelling does not need to take place with the educator at the front of the classroom. Small-group conversations can be very powerful, creating opportunities for personal mathematical discussions.

By using specific prompts we can assist our students in talking about their thinking. Our prompts can encourage them to go beyond sharing the correct answer and to engage in insightful mathematical discourse (Stein 2007). Asking students to explain why they chose a specific strategy or explore the difference between their strategy and the one their friend chose elicits critical thinking related to their own mathematical work. Inviting our students to analyze and create their own mathematical connections is important.

Many of the effective teaching strategies we use in language arts can assist our students in understanding mathematical vocabulary. Including mathematical images and vocabulary in our word walls can help all learners in understanding mathematical language. Many words have different meanings and applied understandings in mathematics than in everyday English: these include square, foot, and translation (Rubenstein and Thompson 2002). We can cultivate an awareness of these differences by ensuring that our students have opportunities to explore and investigate specific meanings of mathematical language.

A supportive and nurturing classroom culture, in which the investigation of mathematics is encouraged and incorrect answers are explored, creates a collaborative sense of sharing and growth. Teachers and students need to undertake what Howard Gardner (1991) calls "risks for understanding" in which teachers encourage their students to take risks in their thinking and try different problem-solving strategies. As they explore and investigate diverse approaches, students may make errors. However, through this process of examining right and wrong answers and different strategies, students can reconcile their earlier forms of knowing, leading to a deeper understanding of the concepts they are learning.

The journey of talk in mathematics takes time. Many of us are teaching mathematics in ways very different to how we learned it in school. With the infusion of discussions and debates related to mathematical concepts, our role changes from one of content provider to one of facilitator and questioner — we explore and investigate with our students. In doing so we can create rich mathematical experiences that will provide opportunities for our students to see mathematics as an important and personal part of their lives. It is hoped that those students who believe that they don't have anything to say in mathematics will find their voice and learn that they can indeed "talk math."

Conducting a Historical Investigation Using Cooperative Strategies

BY JOHN MYERS

For the longest time history has been treated as simply a story: a chronicle of past events. Yet the Greek roots of the word reflect the idea that historical knowledge comes from inquiry, *making history a verb!* Herein lies an approach to developing critical literacy through historical investigation.

I worked with Georgette Sandhu, a remarkable middle school teacher in Ontario, to develop a template for use in any analysis of a historical event. The template combines a specific variation of the popular jigsaw cooperative strategy and the analysis of primary sources for use in diverse classes.

An overview of the jigsaw structure

Jigsaw was originally developed in order to promote academic achievement and positive social relations among students in the then recently desegregated schools in the U.S. Southwest (Aronson, Blaney, Stephan, Sikes, and Snapp 1978). A number of variations have been developed since then, but I have often seen the strategy work as follows.

1. Students are organized into home groups. For a particular topic each member of a home group is given a piece of text to study.

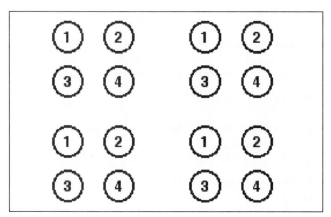

Home groups in the jigsaw structure.

2. Members from each home group meet with counterparts in expert groups reconstituted from the original groups. In Aronson's original model, after considerable practice in leadership skills, a leader in each expert group facilitates discussion so that all have opportunities to contribute to and learn from the dialogue.

3. Finally, the group members return to their home groups to teach their part of the topic to their group mates. Every group member has a unique and necessary part of the material to be learned by all.

New France lesson

In our context, the New France unit is the first unit in Grade 7 history and is taught in the second half of the year. Geography is taught in the first half because its content is more concrete and accessible to students, and can link with content in some of the history units. In the first half of the year, as well, much work is done in literacy to support student work in the later history program.

After a couple of classes on the nature of history as a subject and a look at early French exploration of eastern North America, Georgette poses a question to the class.

"We saw that the early explorers were looking for a passage to India and China, but found this huge land instead: a land with people, animals, trees, and lots of snow in the winter. If you lived back then, what would you do with a land full of snow like this?

"I am the King of France, Louis XIV. I am going to divide you up into groups of four or five. Each group will be a Royal Commission. Your job is to explore the new world and advise me on what to do with these acres of snow."

Georgette carefully selects the teams and mixes the reading levels so that each Royal Commission has strong readers, weak readers, and readers in-between. Students have worked in small groups before and have even done some simple forms of jigsaw. They know the expectations for working in groups. Social skill development has been a key component of Georgette's program.

The home groups are given a few minutes to think about the options presented by their king. These include

- leaving the land to the English
- Christianizing the Aboriginal people in the name of God
- sending farmers to colonize and produce food for the mother country

- taking advantage of the abundant furs and bringing them back to Europe as a valuable item for trade

The members of each home group are reconstituted as exploration groups. Their task is to examine a variety of primary sources provided by their teacher. Because the class of 35 students is large, the groups are doubled: two groups work on the same set of sources.

These groups are not established randomly or heterogeneously, but by reading level. The 1s are the strongest readers and the 4s are the weakest. The primary documents for the stronger readers are text accounts from early French explorers or settlers; pictures dominate the source packages for the struggling readers. For groups adept in math and geography, there are climate graphs. The English Language Learners are matched with supportive teammates of a similar language and cultural background.

The exploration groups meet for about 45 minutes. They work on understanding their packages, making notes, and discussing the king's options. Once members return to their home groups, they discuss the findings from their "explorations" and work on a draft report for the king. In the report they recommend an option with evidence to support their choice.

After about 35 minutes the reports are given orally and followed by a general class discussion. The history class shifts seamlessly into language arts as students begin to write position papers on their personal recommendations — these will be submitted to their teacher. The following organizer is one of the tools they use for assignments of this type.

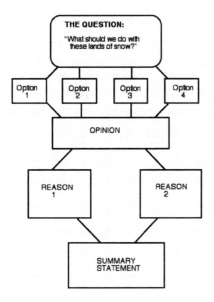

Here are some of the unit's overall expectations:

- Outline the reasons why settlers came to New France; identify the social, political, religious, and economic factors that shaped the colony; and describe how settlers and fur traders interacted with the First Nation peoples.
- Use a variety of resources and tools to gather, process, and communicate information about how settlers in New France met the physical, social, and economic challenges of the new land.
- Identify and explain similarities and differences in the goals and interests of various groups in New France, including French settlers, First Nation peoples, and both French and English fur traders.

The use of homogeneous exploration, or expert, groups allows all students to contribute. Synthesizing information and perspectives to arrive at a single conclusion based on evidence or even a group consensus on a complex issue promotes deep thinking through the medium of purposeful talk.

For teachers, the challenges include the following:

- ensuring students have the required group skills and behaviors to work through complex issues
- selecting the appropriate documents for the appropriate exploration or expert groups

The benefits stem from the power of purposeful talk. Students can take risks with colleagues. They can try out ideas through hypothesizing, verifying, adapting, and revising. When the talk is purposeful, the dialogue among perspectives can result in deeper insights and understandings than can be attained by one student working alone. Finally, quality writing or quality whole-class discussion is more likely after students have talked through the ideas, issues, concepts, and information.

In the end, we have a choice: we can give students a passing acquaintance with surface knowledge unlikely to lead to deeper understanding or something better that will make powerful content more meaningful and more memorable.

9

Deepening Understanding through the Arts

With each new understanding the Arts bring us to, we re-invent ourselves.

The Arts take us more deeply into every text we meet, and they become texts that affect our lives. Through the Arts — music, drama, movement, and visual arts — we imagine ways towards a better social order, towards alternative realities. The Arts bear on our emotional intelligence.

What role does emotion play in becoming a literate human? Why are we so afraid of tapping into this form of intelligence? If students are passionate about their discoveries, if they are engaged in examining the implications of their findings, and if they give them to me with trembling hands because they care about what they have written, then I will read and be involved with both texts and writers. I appreciate the struggle to capture with print and image what enters our minds as we assimilate, interpret, and represent what we think we have found.

In this chapter, contributors present a range of ways to use the Arts to deepen understanding. Kimberly Bezaire says we have much to gain from observing and documenting children's literacy play practices; we also have much to offer as thoughtful play partners and participants. Lynda Pogue invites children to create Storyboxes, representations of their thoughts about a book read. Milica O'Brien selects an author, Barbara Reid, and incorporates her books into classroom literacy events: she promotes discussion and response, as the students employ Reid's art material, Plasticine, to create artistic interpretations. Marni Binder explores students' imaginations through their work with picture books. Wendy Agnew describes the themes that different classes selected to be interpreted and represented through amazing art. Leslie Stewart Rose describes a music class where the teacher shows the students a means of representing musical notation with symbols and deepens their understanding of how music works. Krysten Cameron uses drama strategies to extend and elaborate folk tales and demonstrates how authors have used this strategy to create text versions. In Tiina Moore's story-based school, she can help create a setting for a three-month thematic role-playing exploration of a social studies theme. Nancy Prest takes us to a reconstructed pioneer village where children role-play for two weeks and gain insight into the past. Maryjane Cruise puts her students into the shoes of bullies and victims through drama. In all instances, the influence of the Arts on student lives is apparent.

"This Is the Bestest Day of Mine Whole Life!"
The Power and Potential of Deep Classroom Play

BY KIMBERLY BEZAIRE

The noise level in the classroom rose with excitement when the children discovered a refrigerator-sized cardboard box in the big blocks area. The group spontaneously and cooperatively spent their entire morning designing and negotiating with each other to build and play in the "city" they built around the box. They used every single block in the room. While their teacher photographed this creation, with an aim to include it in her weekly parent update, the Grade 1 class was toured through by the builders. As four-year-old Justin exclaimed, times such as these truly do make for the "bestest" play and learning.

When teachers value, attend to, and take part in classroom play, they open the door to opportunities for children to think and act in profoundly critical and complex ways.

In Kindergarten classrooms, the big block and house corner centres are perennial favorites for freeplay time. Children act out roles, assume favorite characters, retell and re-imagine storylines, and re-enact the drama of their everyday lives.

"You're the baby and I'm the Mamma! And I can't find you, and you're scared," four-year-old Hanna declares as freeplay time begins in the Kindergarten house corner. Over her shoulder, she tosses a gold lamé purse, a favorite prop among this group of Kindergarten players, indicating her grown-up role.

"No, I'm the teenage sister!" counters five-year-old Emily, as she grabs a purse of her own.

"But you're lost," asserts Hanna.

"Yeah, and then you find me and it's my birthday," Emily agrees.

The scene is set for a domestic drama, a storyline these girls have repeated and varied on occasion over the past two weeks. The girls soon add rectangular blocks to their purses, using them as cell phones to send messages and call friends.

A few Grade 3 helpers drift into the classroom. They are friends from the playground and reading buddy time. The classroom teacher, Stefanie, welcomes these play partners, informing them of the current play theme in the house corner, as the players are engrossed in phoning friends for the big birthday party. Passing on some messages pads, new sparkly pencils, and a wipe-off day planner, Stefanie introduces herself and the Grade 3 students as party guests who have arrived early. How can they help get ready for the party?

Meanwhile, with the noise level in the classroom rising, another drama begins in the big block area. "Gonna build a Supercity, cause I'm Superman," four-year-old Justin exclaims with a deepened voice. He stacks large hollow blocks until they tower, wobbly and precarious. He bends his arm to "make a muscle," then grimaces as he knocks the tower to the floor with a stylized punch.

David and Matteo scramble to join in the demolition; then, the trio begins to rebuild. After another crash, they quickly move to the craft table where they begin to fashion utility belts and super gadgets.

"Help! Help!" Stefanie exclaims, sitting next to the demolished block pile, and the players then return to sort through the "rubble" for survivors. Superhero play, too, is a recurring play theme, complicated by the dilemma of whether to allow toys from home or not.

During the "together time" on the carpet, the theme of superheroes is used to promote thoughtful language activities. The wipe-off board records group-time brainstorming on questions such as "What does a hero do?" "Who are our super and everyday heroes?" There are lists of heroes' strengths, weaknesses, powers, and enemies. On the bookshelf and in the block area, Stephanie has included superhero comic books (some added by the Grade 3 reading buddies, who found the topic exciting), as well as picture books, such as *Superhero ABC* and *Superdog: The Heart of a Hero*. Classroom visitors with hero status have included Matteo's aunt, a firefighter, and Hannah's father, who recounted a story of rescuing a lost dog. A bulletin-board displays charts and digital photos taken during freeplay. During one storytime, Hannah exclaimed, "Hey, Jillian Jiggs is a hero!"

With a December birth date, Hannah is among the youngest in the group, yet she makes this connection between texts, linking a new fictional character to classroom discussions and documentation about heroism. Fashioning a superhero cape during make-believe, Hannah tries on the role of a hero, deepening her understanding and exploring her own powerful potential in the process of make-believe. "Heroes save the day," she says. "Heroes do important things."

Make-believe during freeplay — often the favorite, most motivating time of the day for young children — can also be recognized and valued as an optimal time for rich, deep literacy learning and practice. Research evidence (e.g., Kavanaugh 2006) clearly indicates that, as children imagine and act out invented stories and scripts, they are engaged in complex mental, verbal, and social processes. In our peek into this classroom's daily play, we see children engaged in make-believe, composing play narratives, and symbolically transforming objects and play settings in personally meaningful, interesting ways — a block becomes a cell phone, and pieces of cardboard and pipe cleaner become life-saving tools and gadgets. And so, pretend play activities are important and contribute to literacy, for as children spend time fully and enjoyably engaged in such abstract, higher order thinking, they come to practise and someday master the use of representational media.

Students learn to view a scenario from multiple perspectives, perhaps as the baby and the mamma, or as the victim and the hero. As they repeat, revise, and re-vision their play narratives again and again, they engage in processes that enable deep comprehension and meaning making — literacy! By offering multiple texts, in the form of various personal stories, interesting books, props, and toys, and through her documentation of classroom talk, Stefanie is creating excellent conditions for deep, critical literacy play.

Research also tells us that pretend play becomes more frequent, social, and complex when children are in classrooms where their play is valued and supported (Kavanaugh 2006), and where an adult is engaged and thoughtfully models role play (Podlozny 2000).

Stefanie "reads" and responds to the children's play as a text by which she learns more about her students — their interests, strengths, and needs. She applies this knowledge in her choice of classroom teaching materials and choice of teaching strategy. Play props for the house and big block play areas, dress-up clothes, books, maps, charts, posters, writing and drawing implements . . . Stefanie provides these materials as play-literacy objects, as well as allowing play objects from home, valuing their potential for inviting children to expand and extend their favorite play narratives. She offers invitations to deepen role play by cueing make-believe, by acting in role with a supporting or alternate point of view, thoughtfully entering the play at times and at others, observing and valuing the play through documentation with classroom notes, digital photos, and audio recordings.

Principles for deepening play

- *Knowing the players.* Through participation, observation, and documentation, teachers gather information that reveal children's strengths, needs, and interests, as well as demonstrating to the children that make-believe play is valued.
- *Providing multiple, interrelated texts.* Teachers offer multiple texts that relate to the children's interests and support the children in considering varied perspectives. The goal is to develop textured, complex understandings. Possible texts include a variety of play props, toys, oral stories, picture books, information books, how-to texts, websites, video games, collector cards, movies, and music.
- *Scaffolding — Building a play-literacy classroom community.* Teachers offer invitations and enter the play through imitating and improvising from children's play scripts. Teachers prompt make-believe by cueing and role modelling. By recognizing the importance of play partners in the form of classmates, parent volunteers, reading or play buddies, and siblings from older and younger grades, teachers build a play-literacy community of many players and perspectives.
- *Finding props that matter.* Teachers provide toy texts and open-ended play items — things that can be used in many ways, such as blocks, scarves, pots and pans, and wooden spoons. These props can be easily used as symbolic objects; they have meaning and relevance to the children's everyday and make-believe lives.
- *Allowing for repetition, replaying, and re-visioning.* Teachers strive to provide the space, time, and flexibility that children need to extend, expand, and elaborate their play episodes. Although finding the time can be a challenge, teachers trust children's natural learning/teaching potential, and do their best to tolerate and embrace the mess, noise, and chaos that often accompany deeply engaged make-believe.

Deepening Comprehension through Building a Storybox

BY LYNDA POGUE

The Storybox can be a powerful learning tool for students as they try to represent their interpretations of a text. Teachers can also use it to instruct, model, motivate, and introduce novels, characters, concepts, issues, poetry, or picture books. The Storybox involves hands-on, participatory learning, and understanding of the text deepens as students respond to and utilize the concepts and ideas of the text in order to present their interpretations.

Use of the Storybox can enhance subject areas, such as language arts or English, math, geography, history, science, and the Arts. It promotes creative adaptation and assimilation, vocabulary development, storytelling or story making, and active learning.

All the ingredients for making the story come alive are placed in the Storybox. The title is on the front of the box and a cue card is glued on the back along with a numbered list of inclusions for the presentation.

The box, usually the size of a shoebox, sits on the presenter's lap or on a low table set before the audience. The presenter finds a way to hook the audience immediately, perhaps by slowly putting on a costume, playing a short piece of music, asking a question, or reading a letter. Somehow, the teller creates a way to set the stage for the story that's about to be revealed.

Once the lid is opened, the story unfolds as the presenter takes each item out of the box and uses it to move the story along. Some items are fastened to the box while others are simply lifted out and used to illustrate a point.

You may wish to create your own Storybox, especially for younger students who then use it as a retelling tool. If a storybook was used as the basis for the Storybox, the younger students will reference the book as they use the Storybox, making the story come alive in their hands.

Students act as detectives to **de**-construct what's inside and to **re**-construct the story themselves. Then, they **co**-construct how they will tell the story to an audience. Usually, a Storybox is constructed and presented by one person; however it may be done with two.

Rehearsing is critical for success in presenting the Storybox. In the early stages, as they move from reading to telling using the Storybox, students return to the story over and over. Eventually, they know the story well enough to simply tell it.

Note: If a story is too long, the teller may just tell the beginning and leave it to the audience to read the rest in the book. This practice creates a high motivation to read. Or, a précis of the story can be told up to the point of the Storybox, and then the Storybox is presented.

Here is a simple example of a Storybox based on a picture book.

Three to five realia, or real objects, make the Storybox have a surprising personal connection with the audience.

Title is clearly visible.

Characters glued or taped to clothespins and are attached to box as story unfolds.

Possible Storybox extensions

After the whole class reads a novel, partners can be assigned different chapters to retell the story by creating Storyboxes. To deepen the experience, one set of partners could be given the task of creating a new chapter to introduce a new beginning and another set of partners could create a new ending. The whole class now hears, sees, and experiences the novel again, as pairs of students present their chapters through their Storyboxes.

Students may interview parents, caregivers, the principal, the caretaker, businesspeople, authors, and others and then create a Storybox on or for the person interviewed.

The Storybox can illustrate a developmental concept, for example, tomato seed to ketchup or Alexander Graham Bell to iPhones.

The Storybox can be used to illustrate a problem or unearth an important issue that's presented to the class. Groups are then given five minutes to come up with a web of solutions on chart paper and return to share their ideas.

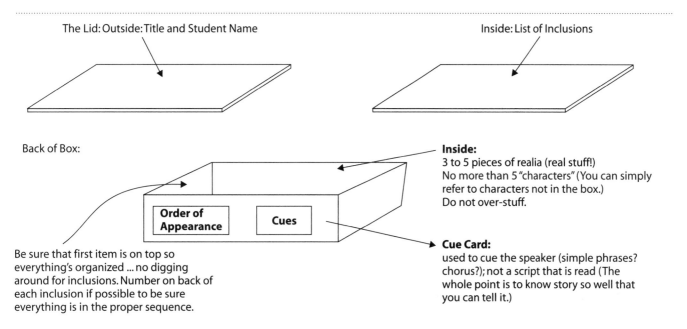

The Lid: Outside: Title and Student Name

Inside: List of Inclusions

Back of Box:

Be sure that first item is on top so everything's organized ... no digging around for inclusions. Number on back of each inclusion if possible to be sure everything is in the proper sequence.

Order of Appearance

Cues

Inside:
3 to 5 pieces of realia (real stuff!)
No more than 5 "characters" (You can simply refer to characters not in the box.)
Do not over-stuff.

Cue Card:
used to cue the speaker (simple phrases? chorus?); not a script that is read (The whole point is to know story so well that you can tell it.)

Creating a Storybox

Instead of a shoebox, what else can you use? A suitcase? Backpack? Briefcase? Lunchbox?

Who's Your Audience?
Friends, classmates, parents/caregivers, seniors, other classrooms, library, younger kids ...

Box is closed at beginning (on lap if possible) and audience is close to speaker.

No more than 2 people do a Storybox together. Perhaps one could narrate while the other moves the inclusions.

Be careful about timing.

Find a unique way of hooking the audience before opening the box.

How could you use it to retell?
pre-tell (a new beginning)?
post-tell (a new ending)?
or to "Tell the story" of a famous person, issue, journey, song, poem, concept, storybook, chapter of a new book, new perspective on an old book?

Magic happens when you open the box and tell the story. Can you use props? music? You are in role.

The Storybox becomes an improvisation box with all the makings of a story inside the box. This could be created either by a teacher or another set of partners. One or two students open the box without rehearsing and instantly create a story. Questioning from the audience while the two characters are still in role could follow the drama. This may be used as a stimulus for writing.

A map becomes a background prop and students refer to it as they use a Storybox to present the journey of an ancient or modern explorer.

The Storybox may become a tool for presenting the findings of a research project, a critique of a film, or a follow-up to what was learned from a class trip.

Intergenerational studies may enhance communication in your neighborhood. Students each create a Storybox of their lives (past, present, and perhaps dreams for the future). The teacher arranges for a visit to a local home for seniors and in advance, pairs each student with a senior. All the Storyboxes are presented at the same time in one room, student to senior.

Creating Texts through Plasticine

BY MILICA O'BRIEN

My primary ESL students were reluctant speakers, withdrawn and hesitant to take risks in their learning, more so than other primary ESL students I have taught in past years. Consistent with all my teaching practice, I decided to motivate and engage them through integrating the Arts.

To stimulate their natural curiosity and enhance their confidence to communicate in English, we embarked on a study of Canadian Plasticine artist and author Barbara Reid. Each day of our study, our read-aloud time focused on one of the author's books. We spent a lot of time exploring the intricate details of her brilliant work, learning about foreground, background, horizon lines, and bird's eye views. My role was to guide the ESL students to look critically at each picture, modelling how to think aloud about details I noticed in each one, encouraging them to do the same.

The students learned to create wonder questions about how Barbara Reid created the textures, shapes, and details in her pictures. As the problem-solving process began, we created a KWL chart (What We **K**now, What We **W**ant to Know, What We **L**earned). Once we had read all of Barbara Reid's books, we viewed her video, *Meet the Artist: Barbara Reid.* In the video, Reid demonstrates many of her techniques and gives students suggestions on ways to create their own Plasticine artworks.

My ESL students' imaginations had been awakened and their motivation to speak in English and have quiet conversations about Reid's artwork had begun. They were eager to create their own Plasticine art — and wanted to talk about it.

First, the students traced on paper the perimeter of a CD cover, which acted as a frame and base to hold their artwork. They chose their favorite animal from one of Reid's books and sketched it on paper inside the traced perimeter of the CD cover, paying attention to details. Each completed sketch was placed under a clear CD lid. The students used their sketch as a guide for their Plasticine work.

Stressing with the students that their most valuable tools were their eyes to see detail and their fingers and thumb to create the details, I also provided them with a variety of working tools. These included a plastic knife, spoon, and fork, straws, textured fabrics such as burlap and plastic netting, and their all-time favorite tool: the garlic press. Upon completion of their artworks, all of the students wrote procedural pieces of writing about their pictures, with teacher support and guidance. They had so much they wanted to say about the process and what they had learned.

The culmination of this study was an art show where each student invited teachers and parents to attend. The visitors were encouraged to ask the students questions about their work. Student artists stood by their artworks and, to the best of their ability, answered the questions. They spoke freely and candidly about their creative Plasticine pictures.

Arts stimulating talk

Two of my ESL students stood out during this study. Nawang, in Grade 3, and Lhamo, in Grade 2, were my newest students to arrive in Canada. Both were reluctant speakers in the ESL program. The Barbara Reid study stimulated their enthusiasm to learn and speak English as well as sparked their imaginations to create several magnificent pieces of Plasticine art. They developed such inner confidence to speak that they began inviting peers from other classes to see their creations, telling them about the process they learned, confidently answering their questions. Their interest in the Plasticine project was so great that they became regular visitors to the ESL classroom during recess and lunch hour, wanting to talk about Barbara Reid's work and making connections with their own art pieces. Their work was filled with extraordinary detail.

During this project the real magic happened when Nawang and Lhamo invited their classroom teacher, Sarah Liscombe, to come and see their work. Their teacher was overwhelmed by their detailed pictures and their enthusiasm, so much so that she invited the two artists to teach their classmates the art process they had learned in ESL class. It was amazing to see such a dramatic transformation in these two students from reluctant speakers to self-confident students, willing to speak in front of their peers as experts on Plasticine art.

The Barbara Reid study was the catalyst to help my ESL students gain confidence in their ability to speak. They wondered about and questioned Reid's techniques, problem-solving together the challenges that their Plasticine art pieces posed. As the ESL students' curiosity peaked and their self-confidence strengthened, they began to find their voice. They asked advice from one another and made decisions together. They became teachers, freely speaking English with each other as they discovered new techniques and shared them together. My role was to support their learning by encouraging them to take risks in their work and asking higher order questions to help them think creatively.

Teaching through the Arts helped my primary ESL students to express themselves artistically and then use their words to reflect about their experience in a procedural piece of writing. The Arts levelled the playing field for these students, as they all found success in their exploration of Plasticine art.

Experiencing Multiple Literacies through Picture Books

BY MARNI BINDER

"What is the imagination?" I asked a Grade 3 class. A multitude of responses rose excitedly.

- Make up stuff that is not really real.
- It is in your mind.
- It allows you to create things — anything.
- You can have your own little world in your mind.
- When you are bored, you can play stuff in your mind.
- You can make up a friend, an imaginary friend.
- It allows you to go anywhere.
- You can do anything you want to.
- I use it to write fiction things.

This was the beginning of a wonderful project with an inner-city Grade 3 class based on the breathtaking images and concepts of *Imagine a Night* by S. L. Thomson and illustrated by Rob Gonsalves. We were exploring what the imagination is and how we could apply our understandings to creating a class book. The teacher in this class used art as a way for the children to express themselves in their literacy work. Book publishing that built on use of the writing process was a regular practice. At the time, the class had been exploring the ocean, underwater creatures, and habitats. Collectively, the class decided that they would make a book, *Imagine an Ocean*.

In my experience working with children, I find that multiple forms of expression unfold when the window is opened for imaginative and creative work, strengthening the contextual richness and the understanding of their socio-cultural landscapes. When children imagine and draw, paint, play, dance, and write or talk about the text, a depth of awareness in their learning emerges. Their inner speech is made more personal and public. Part of the beauty of working with children is that we, the adults, are allowed to explore our imaginative processes too. Isn't that what education should be about?

Kieran Egan (2005) and Karen Gallas (2003) conceptualize the embodiment of the imagination as an essential part of learning. The unfolding of the imagination transforms into a tangible view of how children think and see the world. Its centrality to education should be woven into the fabric of the teaching and learning process. One way to thread imaginative texture into the curriculum is by engaging children's multiple literacies through quality picture book use.

Ways of imaginative talking: The Imagine an Ocean project

On the first day of the month-long Imagine an Ocean project, I asked students: "What is the imagination?" As described previously, many ideas emerged. I then read *Willy the Dreamer* by Anthony Browne. Soft music played in the background; lights were dimmed. After the reading, the children were asked whether they had anything else to add to our list. Among their eager responses were these:

- You can do things that are impossible.
- You can picture how it will be when you grow up.
- When you hear a story, you picture it in your mind.
- Daydreaming
- What grownups were like when they were younger.
- Ideas come from the imagination.

On the second day, with quiet music again playing, I read *Imagine a Night*. I first read the book without showing the illustrations, allowing students to visualize their own images — I view the use of visualization as an essential practice in the classroom. Heightening imaginative capacities empowers children to take control of their own images, where sensory experiences enhance embodied knowing. Discussing what the children picture in their minds from the words alone validates personal interpretation and meaning.

The book was then reread, the illustrations shown. The artwork was discussed, as well as the artist's approach to conveying meaning. This segued beautifully into ideas for students' own class book. The discussion continued with their classroom teacher and through consensus, a decision on the focus of the book was reached: Imagine an Ocean.

Watercolors were selected as the medium for students to work with. Grade 8 students who had skill with this medium came to the class and worked with small groups of children. They first played with the watercolors before creating their final images. The accompanying text emerged from the paintings, very much like the Thomson and Gonsalves book. This progression enhanced the concept of process in the imaginative and creative endeavor.

Once their book was laminated and bound, I returned to the classroom. *Imagine a Night* was once again read. I then pulled out the children's completed book, *Imagine an Ocean,* and read it to them. Their eyes were filled with wonder and pride over the work they had done. The underwater images floated off the pages. Knowledge of the ocean, its delightful creatures, and habitats came to life in meaningful ways. Image and text merged within a multi-modal lens. The teacher contributed by creating the cover of the book. "Teachers need to be creative, too," she said.

The Imagine an Ocean project reflected the significance of being able to understand, communicate, and think in alternative ways, using a variety of symbols that characterize a particular form of expression.

Turning the pages to multiple literacies

I have watched for many years the joy in children's eyes when a picture book is opened and they are drawn into the story. Worlds are often reconstructed when they place themselves in the story and relate it to their reality. From experiences with images, children are able to construct meaning that can empower and transform events in their lives. Symbols of expression that move beyond text offer the possibilities to children of new literacies that can speak to others and nurture expression in alternative ways.

Bob Steele (1998) believes that "children think words while planning a drawing; they conduct internal monologues or talk out loud to themselves as they draw, and put thoughts, words, and their drawings together on conversation with adults when drawings are finished" (p. 149). I have witnessed internal and external monologues when children are creating.

As a teacher, I want to promote the significance of the imagination, the use of quality picture books, and the multiple forms of expression that unfold in children's lives through such encounters. The contextual qualities of picture books create the possibilities for meaningful artistic narrative experiences, informing and shaping children's literacy acquisition through multiple ways of knowing.

Here are a few ways to help children think creatively and imaginatively by working with picture books.

Honoring multiple literacies

Mikhail Baryshnikov with Vladimir Radunsky created *Because . . .* , a whimsical book with captivating visuals about being yourself and allowing your creative energy to flow. In the story, a young child describes his grandma's antics leapfrogging, rolling, and flapping outside through a week. Everyone in the neighborhood, even the cat, asks: Why? Why is she moving in such unusual ways? "Because . . . I-am-a-dancer!" she exclaims.

Many activities, such as the following, can emerge from reading *Because . . .* :

- letting the children leap, flap, and swing outside or in the classroom, having them imagine different ways they can move their bodies, and having them draw different actions, games, and movements resulting from their explorations
- creating their own personal "because" in drawing, painting, or a collage of images and words
- composing acrostic poems related to the story and using the word BECAUSE
- exploring the world of dance or pictures of movement (also from the natural world) through the Internet
- designing collages of different forms of dance or movement from pictures and words found on websites

These ideas foster and honor multiple literacies in the classroom. All children are provided with the opportunity to "speak" their own expressive language.

Fostering the imagination

In the wonderful story *Jeffrey and Sloth* by Kari-Lynn Winters, illustrated by Ben Hodson, Jeffrey doodles a sloth into life and Sloth encourages him to draw his thoughts instead of struggling to write them. Sloth baits Jeffrey, stating that he doesn't have any good ideas. Sloth gets Jeffrey to draw things for him until finally Jeffrey bursts with ideas to keep Sloth busy and prove he has ideas to draw and write about.

This book lends itself to many engaging activities, including these:

- creating a digital collage of countries and images from the places Jeffrey sends Sloth to visit

- having children create versions of where Sloth will go, what lakes he will swim, what mountains he will climb, and so on
- creating a Readers theatre dialogue between Jeffrey and Sloth
- re-creating, in pairs, the story or sections of the story in movement
- developing a visual story map of the book and extending it to the continuing adventures of Jeffrey and Sloth
- discussing why Jeffrey changed or what would happen if he joined Sloth

Conclusion

Quality picture books are a gift to the world of the imagination. Experiencing picture books in meaningful ways allows children to retell, reinvent, or express their own visions of what the books become for them. These deeply personal and mindful engagements cultivate a wealth of creative and imaginative activities in the classroom. Picture books allow for drawing, painting, play, dance, poetry, and other forms of multi-modal expression to interweave the imaginary and real worlds of aesthetic experiences. Not only do the intricate details of how children construct this lived meaning emerge, but also unveiled are the multiple ways literacy is construed through artistic forms of expression. From reading pictures, to reading text, to reading the world of the child, teachers deepen their own learning constructs through collaborative imaginative engagements with the children they teach.

Thematic Explorations through Visual Art

BY WENDY AGNEW

Curriculum is fluid —— its ripples emanate from pebbles of desire.

At my school, the year begins in June. At that time, we collaborate on the next year's theme, and this theme gives shape to a year of research projects created by the Grades 7 and 8 students and their environment. Through the arts of narrative, theatre, visual artifacts, and film, we attempt to create complex and powerful media representations of our developing school community.

Our brainstorming sessions all aim to be a democracy of dialogues. Ideas spark and flare: "I have some old plywood." "I want to do plays about the witch trials." "I want to do thousands of hand prints on the wall." "I want to make a mess . . ." "I want to make a movie." "I want to go to the forest." And so on. A litany of wants ensues from this community of student artmakers. We are preparing for the following year's program of projects that will help our students examine, portray, and reflect upon their values, their ideas, and their futures through the deepening perceptions of artistic experiences. It is my job to frame their learning explorations through the Arts, and from their discussions, I create an overriding prologue to act as a guide for the experience.

For the artmaking projects this past year, each class chose its media and its texture to work with. Through this chaotic and sometimes frustrating process, the artistic dialogues of the students evolved into the artistic texts that follow, and the the students' collaboration resulted in significant artistic and living-through experiences.

Class one: Three hundred suns

Prologue: *Once there was a school without a face. A whispering wall cries: "Cover me with your loving marks. Define me with your imaginations. Make of me more than a utilitarian barrier and prove that life is an aesthetic poem on the kneecap of infinity."*

We proceeded to create a series of panels to hang on the walls of the school. This project grew from a suggestion to create handprints inspired by artist Richard Long. The tile project evolved using as a theme anything to do with sunlight, but with a strong ecological flavor. This project provided a visual signature for everyone in the school — from the daycare infants to the teachers.

Materials: 300 bisque tiles, 10 bottles of underglaze, three glazing pens, small paintbrushes, sponges; materials, guidance, over-glaze, and firing provided by The Art Studios

Mounting materials: 2 sheets 4 by 8 half-inch plywood, tile adhesive, moulding, white paint, stain, glue gun, concrete screws

As a constructed text, the tiles create a symphony of individual images that "speaks" every day as long as we are there to visually "hear." Each tile acts as a window into the artist, thereby permanently texturing external and internal space.

Class two: My Mona

Prologue: *Then the Gods of Waste were flummoxed and swallowed their trash and were reborn in glories of sandpaper and sweat. And would became wood and the trees were joyful to see what they had done.*

The students ripped apart old plywood; they lovingly cut, sanded, filled, and stained the wood to enhance the grain, and they sanded and filled bigger cracks. Next, they researched and designed their explorations on paper. They then applied base stain and pencilled in the

artwork; they commenced painting. We then used old nail holes as punctuation to our efforts to recycle the ghosts of trees into artistic tributes and completed the artwork. We treated all the pieces with overcoat. In April, the artwork was installed.

Now, as we walk along the hallways, our permanent installations fill our minds with textures of toil, triumph, tenderness, and gratitude for artists of the past.

Materials: approximately four trash pieces of 4 by 8 plywood, sandpaper, wood filler, stain, art books for research, pencils, acrylic paint, UV inhibiting varnish, washers, and concrete screws

Class three: Glorious galleries

Prologue: *We move backwards, our signatures, shining like Hansel's breadcrumbs in the forests of art history. We step lightly, stopping to admire the view, but completion makes us hungry for more, that and the deadline, that final period of time after which there is no pressure. We nudge the presence of the dead with our memory stories and through our re-creation of the lives of artists, we create a café of ghosts in our performance.*

Amid the galleries that extended throughout school and playground, we told our own stories through our research. (Or did we tell the stories of others through the context of ourselves?) We chose and researched art-

ists for our dramatis personae projects. We created a video of interviews and vignettes, role-playing nine artists. Then, we developed portfolios and began filming *Art Talk*; we finished and edited the film, and screened the DVD. We projected this on a bedsheet hung at the end of a hallway, and the images looped throughout the day, reminding us of the gifts of the past.

Materials: art materials, camera, blank tapes, computer, projector, and bedsheet. Students created costumes and artifacts as well as a potluck feast.

Class four: The Tempest

Prologue: *What does literature tell us about history? Who are we and how much deeper can we become through our language explorations? What is the gift of performance? And how is nature the greatest stage?*

Using Shakespeare's *The Tempest*, the class explored and researched colonialism through the lens of the islanders in the play. The students created a court case, charging Prospero's descendants with imprudent stereotyping and theft. We went to the forest in May and filmed the play there. The film was later presented while a video of the students' Renaissance research looped in the foyer. At the end-of-year celebration, each student was presented with a DVD.

Become your Ancestor Project

Some members of Artists' Café

Shipwreck on the Banks of the Stream

Discovering Symbolic Ways of Transcribing Music

BY LESLIE STEWART ROSE

It is Fun Friday, the afternoon of the weekly surprise. Twenty-eight Grade 7 students tumble into the classroom from a rainy afternoon recess. They are curious about the unusual materials that Mr. Benjamin has set out before him. They wonder what is in store for them today, as they group themselves on the carpet, around the strategically placed piles of prepared materials.

"Mr. B" draws upon his passion for listening to music and his understanding of dialogic inquiry to engage the class as a community of learners towards student-constructed deep understandings. Students are responsible for the construction of communal knowledge by imagining possibilities, considering perspectives, offering insights, comparing and analyzing ideas, building on their ideas in order to develop listening skills which deepen their understanding of music and their personal musical experiences.

The central activity of active musical engagement, whether it is performing, composing, creating, or responding as an audience, is listening. MRI studies of the brain's ways of experiencing music reveal that listening is not passive, but active and complex (Jourdain 1997). The *listening brain* processes variability in pitch patterns, rhythmic patterns, tone colors, dynamic levels, and tempo and the relationships among them. One aspect of listening is simply the brain comparing and categorizing: "Have I heard this before? "Is this familiar?" In order to do this, the listening brain is always seeking patterns and then anticipating patterns, on micro and macro levels. Hearing the chorus, or refrain of a song, over and over can be an experience of great satisfaction.

Though we might think we seek comfort in familiarity, the brain attends to what is new. Too much repetition without enough contrast leads to boredom and disengagement. This skill of comparative discrimination is why the old and repetitive sounds of the construction next door or the unchanging bass drum pattern fades to the recesses of consciousness. It is also a key piece to developing deep understandings about music and passionate responses to music. I believe that it is in the active state of expectation and anticipation, when we are processing just ahead of the actual sound of music, that we derive inexpressible experiences of ecstasy, the deep, powerful, overwhelming, and mysterious emotions and fulfillments from music.

One major challenge in developing these listening abilities lies in the nature of music itself, as perceptible to the brain and body through vibration in a somewhat ephemeral event tied to a moment in time. This characteristic makes engagement, observation, description, feedback, and evaluation challenges for music education in schools. In this invisible, temporal world of sound, how can a teacher understand the listener's experience and support the development of listening skills? How can we know the hidden world of what and how a person is hearing? The following presents a strategy with manipulatives and dialogue as informative ways to make approximate representations, to make visible and stable illustrations of what and how we hear, interpret, and experience music.

Representing music through shapes

Mr. Benjamin lays out the rules of the game.

"I am going to sing you a song; one of my personal favorites. When you hear something, a unit of music, you represent it with one of the symbols from the pile of shapes that I have set out for you. Every time you hear that *something*, that pattern, that *something similar*, you use the same symbol to represent it. If you hear something new, you represent it with a new symbol, like we did when we had some lemonade. And again, when we had some bacon, we used yet another symbol. Each *something* gets its own symbol to represent it. Are you ready? Listen carefully!"

Mr. Benjamin sings a dramatic rendition of "Twinkle, Twinkle, Little Star," and the students listen, think, and represent.

"Do you think it will be a top-10 hit? Does anyone want to hear it again?" Mr. Benjamin, though a bit of a comedian, performs with seriousness and focus. He sings again, adding conducting-like gestures. Some students join in. He works hard to re-present the familiar melody to engage the critical Grade 7 audience. Choosing the child's lullaby is a risk, but he needs a simple melody to begin this work. Most of the students have come to trust "Mr. B's unique sense of humor" and know that he won't treat them like babies, even though it is a nursery song. Some students continue thinking and manipulating their colorful cut-out shapes.

Next, the students find a *shoulder partner*, someone close by with whom they can share their representation. As the song is sung again, the students each use a finger to point to the shape that was used to represent it. Everyone notices that some representations are the same and that some are different. Fatima offers a representation of how she interprets the music. She points to the shapes as she sings and explains.

"I used two circles to represent the middle part [sings] "up above the world so high, like a diamond in the sky" — you can hear it goes from high to low. [She moves her hand to show each note as it descends lower in pitch.] See, they are exactly the same!"

ABBA

Joey offers his own interpretation based on his experiences playing guitar: "Yeah, but I put those two as one. I think the middle section should be represented by one shape. That's how I heard it, anyway. You see that repetition, that pattern, in the music I play on my guitar."

ABA

Mr. Benjamin wonders aloud whether "different" means wrong.

Melissa doesn't accept that just any answer is correct, but does see how two answers could both be accurate representations. She says: "Well, you *could* be "wrong" — but not just because it's different. You could have different patterns for the same music but they are both right. But in the case of being wrong, well, someone could have not heard — could have not picked out what was the same or what was different. If they listen to it again — they might hear it differently and fix it."

Karleen agrees: "Me, too. I didn't hear it [Fatima's] way. I heard that those two parts combined to be one section — like Joey says. But I totally get what you [she is talking directly to Fatima] are saying . . . but it's like the next level down. If you think about the next level down, you could show it like this . . ."

Karleen grabs more shapes and constructs a new "layer" of meaning. She has taken ideas that her peers have suggested and, on the spot, explores a new perspective of listening and thinking about "Twinkle, Twinkle":

Creating a space to generate multiple ways of hearing

ABCCAB

the same piece provides a context for students to build knowledge together. Each student's personal interpretation is shared and valued, as everyone in the class attempts to hear it through each others' ears. Armed with sticky tack, Mr. Benjamin posts the three representations on the board and plays a devious game.

"We can't have *all* these different answers and they all be accurate, now can we?!" he asks. "Which *one* is correct? Don't we always have to have one right answer?"

The class asserts all at once: "No, they are accurate, but we just heard and represented them in different ways."

Mr. Benjamin listens in on the small-group discussions, commenting on the notion of playing with multiple possibilities. "We can actually see the students thinking, changing their minds, making their decisions. Because we are using manipulatives, they can *play* with the ideas; they explore and change their minds. Or show that they see it many different ways all at once. It's great because there is no one answer — there could be 28 different 'right' answers, 28 ways of hearing it."

Psychological experiences of listening

Next, the rocking rhythms of Elvis Presley's "Jailhouse Rock" fill the room. The students seek out the shapes they need to represent what they hear. Jamal hears this:

Intro ABABAB*B(solo)*ABABtag

Jamal realizes the simplicity of its form and exclaims: "Are you telling me that Elvis made millions of dollars with a song that is just two parts? Are you serious? Hey, I can do that! All you need is a good hook, a good chorus that everyone can sing along to!"

Further questions prompt conversations about the *psychological experiences of listening* to music. What is a "hook"? What are your criteria for an effective "chorus" in a song? What songs do you know that have an unexpected part in them? Do you know songs where another song shows up in them? Do you know a song in which the drums stop playing for a few bars and it sounds great? What was the pattern? How did the performer or composer trick your ear or deceive your expectations? What were you expecting? What song would you identify as ineffective? How would you change that song to make it more effective? Using their experiences and own terminology and language, the students are discussing, among other things, unity — the tensions between repetition and contrast, or as curriculum writers label it, *form*.

Mr. Benjamin summarizes what they have already discovered: "We could call these sections that we are hearing *square* and *circle* or we could call them *verse* and *chorus*, in this case, or we could call them *A* and *B*."

He asks the students whether ABA is truly possible. Is the second *A* ever heard and experienced in the same way as the first *A* is? The talk centres on the music experiences of repetition and anticipation, and how music makers deny or fulfill listening expectations.

Jamal moves the class beyond thinking about *what* is heard to an exploration of how we psychologically

experience listening to music. "The chorus feels different every time. The more you hear it, the more you feel part of it — everyone sings along at the chorus."

Joey returns to the idea that "musically though, the music is just plain ABA."

Multiple lenses of analysis

These discussions are interrupted by a passionate debate building at the back of the classroom. André has added another shape to represent the section that is "all instrumental" and "has a guitar solo." Joey, our resident guitar player, says: "No, if you listen to it, the chords are all the same; the background is all the same. It's just a guitar making up solo, and it has replaced the vocals, but it is the same!"

André justifies his position, explaining how it is different enough to warrant a new shape. "But the whole experience of listening to it is different. You notice it because it's not the same ol' blah blah of the lyrics. It has a new job to do — otherwise, the listener is going to get bored and tune out." Joey, recognizing that it has a different function, acknowledges Andre's point, but also sees that it's the same harmonic progression.

Joey is able to deal with the tensions between the two ideas by recognizing that there are two lenses of analysis: one, the harmonic; and two, the listener's experience. He creates a way to represent both ideas:

For the final tune for the day, "All Shook Up" by Elvis Presley, the groups of four are given the challenge to brainstorm and create as many different representations as they can, to explore the diversity of possibility, to think on many levels through many lenses. Approaching the tune this way steers students away from possibly becoming attached to their personal ways of hearing. Key to brainstorming is avoiding judgment and making a long list of possibilities.

Karleen hears it this way:

Jamal hears it this way:

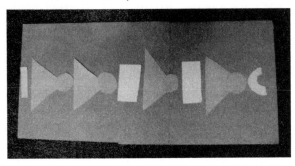

Later, groups are asked to come to a consensus and explain how they represent the song and why they made the choices they did. These perceptive young musicians hear the piece in many different ways. Balancing the emotional and analytic experiences, they apply previous knowledge, they explain and justify, and they make value statements about personal experiences of listening to the song.

Students link this learning to personal experiences.

Fatima has played the piano for five years and is practising for her Grade 3 Royal Conservatory of Music exam. She is shocked. "I've never listened to music this way before. This is crazy! I never knew!" She strikes up a conversation about a piece she is playing on the piano.

Students in another group announce that they will bring in their favorite songs for next class to give "Mr. B" an education and bring him into the 21st century!

As Mr. Benjamin watches his students work in many different ways, he wonders about the different ways that popular musicians and classical musicians are trained to hear music and what that might mean to him as a classroom teacher. He relates these ideas to his own life, saying: "Can you imagine trying to analyze a Bach fugue this way! Or can you imagine analyzing a complicated art rock piece by RUSH? It would blow your mind!"

Mr. Benjamin then moves everyone's attention to the big questions written on chart paper posted on the chalkboard:

- How might my experience of eating breakfast be like the experience of listening to "Twinkle, Twinkle, Little Star"?
- What is it about a song that makes it rewarding to listen to?

In small groups, the students develop possible answers which they are eager to share with the whole class. A burgeoning game of Jeopardy is redirected by skillful questioning towards inquiring conversations about time as a type of space, about reasons to want to be able to stop time, problems with time travel, and back to the challenges, limitations, and practicality of using words to represent sound and the general questions about music as a language and whether music can have meaning.

Mr. Benjamin attempts to capture all their ideas and new questions on the chart paper. As the learners connect their understandings and ideas, a mind map begins to emerge. Mr. Benjamin brings in the class talking stick to help the students take turns. He moves the class seamlessly between large and small groups. He uses paired talk so that everyone gets a chance to share their ideas — the students are constructing their own understanding of musical *form* and the psychology of musical experience. He measures the lesson's success, in part, by the new questions that arise. At this time, he is less worried about the answers, and nobody else seems to mind that there is no singular safe conclusion, but rather more questions and a mind map flowing off the 36 by 24 inch chart paper.

Expanding Folk Tales through Role Playing

BY KRYSTEN CAMERON

As a classroom teacher, I have always used drama to invite students to interact with literature. Drama focuses on the process of the enactment for the sake of the learner, not the audience, which can be a later project of presentation. I have found that drama aids reading comprehension and critical reading as it develops the ability of the readers to go beyond the text to a place where they are engaged with the story, the characters, and ideas. Through drama I have been able to witness my students' ways of thinking, their abilities, and their feelings. Drama has provided clarity in comprehension and has made public the meaning-making process.

Using drama did more than improve the reading comprehension of my students; it expanded their schema and bonded our community. The closer we were as a group, the more we could play with drama and literature together, and the more we learned. Drama provided my students with the concrete experiences that create personal meaning. In the safe environment of the classroom, it has given my students time to interact with one another, to create and share new experiences and build on past experiences; it has brought their schema to the forefront to assist with expanding and creating new knowledge. Drama has helped make my students enthusiastic about reading.

I want my students to be able to think critically about what they are reading and to challenge the text in a way that deepens their comprehension and connects them to the text. I fear too many of my Grade 8 students take what they read for absolute truth. My grade partners and I work hard to remind the students that there is always another perspective or another voice to be heard and considered — be it their own or that of the villain or victim or character other than the narrator. Even non-fiction texts have perspectives, agendas, and issues of focus that need to be considered.

To start the process of reminding students of other perspectives, I began with a familiar text: the tale of Snow White. I entered the room for a round of Hot Seating and told the students to ask me yes or no questions to figure out which famous character I was. This activity often begins with simple questions, such as "Are you a boy or a girl?" As students begin to think they have figured out the character, the questions become more complex. Once the class had established that I was

a girl, not married but in love, and a princess, they began to ask questions about princesses they all knew. One student asked if I had ever worn glass slippers, while another asked if I kissed frogs. Eventually, it was uncovered that I was Snow White. This activity stimulated our schemas, or prior knowledge, about who we thought Snow White was.

After the Hot Seating, I read aloud the traditional tale of Snow White and the Seven Dwarfs. Students were asked to use a graphic organizer with their groups to summarize the story and describe the characters. All of the groups shared with the class: it was decided that the stepmother was evil and Snow White was the victim.

I reminded the students that there are always two or more sides to the story. We brainstormed who else in the story might have a perspective or an opinion: the stepmother, the prince, the dwarves, the hunters, the father, and even the mirror. What might their perspective be on the Snow White situation — and why are we so willing to trust Snow White? My students responded to this statement: *Stepmothers are always mean and evil.*

- Snow White is pretty and young and seems innocent.
- Since when are princesses bad? Give me one example, Ms. Cameron.
- If the stepmother was good and Snow White was evil, then why did the stepmother try to poison her?

The last question evoked a discussion of possibilities and ideas. I heard statements about bribery and threats, fear of losing the king, and many other creative suggestions. I stopped the class and read aloud Alvin Granowsky's *Snow White: The Unfairest of Them All.* This version paints Snow White as deserving of her plight and her stepmother as worthy of praise. I asked students to write a response to or give an opinion about the fractured version I had just read.

It makes sense that Snow White is protective of her dad and that she didn't love her step mom. My parents are divorced and my mom is always taking her boyfriend's side of things.

I think lots of people get away with bad things because they are seen as good by other people. It's like you tell us that story about crying wolf or about how sometimes when we do bad things people see us as bad even when we aren't. I never would have thought that Snow White was bad or mean. Is there one of these for all the fairy tales?

Our next exercise in perspective involved the tale of the Little Red Hen. In this story, the cat, pig, and duck are lazy and do not help their friend the hen make bread. As a result she does not share any bread with them.

I prompted students to act out the dialogue in the book, but as they presented in front of the class, we stopped for some Thought-Tracking, where students are asked to speak out loud the private thoughts of their characters. I asked different cats, pigs, and ducks to explain how they felt when the hen asked for help. I asked how they felt after they said no to her and I asked why they said no. I also had different students explore how they felt when the hen wouldn't share with them. The hens were asked why they wanted help, how they felt when their friends wouldn't help, and if they were happy at the end when they ate their bread alone. Each student had to justify his or her answers. One pig told me that he didn't help because he is a pig and it would be wrong to help because it is his heritage to be lazy. Another pig told me he regretted not helping because pigs like to eat and he couldn't stand not eating the bread. A duck didn't help because she didn't have teeth and couldn't eat the bread so who cared, and a cat said she was too busy cleaning her fur. Many of the hens felt attacked or abandoned by their friends, and although they were supposed to feel good about not sharing in the end, many hens wished they could have shared.

I read Alvin Granowsky's version of this tale, *Help Yourself, Little Red Hen!* Students compared their earlier experience to that in the second book and commented about who they were most like in the story. The following are two examples:

At the end of it I realized the hen was the lazy one and the pig was the hard working one. The cat and duck are followers and the pig should tell them off unless they are scared and the pig is really a bully. I wonder which one will tell the hen how they feel. I think I am like the cat because I am kinda a follower and do what my friends tell me even if I know it will hurt someones feelings.

I was surprised that the hen was selfish and lazy. I should have thought that because why would three friends say no without a good reason. If it was one friend then it could be the friend's problem but three friends should have been a sign to us that she was the problem. I think I am like the pig because I don't listen to what other people say but I do what I think is right.

My students have begun to use what they learned though drama to think critically about the perspective of the author and the other characters when reading a text. They are able to put themselves in the story and see things from a different perspective. They are asking questions of the narrator or author and are looking for motives and agendas.

When my students read an article about climate change, one student commented that this was obviously not written by anyone in the car industry. When I asked why he thought that, his response was as follows:

"Well, because the article is blaming cars a lot and if I was in the car business I would say that people do need to walk more but we are making cars better. There are cars now that use solar power and batteries and we will make more. It isn't all our fault and what about the factories that make smoke?"

This student was considering the other side of the story, putting himself in someone else's shoes and going beyond the text. Drama lets us slip between the words on the page and disappear into the story; it allows us an understanding that goes beyond the literal to something deeper. Drama brings the text to life and to heart.

Building an Environment for Dramatic Role Playing

BY TIINA MOORE

Eighty students looked up as Anne, the school receptionist, carried a parcel into the centre area of the Years 3 and 4 teaching block. It was addressed to Mrs. R from the Cairo museum, a place we knew she had visited on a summer holiday. Perhaps she had forwarded some souvenirs. Mrs. R, however, seemed to have no knowledge of the contents and seemed concerned about opening the package publicly. She sought advice from the other teachers who looked at each other and shrugged. The students started to chorus, "Open it!" Tentatively, she began to do so. First came the unravelling of the string, then the meticulously taped brown paper. Mrs. R removed the lid of the box and lifted out a letter and a scroll. There wasn't a sound in the room.

The letter, from the curator of the museum of Cairo, had remembered Mrs. R from her visit to Egypt. He had recalled that she was a teacher with a passion for ancient history. A scroll with a strange plea for help had crossed his desk and he somehow knew that the four classes of 8 to 10 year-old Australian students and their teachers were the right people for the job. After all, they worked in a teaching and learning community known as The History Centre. Mrs. R turned to the scroll and slid it out of its ties:

Hi, my name is Hermon. I am 12 years old. I live in a small village close to the pyramids. It is 1435 BC. I have helped build these pyramids with my father and we will share in the Pharaoh's life after death. It has taken thousands of men more than 20 years to build the pyramid and it needs some finishing off to make the Pharaoh's inner chamber complete. Today I am worried. My father has not returned from his work in the inner chamber and unless he is able to complete his work, my family will not have passage to the afterlife. If there is anyone who can help me I can assist in your travel to my time. You will need to solve the coded message and use the power of the red stone to unlock the secrets of the afterlife. Thus you will set the spirits of my family free.

Inevitably, many questions followed. How had the parcel come to Anne? Was Hermon real? Would it be safe? What work would be required? Where was the coded message?

The History Centre is the name of the Years 3 and 4 learning paradigm that has been developed at ELTHAM College of Education in the urban fringe of Melbourne, Victoria. It is a K–12 non-denominational independent school with a history of integrating curriculum through storied frameworks. Since the 1990s, teachers have applied Kieran Egan's "story form model" and David Booth's story drama principles in a variety of ways. In its seventh year of operation, the school's administration supported the shift from a weekly drama specialist model to a learning community model wherein four classes, four class teachers, and the drama specialist have an uninterrupted full day each week to engage with a particular community's problems and tasks.

Broadly speaking, the two-year curriculum is framed by issues of colonization and conservation. Each unit of work is designed as a 10-week story block with built-in flexibility for extensions and interruptions. All participants work in role as characters inside the story. Teachers less comfortable with the notion of managing students-in-role adopt characters similar to the teacher role. At times we have assigned a teacher/floater to sort out those out-of-role moments like music lessons or upset tummies. Once the riddle (spelling ELTHAM) was solved, preparations for time travel began in earnest.

How did you create the living setting?

Student familiarity with alternate realities is an enormous advantage to classes interested in completing inner tombs of pyramids. In the first year of time travel, we started with a large sheet of calico on which we pencilled a rough outline of distant pyramids. In class groups, students took turns alternating with researching facts about pyramids and sponge-painting the backdrop that signified the entry into our ancient world. It was hung as a split curtain in the middle of a room as a way of keeping 2008 and 1435 B.C. separate. In shared spaces and small areas, transporting options include these:

- stepping over a rope
- closing one's eyes and saying a chant

- placing one's hand on the eye of Horus and counting backwards (3, 2, 1 or 2008, 1908, 1008)
- hanging a cartouche (an oval ring enclosing Egyptian-like hieroglyphs) around one's neck
- walking under a "papyrus" arch
- walking into the classroom "portal"
- whispering the name of a pyramid three times

The first visit to ancient Egypt was highly ritualistic. One by one each student placed a hand on the red stone, cited Hermon's name, and slipped through the calico curtain into an empty inner chamber. The master artisan Jani (teacher-in-role) met each in turn and offered students a choice in the role-appropriate tasks for the completion of the tomb. In subsequent visits it was enough for time travellers to put on their cartouches (their names in hieroglyphs) to transform into work groups, such as the following:

- **priests, viziers, and nobles** who undertook research and practical work connected to creation myths, local gods, mummification processes, charms and amulets, offerings for the afterlife and the weighing of the heart
- **scribes** who prepared reports and visual materials on tools for writing; hieroglyphic symbols; letters of praise and safe passage to the afterlife; Osiris, the god of the Underworld; Anubis, god of the Dead; and the social hierarchy
- **artisans** who researched and created Canopic jars for organs, panels for the inner chamber, death masks, and stylized images of the gods
- **builders/peasants** who were responsible for sharing knowledge about tools and materials, crops and irrigation, pyramid construction, statistical facts, temples and obelisks, and the building of a sarcophagus

Research projects tended to develop over time in the four discrete classes. The information was shared to all classes in such forms as posters, booklets, PowerPoint, models, and dioramas. Each class also enjoyed specialist drama sessions in which a simplified version of the delightfully gruesome story of Isis and Osiris unfolded.

During the communal time, students worked under the teacher who was head noble, priest, scribe, artisan or builder, focused on the creation of artifacts for the inner chamber. The building of the sarcophagus with timber, chicken wire, plaster of Paris gauze, paint, and

decorative features unfortunately took an entire term and forced the other masters and apprentices to supplement their original research and practical tasks. However, the calico backdrop and the gilt sarcophagus are now part of the permanent design elements available as set features for concerts, assemblies, and future tomb restorations, such that our socially hierarchical tasks can henceforth be more equally distributed.

Once students were comfortably used to the routines established for time travel, research projects, and creative projects, teachers folded the pressure of time into the story mix. We deliberated with students whether there was a time beyond which Hermon's family would miss finding the passage to the afterlife. The eye of Horus somehow magically appeared in our room. We worried whether it represented protection or danger. We shared our knowledge of the evil eye and decided to remain wary. Not long after the appearance of the eye, certain messages were posted in the half-completed tomb:

Beware the Evil Eye

Who Dares Disturb the Peace of This Tomb?

The Secrets of the Afterlife Are Not Yours

We held a community meeting and got advice from the nobles, scribes, artists, and builders. We took that advice to the year 2008 and as school students and teachers decided on a way to assure the spirits/messengers that we were not tomb robbers. We offered a culminating burial procession in honor of Hermon's family and the Pharaoh for whom they worked. The procession would bring the two worlds together for one final time.

On the day of the ceremony, teachers and students came dressed in accordance with their place in society. Each social group had written burial scripts, had chosen representative speakers, and had selected appropriate offerings to be placed in and around the chamber.

The priests led the way to the beat of a drum and the builders carrying the sarcophagus followed. In all, 80 students, five teachers, and many respectful parents processed through the school grounds.

At five nominated stops, the speakers came out of the procession to say:

Priest: We the priests believe that through death the Pharaoh can be renewed and live an eternal life. We wish our pharaoh a successful journey so he can reunite with this spirit. . . .

Builder: We the builders have purified the grounds, driving the evil spirits away. We have dug the foundations and cut the stone. Your place of rest has been made of solid limestone to cast you into the afterlife. . . .

Scribe: We the scribes have studied the detail of your life. We have noted your bravery and courage and the kindness you have shown to your people. . . . .

Artists: With the guidance of Jani, we the artists have created treasures of gold and murals telling your life story. We hope these humble offerings are worthy of your greatness. . . .

Once the sarcophagus was back in the inner chamber of the pyramid, offerings of tablets, parchments, Canopic jars with organs, images of the sons of Horus, food, scarabs, jewels, and ankhs (symbols of life) were placed around the tomb. The final speaker made this pronouncement:

Final speaker: May the eye of Horus protect you throughout your journey . . . You will live again. . . . You are now united with your lived ones forever.

Building communities

The communities that we build in the History Centre are at times simple (a village well, a flag planted in the soil of the great southern continent) and at times elaborate (Sydney Cove, a fishing village). In each case, the fundamental principle is to find a way to invest children in the problems and the issues of each community. Using Dorothy Heathcote's Mantle of the Expert approach, we take on the responsibilities of adults within a framed story. The stories we take part in could be deepened in other ways, many of which are discussed in this text. At the time of writing, we are privileged to have a centre area for building which can accommodate four classes and their teachers (albeit less comfortably when the pyramid is erected); however, each of the units of work has evolved from environments that were first conceived and created by a single teacher in a classroom. They can be simplified by using signs (Single File for Tomb Entry), cloths (the river, the mummy), and rolls of paper (hieroglyphic panels).

Building an environment represents building belief. There are opportunities for taking pride and for under-

taking tasks that somehow matter — Hermon simply needed our help.

Reflections in writing

From a priestess . . .

I am a priestess and my role is to preserve the body, get it wrapped up, and also to get the small and big intestines, lungs and the liver in the four canopic jars which are guarded by four gods. The gods are a jackal-head named Anubus who guarded the stomach and the upper intestines, the human-headed god called Imsery who was the guardian of the liver, the baboon-headed Hapy guarded the lungs and the falcon-headed Qebehsenwef guarded the lower intestines.

As a priestess I have participated in many groups: illustrating the book of the dead, a story and play on the sun god Horus, and the opening of the mouth ceremony.

At the Egyptian Burial Ceremony . . . I felt like a very important person. I enjoyed wrapping up our king, leading the procession of the death of our king Azura. . . .

From a scribe . . .

Many Egyptians could not write so scribes hired themselves out to people who needed them. . . . The major jobs that the scribes need to finish [is] the writing of the king's life and the hieroglyphics on the sarcophagus lid. It'll be a lot of work but we'll finish it. I think we are the luckiest school in the whole world because [who else] would let their students recreate an inner chamber of a pyramid and use proper tools.

From an artist . . .

I've had very big opportunities in the artist group; we made canopic jars and painted on canvases. I've achieved many things including laughter . . . [and] fixing my art work that has broken. I learnt that pottery takes over a week to dry. . . . We have learnt how to draw extremely hard drawings of Egyptian creatures.

From a builder . . .

I felt very excited before the ceremony. My favourite part was when we entered the tomb. I liked my character because it involved carrying the sarcophagus. . . . I will always remember when we farewelled the pharaoh to the afterlife. I wish that [our] place was really Egypt. That would be so cool! I wondered what it would feel like to be a slave or a mummy. I also wondered what it would feel like to rule Egypt.

Eighty people processed through the school grounds the day of the burial ceremony.

Students find a way to enter Ancient Egypt.

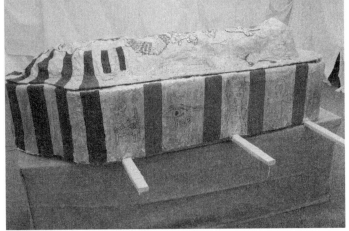

Building the Pharaoh's sarcophagus took a school term, but it remains as a reusable prop.

A Historical Setting for Role Playing

BY NANCY PREST

The Young Interpreters program at Upper Canada Village in Ontario provides participants with the opportunity to assume the roles of typical 19th century children. Children come to Upper Canada Village for nine days to help portray life in the 1860s and to learn about the skills and techniques involved in being a historical interpreter. Each child is lent a period costume and instructed in the proper manner of behavior for a child in the 1860s.

As Young Interpreters, children are assigned to locations where, under supervision, they observe and participate in the historical interpretation, performing tasks and learning the skills appropriate to the time period. These locations include tenant farms; the shops of the cabinetmaker, tinsmith, and blacksmith; the bakery; the home of the dressmaker or the weaver.

Children from ages 10 to 15 become the pioneer children of the 1860s. As they arrive to work each morning, they relinquish modern-day jeans, T-shirts, running shoes, knapsacks, watches, and MP3 players for breeches, petticoats, frocks, hair ribbons, white gloves, sun hats, suspenders, and lace-up boots. They also leave in the parking lot their modern-day language and behaviors. Children at Upper Canada are to be seen and not heard unless spoken to.

In role they learn valuable lessons about daily pioneer life and chores. They churn butter, tend the animals, spin wool, make food, garden, sew, make bread, make cheese, do carpentry, make barrels and brooms, and become apprentices to the tinsmith and the blacksmith.

Children attend a one-room schoolhouse and church — quite an eye-opening experience for them! They also learn how to play the childhood games of the 1860s, such as baseball and tug of war. They work as a team and play as a team. Once they are enveloped in their clothes and surroundings, it is truly amazing to see how they transform. The children really authentically become Canadian pioneers — a life-altering event!

Volunteering as a young interpreter at Upper Canada Village was an unforgettable learning experience. It involved participating in an authentic pioneer community in full costume. A typical day began by donning petticoats, a dress, hair ribbons and a sun hat and from that moment forward we were the children of the village, helping out with daily tasks such as churning butter, spinning wool, and going to school at the schoolhouse. We were expected to stay fully immersed in the period, interacting with tourists in character.

Actually partaking in the activities of the 1860s was a better history lesson than I can ever remember from elementary school; the meticulousness of placing each letter in each column at the printing press, the humiliating tactics used by teachers to maintain order in the classroom, the division between suitable jobs for girls versus boys, the food we ate (straight from the garden), and all the hard work that went into producing things we take for granted in modern times. Experiencing rather than observing or reading about these things made it easy to relate the pioneer experience to questioning tourists, and at the same time it fused the historical information with personal experience.

Kaitlin

Bullies and Victims: A Drama Experience

BY MARYJANE CRUISE

With my Grade 4 class, I wanted to address the bully issue. In the past I have dealt with this topic by doing exercises, tableaux work, bully stories, and so on, but this time I wanted the students to create an original work that would have a lasting effect on them.

We decided to create a dramatic play about bullying for Smith School. We would incorporate movement, music, and dialogue into it and everyone at all times would participate. It would be a true ensemble piece. In the past, I have done this only with high school students because it is a challenge, but since I had worked with these students for over four years — I had been their Kindergarten teacher, too — I knew that they were a delight to work with and knew my expectations. This experience required focus and commitment from every student in the class.

We began the work of building our production in February and completed it in late April. We met twice in a 10-day cycle and the class gave up many lunch hours and gym periods as well. The process took many twists and turns. The class was divided into two groups: the bullies and the victims.

One student, Tyler, became our drummer who helped with the transitions. Tyler had always been a student who lacked confidence and so having that drum in his hand was power. He would come to class and drum everyone into their opening positions. He gained respect from his peers and as a result began to have more respect for himself.

The students were full of ideas on how the play should sound and look. They would constantly stop and gather together to make suggestions on how to proceed. Sometimes we would throw out something we tried. The period always ended with a groan as the students would want to continue into the next period.

We gave voices not only to the victims, but to the bullies. Students had to walk in the shoes of the bullies as well as those of the victims. There is a scene where the bullies explain why they became bullies. It turned out to be so powerful that a few of the students choked when they said their lines. Our drama classes became electrifying. We couldn't wait until our next class and see what would evolve. Students would meet me in the hall and tell me they had a new idea they wanted to try. One of my most timid students became one of my most confident. And one of the students who had bully issues at home became the most focused at the end.

Here are some of the reflections the students wrote to me about their experience.

Julie:

> This play is an important play. It is about bullies against victims. In the end the bullies and victims become friends and live in harmony because they form a bridge of friendship. This play can change lives. It changed mine. That's how important this play is to me.

Teresa:

> We have been working really hard on our bully play. Except it's not just a play — it is a lesson to teach people that have been bullying how wrong it is. It means a lot to me because I learned lots of important things. The exciting thing is it is not in a book. It is our play and you can see so many emotions.

Thomas:

> The play really helped me understand bullying. Before I thought bullying was just people kicking or punching. But now I know that words can hurt more than violence. It also helped me learn a lot about friendship. I won't forget it.

Quinn:

> It is really sad how people can feel when they don't get treated nice. So I think our play changed everyone. Can we do it again?

Siera:

> I am not a bully but I did not know how much people get hurt and how bad it gets. I hope our play touched people's hearts just as much as it did mine. I wish that we could perform it for the world.

10

Deepening Understanding through Media

In today's schools, we see students of all ages using photographs, digital cameras, video cameras, taped recordings of commercial programs for reviewing, and computers for Internet searches and graphic publishing; creating and listening to audio books; and using PowerPoint and SMART Boards. The age of technology is here, and it has entered many classrooms with great impact.

As teachers, we need to understand each medium's strengths and difficulties, and as we incorporate each of them in our teaching/learning situations, we must be certain that our literacy goals with these types of texts are clearly defined. We must also remember that all text types require exploration, interrogation, elaboration, and interactive response modes that extend, expand, and enrich the experience of the text.

Once we accept that different media forms are indeed texts, we can have our students approach each text form with a set of strategies that promotes deep and critical understanding. As well, we can have students use different media to interpret and construct responses, increasing their repertoires for expressing their thoughts and opinions — both cognitive and aesthetic; through the process of responding through a different medium, they can come to rethink and reflect on their understanding of the original text.

Facets of various media are explored in this chapter. Anne Burke reminds us that text messaging is an act of literacy and connects it to the developing linguistic choices of young people. Recognizing the newspaper as a collection of genres, Joan O'Callaghan focuses on opinion pieces that present opportunities for critical reading and thoughtful responding. Chris Grady uses videotaping with his students in different grades, teaching them the simple required techniques and observing the learning that takes place when they both produce and reflect upon the product. Selia Karsten works with technology and offers a guideline for incorporating Web pages in classroom work. All of these media open up avenues of critical and creative expression that take us in different directions from our original intentions and surprise us into learning.

MSN Is Real Talk, Real Text

BY ANNE BURKE

During my time as an English teacher and as a classroom researcher, I have observed how new literacies, such as blogs, wikis, and instant messaging, can motivate and engage students' interests — particularly in comparison to the typical canonical texts taught in our everyday curriculum.

Listening to colleagues grapple with challenges introduced through technology has caused me to seek out opportunities to observe how new literacies are being introduced and used within classrooms. The novelty of new literacies often requires moments of critical reflection for both teachers and students. The following is a critical learning moment observed in the classroom of Carol Roberts. It shows how she engages her Grade 8 students in a discussion of contextual use of MSN language (an instant messaging service).

> *Carol:* So, do you think that using abbreviated language forms such as "u" for you and "ur" in a formal essay is correct?
> *Bruce:* You need to know how to use language because you use some language in some places and other in other places.
> *Carol:* If someone writes it and lots of people use it — is it really language?
> *Meredith:* I think it is language when it is used where it is supposed to be.
> *Derrick:* If it is on Wikipedia [www.wikipedia.com] as a word in their dictionary . . .
> *Sela:* It is language when it has good writing and the words are properly spelled.
> *John:* Why bother writing it out when you can use an abbreviation and people know what you mean?
> *(Students share similar ideas in contexts of their own use of MSN. Carol, seeing this as a critical learning moment, moves into an opportunity for all students to engage in reflection.)*
> *Carol:* I think that we have touched on some interesting ideas about language. I think this is a good place for all of you begin to write your thoughts on how and when we use language. What do you need to know? How do you use it? And when? Let me jot that on the board . . .

This brief exchange shows how adolescents perceive and use language forms differently, and for different reasons. First, Carol situates this discussion about language in a form and sphere that her students understand — the world of MSN. She then challenges students to think critically about how language is formed and used. Bruce's response shows understanding of the importance of register and context when communicating. Carol's challenging question about contextual use of language is addressed by Meredith's comment on how language is situated in particular ways, through both its use and user. Derrick's comment about users of Internet wikis (sites that allow contributions from multiple authors) suggests an authority associated with online texts. Sela, an English Language Learner, sees language as power: proper language will give access to better grades, better education, and a better life. John's comment shows how language carries cultural meanings that give greater understanding of the context in which conversation takes place. In particular, students, such as newcomer Selena, are further challenged through decoding and encoding of vocabulary, as well as the implicit social meanings attached to the choices representing language on MSN.

Carol's encouragement of a critical discussion of language use and representation characterizes the potential of new literacies, with their possibilities to motivate the learners. Carol makes use of an opportunity to make a bridge to the world of technology, which addresses her students' communicative needs. The multiliteracies framework is concerned with *what* students need to learn as a result of the new semiotic landscape and *how* students should go about this learning. Carol engages the four forms in her classroom:

- *situated practice:* She asks students how they would use language.
- *overt instruction:* She questions whether the use of language makes it language.
- *critical reflection:* Through debate students discuss ideas about the use of language.
- *transformed practice:* Students are asked to write about how they use language in context and for what purpose. Carol's invitation to students to think critically about their language use engages the very essence of new literacies, which value the multiple forms with which we make meaning.

Interpreting Multitexts in the Newspaper

BY JOAN O'CALLAGHAN

Newspapers publish a variety of opinions. The most obvious is the editorial, which presents the collective opinion of the newspaper's editors on pressing issues. Another popular feature is the editorial or political cartoon. The topic of the cartoon should be easily recognized by readers. Symbolism, caricature, and exaggeration are the main tools used to convey an opinion about the issue.

Columnists and feature writers also express opinions and provide information. Columnists have a special place in the newspaper. Most of them are experienced journalists. Some are specialists in certain topics, such as politics or the Arts. Others are generalists. Columnists have a great deal of freedom in what they choose to write about. They may range over many subjects, but their columns appear at regular times. They always write over their own byline, meaning that their names appear with their stories, to signal that the opinions expressed are their own.

The headline often gives a clue as to what an article is about and what the writer thinks.

Columns and features

What does the headline tell you?

What does the headline infer or suggest?

Does the headline suggest what the columnist's opinion might be?

The opening paragraph is called "the lead." Does it tell you what the article is about?

Using a marker, underline any words or phrases that suggest what the columnist's position will be.

Once you have read the article, identify the columnist's purpose in writing it.

Use your marker to draw a box around the thesis or main point of the article. Share your ideas with a classmate.

Use a marker to circle all the arguments and points the columnist presents to support a certain point of view. Share your findings with a classmate.

Examine the columnist's arguments. Are they convincing?

Are they valid?

Does the columnist use any other strategies to persuade the reader to a certain point of view?

Do you agree with the columnist?

If you were to write an article taking the opposing point of view, what arguments would you present?

How would you present your arguments to make them convincing?

Conduct some research on the subject.

Does knowing more about the subject change your point of view?

Write a paragraph summarizing what the article is about.

Editorial cartoons

Not all points of view are presented in words. Editorial cartoons, a staple of all newspapers, are intended to present a particular perspective using visuals. There are few, if any words in an editorial cartoon.

Source: *Toronto Sun* 23 June 2008.

Examine the cartoon carefully.

What is happening in the cartoon?

To what newsworthy event is the cartoon connected? How do you know?

What images has the cartoonist utilized?

Is there a caption? Is it necessary?

How has the cartoonist used perspective in the cartoon?

What seems to be the cartoon's message?

Does the cartoon convey its message effectively?

Would the cartoon be as effective if the cartoonist had selected a different vehicle (e.g., a car or train)?

Write a short opinion piece — a column or an editorial — on the same subject as the cartoon.

Do you prefer words or graphics to convey a message?

Using Video Production in the Classroom as Texts

BY CHRIS GRADY

I am often shocked when I hear adults say they can't believe kids would rather spend their time inside, on the computer, than outside on a beautiful day — it does, however, seem to be true. When I take a walk to the community centre near my house on a cool spring day, few kids adorn the outdoor hockey rink or the skating park nearby. Most of them are huddled around computers in the community centre lobby, surfing the net, playing games, and watching videos on YouTube.

Technology is cool. I'm certain that, if all of us had grown up with high speed Internet, Xbox 360s, cell phones, and video cameras, we would have used and love them too. Today, the combined influence of media and the Internet is changing the way our students live, learn, and interact with each other.

I feel extremely lucky to be a teacher now because I have culturally relevant tools that will help excite students about learning. Part of the teaching job is to identify culturally relevant tools and figure out how to use these tools to deepen student comprehension of curriculum, which ultimately will lead to increased success inside and outside the classroom.

Playing back a videotaped lesson

I first introduced video equipment into the classroom while teaching a Math Equity/Social Studies project for a Grade 2/3 class. Students had to build their ideal community using geometric shapes. Even though I believed my lesson to be strong, I thought that I could make it more exciting by videotaping the students during their work, then sharing their ideas about the unit and the final outcomes of their projects with them through a movie. Introducing the camera would also communicate to students that their work was important enough to videotape; it would give them more confidence and encourage them to take the work seriously. Most important, the introduction of the camera into the classroom would help to deepen students' understanding of the work they were doing. Videotaping a lesson and then playing it back would allow the students to review their work, reflect on it, and discuss it, which would lead to a better understanding of the lesson.

I think it is important to note that I am not an expert in video production, editing, and cinematography. I learned how to edit the same way every kid learns how to use a computer: by experimenting with programs, asking a friend, and yes, even typing in "how to edit a movie?" at youtube.com. Basically, the editing process for me involved taking the most relevant clips of the student interviews and combining them with clips of the students hard at work. I added a basic title as well as, a recognizable song at the start and the end of the film, and voilà! Amateur movie magic!

Watching the final video is the most valuable part of using video production in the class to increase student comprehension. In the case of my Grade 2/3 class, we watched the film twice because the first time, the students were so eager to talk about what they were hearing and seeing that they would excitedly turn to whoever was talking on film and start a discussion. My favorite line from the first viewing of the film happened when one of the more energetic students was shown on video creating a structure out of a rectangular prism and a classmate asked, "What are you doing?" To which he answered, "I think I am actually doing work."

My Grade 2/3 students were not distracted by my amateur editing; instead, they were more excited to see themselves on TV. Best of all, they were engaging and deepening their comprehension with the issues presented in the lesson. The film deepened the students' comprehension in the following ways:

- It offered an opportunity for the students to review their work.
- It offered the students an opportunity to review the main learning points in a lesson.
- It gave the students an opportunity to hear their classmates' opinions about the lesson.
- Finally, it presented a lesson in a format that was culturally familiar, appropriate, and interesting to the students.

Teaching critical media literacy skills

I built upon this idea of using video equipment in the classroom, while teaching a Grade 6 class at Oakridge Public School. I introduced the camera during two separate science lessons on vertebrates and invertebrates. Both the vertebrate and invertebrate final projects were to involve a performance. In groups, the students had two tasks: (1) to write a script for a play that would be performed in front of that class on a particular vertebrate; and (2) to write and then perform a rap about a particular invertebrate. During the final performances students' work would be filmed and then all of the footage would be put together in a film. The film's purpose was to reinforce what students were learning as well as teach other students. In this class, I did not do the editing on my own; rather, we did all the editing as a class.

The motivation to using video cameras in this lesson was, in a way, to create the same level of excitement as had arisen in my Grade 2/3 class; however, my main goal was to teach extremely valuable critical media literacy skills while teaching science, music, and drama curriculum. I began this lesson by showing students a television commercial for a fast food chain.

For the first viewing of the 30-second clip, I told the students nothing, just to watch. This being a popular fast food chain, most of the students had seen this particular commercial before. Some said they ate there on occasion, others said it wasn't as good as other places, and some said it was disgusting; however, all of them seemed to know the jingle at the end of the commercial. No one said anything about the actors chosen for the film, about the choice of music, sets, or props, or about what images were used and why.

In subsequent viewings, students looked for specific things. On second viewing, I told them to forget about the product and watch how many times the camera angle switched. On third viewing, we talked about the actors in the commercial and why they were being used. After a few more viewings, most students were sick of the commercial (one student sang that jingle for a week afterward), but all the students were no longer looking at it as just another flash on TV. Instead, they were starting to become more cognizant that everything we watch is there for a reason. They were beginning to develop the ability to critically analyze media messaging. After this lesson I gave the students the homework of watching TV and writing about what they were seeing using their new critical lens. Most students did not complain.

Once the students began working on their plays and raps, I asked them to consider the same things. They couldn't just film their plays or their raps — they needed to draw out basic storyboards, highlighting where they wanted to put the camera, what angle they wanted it at, what props they would need, and about how long the scene would be.

Only after all the students had properly prepared for their videos could the filming process begin. All this detailed preparation not only enhanced the students' ability to think about their work and their roles as both creators and observers of media, but also helped to move work along efficiently, keep students on task, and have students constantly working together to come up with and discuss ideas.

Editing for comprehension

The process of editing these carefully planned-out vertebrate plays and invertebrates raps was the most powerful tool in helping students to comprehend their work. By asking students to examine the footage of their thought process, production, and presentation of a piece of work and then edit it into a more concise work, I was forcing them to choose the most important portions of their work. Essentially, I was teaching them summarization skills. The editing process also taught the students to reflect on the areas of their work that were not clear and still needed attention. Reflecting on their work helped to strengthen their ability to further comprehend the main points of the lesson.

Since we were editing these videos as a class, different groups were given the chance to examine not only their own work, but that of others as well. We did this by showing all the footage filmed for a group, then together having the students discuss what parts they thought were most successful in teaching them the information they needed to learn about vertebrates and invertebrates and what parts maybe distracted them or were less useful to the overall learning objective. Once they had agreed on two or three key scenes, we would list them and move on to another group's footage. After each group had gone we were left with a series of scenes that could make up a short video that contained about six plays on vertebrates and about six raps on invertebrates. All that was left was to put them in order in the classroom's computer editing program.

When introducing the editing equipment into the classroom, it is important to show the class how editing works. Basically, you are taking existing footage — say, five minutes of a group of students acting out a play — and cutting out parts you think are unnecessary. The way most editing programs work is you open up the video your group has taken. You can then select portions of that video by determining the start point and an end point.

For example, imagine all the footage a group of students filmed is represented by a candy bar. One end of the candy bar is the beginning of the film and the other is the end of the film. In this case, you want to eat only the middle of the candy bar because the ends aren't up to your standards. So, you would select the part you want to keep and cut that out.

The same applies with editing in class. Taking the total footage, we would simply cut out the portions the students didn't want. The way most of these programs work is simple, and I would be surprised if by Grade 5 or 6, at least one of your students didn't know more than you about editing. One of my students helped teach me how to upload something onto YouTube.

This process has many advantages. It teaches students how to use computer programs and allows those students who are familiar with the programs to share their knowledge. It also allows students to work together, foster positive discussions, and look at things with a critical lens. Since these videos dealt with the Diversity of Living Things unit, the more time we spent editing and discussing the footage, the more time students had to become familiar with the concepts, information, and learning objectives of that unit. At the end of this process students had created an engaging science video that they could be proud of and could share with another class beginning to learn about vertebrates and invertebrates.

After the vertebrate/invertebrate project was finished, the students were eager to create more videos. Although that project was enjoyable enough to warrant a desire for similar work, I knew that the next project had to be bigger and more involved. Now it was time for me to step back and let them explore the world of video production.

Movie trailers with purpose

We decided that we would get into groups and create movie trailers. Each group decided upon a subject to pursue. One group decided to make a trailer for a horror film, another decided they wanted to make a sports movie trailer, and one ambitious group decided to make a trailer for the greatest action movie of all time entitled "Friend or Foe?"

The first thing I did was explain to the class the role of a movie trailer. Just like a fast food commercial, every second of trailer has a purpose. A movie trailer takes the important scenes of a full-length movie and weaves them into a coherent and concise summary of what the

story is about. The students were required to identify the main themes and ideas of the work they would be adapting/creating and decide with which angle they would approach their trailer. For this portion of the lesson I showed the students two trailers for the same movie: *Star Wars: Attack of the Clones*. One trailer presents the movie as a love story, while the other trailer presents it as an action movie.

Once students figured out what angle their trailer would take, they created detailed storyboards for each scene. They also had to consider scripts, music, props, sound effects, filming locations, camera angles, and actors. The breadth of this undertaking forced students to really examine and understand the piece of work they were creating because everything included in their work had to be part of the plan and serve a purpose.

Often, we would begin each day with a 15-to-20 minute update from the groups on how the planning was coming along. I found this worked most smoothly once different roles were chosen (or assigned) to each group. For example, someone was in charge of filming, another person was in charge of the camera, and some people took on the task of editors. It was important to me to show the students that the actor of a film is not the most important part; rather, the people behind the scenes working the microphone, honing the script, holding the camera, editing, and so on really make the project come together.

During this planning process, it is important to take things in steps. For example, spend week one on just the script and throughout the week integrate other lessons with the video project. So, in week two, when we were focusing on storyboarding, I was able to integrate a visual art lesson on perspective drawing, a language lesson on how to draw a storyboard, and a math lesson that involved the students in creating fraction word problems about editing.

One great way to keep students focused on thinking and planning good material is to tell them they have limited time with the camera. One scene for a trailer needed to be filmed in a five-minute period. In most schools that have cameras for student use, they can be signed out only for a short period. When I was using my own camera, only one group could film at a time. Since students had only a short time to work with the camera, they needed to make sure that all their camera layouts, props, and scene locations were planned and discussed before filming.

The most difficult part of the filming is finding the time to do it. If the scene took place indoors and could be done in the room or the hallway during silent reading or when they were finished with a project, then there weren't many limitations. However, with most groups I found I would have to spend 10 minutes at lunch or during a recess, supervising their filming outdoors or in the location they had chosen. None of the students seemed to mind missing out on their recesses and in the end I didn't mind losing a bit of my break time — my students were excited about their work.

Once all the filming is done, the editing process once again serves as a good tool for reinforcing what a student already has taken from the novel or story and for bringing to light new pieces of information and ideas that may have been missed during the pre-production. Deciding which scenes should be cut and which should be part of the final project helps students better comprehend the work they are analyzing and creating. In most cases of editing, I had students working on the one class computer or on my laptop when they had finished their work. Since the class had five groups, I gave each group a class period to meet and edit on one day a week. So group one edited their movie while the rest of the class worked on a Social Studies project. Each day we would rotate. Originally, I was worried there would not be enough time for each group to complete their projects, but in many cases, students willingly met during lunch and during After School Homework Club to work on their videos.

The role of "private screenings"

Once all the videos were complete, the students provided a "private screening" for their classmates.

These private screenings are really important because they give each group a chance to discuss how members contributed to the project (which helps for assessment, as well). They show all the work they have done up to that point. Storyboards, scripts, and ideas are all put on display for the class. The video is shown and then the group can discuss why they did what they did. Finally, the class can ask questions about what any of the groups did or make any last-minute suggestions.

This process is about letting the students show all the hard work they put into the project, but it also helps in reiterating key points that further lead to deepening comprehension among the students. When the "private screenings" are complete, the students can take their videos to show to their friends and families. Usually, this is the moment they have all been waiting for: a chance to share a project that one of my Grade 6 students said "was the reason she wanted to come to school each day." The things you can do with video production in the classroom are amazing. Simple movie trailers and science videos are just the beginning when it comes to creating engaging lessons that lead to deeper comprehension of information and better understanding of how information is given and received. With each project students build more on what they already know, while creating projects that have relevant purpose and implications. Students can also be active teachers in their classrooms, teaching both their classmates and the teacher.

Imagine a class creating meaningful and educational videos for the library to replace the outdated ones that make students drift off to sleep. Imagine students using this technology to create powerful documentaries about issues in their communities and sending those documentaries to their local and provincial or state officials. These things can happen — and already are happening — in schools across the country.

Designing a Web Page

BY SELIA KARSTEN

A Web page is a collection of words and images on the Internet in the form of a page. It is a document with words and images written in hypertext markup language (HTML). Words on Web pages can be links to other words and pages on the Web. Web pages also include images, some photographs and some animated.

Ways to create a Web page

- A Web page can be written as text with added code in hypertext markup language.
- It can be created with a Web editor program that provides help in building the page.
- It can also be created with templates, where some elements are selected from a collection — for example, a page banner.

Plan for your page

Approach creating a Web page in much the same way you would plan for a hike. Make a checklist. Consider what you will need.

Come up with a few ideas for your page. Will you present a true story or fiction perhaps?

Do a mind map to generate ways to think about your page. (See the example below.)

Find a theme and the subtopics of that theme for each page.

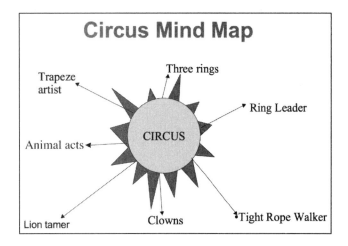

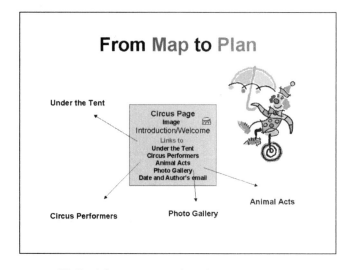

You will find four types of Web pages:

1. *A page made using HTML* (Selia's Cooking page) This page offers an activity where learners will substitute their names for Selia's name and their topics for her topic; they will also include their e-mail addresses and dates. Two examples are given: Mark's scuba page and Mary's snowboarding page. Learners visit http://www.google.ca and http://images.google.ca to find appropriate sites on the topics to link and to find good graphics for the page. (It's important that they cite these sources on their pages.) To complete this type of page, creators need to have the page file(s) and image file(s) transferred to the school server so that the finished pages could be viewed on the Internet using a Web browser.

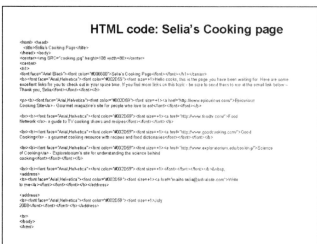

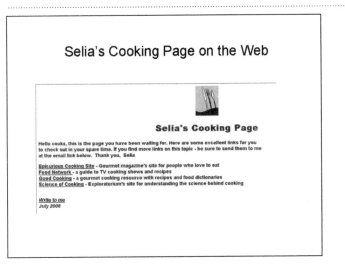

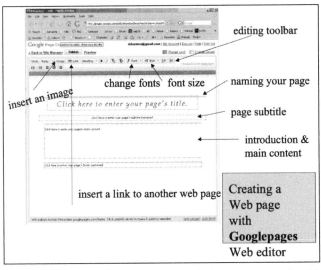

Images (photos taken with a digital camera or scanned-in and digitized pictures) can be inserted in the page to illustrate the story.

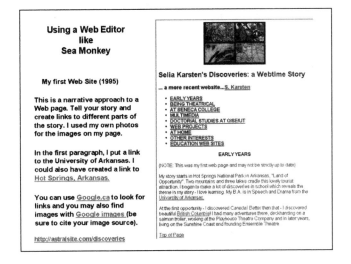

2. *A page made using Googlepages Web editor*
In order to use this free Web editor, the page maker registers for an e-mail account with gmail (http://gmail.com). The completed page can be published to and hosted by Google.

3. *A collection of pages — a website — created with Freewebs Web editor*
This program is free as long as you don't mind banner ads at the top. (For a few dollars a month, you can eliminate the ads.) To register for a Freewebs account, you need to have an e-mail account. Freewebs tools can be used for creating team sites as well as individual pages.

4. *The narrative version of a Web page done with a Web editor (the free browser Sea Monkey:* http://seamonkey.com)
In this approach, a story (truth or fiction) is told and words are hyperlinked to appropriate external sites.

Tips: In creating page and image files, it is always best to use one-word file names without spaces. Small image files load fastest and take less space. All text must be checked carefully — Web browsers can't find links that have been misspelled. Use common fonts (e.g., Arial). Fonts that aren't found will default to Times New Roman.

You have seen different approaches to creating Web pages.

- What approach will you take?
- What tools do you plan to use?
- What stories do you want to tell?
- Are you ready to start?

Prompts for Deepening Comprehension

Connecting to Previous Experience
- What do you already know about this topic?
- How does the information in this text fit with what you already know?
- What have you experienced that helps you understand this topic?
- What does this book make you think or wonder about?
- What surprised you?
- How does this text remind you of other texts you have read?
- Does this text provide information that you personally find useful?
- Why did the author think this subject was important?
- From this book, what did you learn about life, about different places, about history, about science, about religion, and so on?

Extending Meaning
- What is the author's message?
- What is the story really about?
- Do you think the title is appropriate?
- Why do you think the author wrote this story?
- Are different points of view presented?
- What are some of the most important ideas?
- Were there parts of the book you didn't understand?
- What questions do you still have?
- What does this text make you want to learn more about?
- What lessons does this story teach about life?
- Did this style work well?
- What was more important: the plot or the characters?

Considering Setting, Time, and Mood
- Where and when does the story take place?
- Where else could the story take place?
- Could the setting be a real place that exists now?
- How much time passes in the story? A long time or a matter of days?
- In another time and place, how would the story change?
- How did the author control the passing of time?
- Does the setting change over the person's life?
- What was the mood or atmosphere of the story? Did it change as you read the book?
- If a friend planned to read the book, what music would you recommend as appropriate?

Thinking about Characters
- Are there any powerful characters in the story? What makes them that way?
- Who is the most important character?
- Who is the most interesting character?
- Which character taught you the most?
- How does the author/illustrator reveal the character? (Look at what the character does, thinks, or says, or what others say about the character.)
- Which characters changed and which didn't? Is character change important in the story?
- Who is a character who plays a small role? Why is this character necessary?
- What did you learn from one character in the story?

- Would the story have been different if a particular character had been omitted?
- Which character did you dislike? Were you ever frustrated by a character?
- Were there any characters who were not described at length, but who could have been important in the story?
- Did the characters remind you of other personalities on television or in films?
- How are minority roles depicted?
- Are there examples of stereotypes or tokenism?
- Are there strong and independent female characters?
- Whose story is the book really telling?
- Could the story be told if gender roles were reversed?
- How did the characters feel about one another?
- Are the family relationships presented in a stereotypical way?
- How do a character's actions affect other people in the story?
- What changes do the characters encounter and how do they deal with them?
- What choices did the characters have?

Thinking about Storyline and Plot
- How did the author begin the story to engage the reader?
- What is the "story problem"? How did you think it would be solved?
- What was the most important part of the story?
- What clues did the author give to allow the reader to predict the ending?
- What two or three sentences could summarize the whole story?
- Do you think the story really could have happened?
- How does the author help you feel that you are really there?
- Did you find out about events in the order in which they would have happened?
- Were there any plot shifts in time, flash-forwards or flashbacks, or two stories told at once?
- Were there twists and turns in the story that surprised you?
- Did you wonder what might happen next? Were there any clues about what was going to happen? Was it too easy to predict the plot events?
- When did you first know that you had to finish the story, no matter what?

Exploring Point of View
- Who was the voice the author chose as narrator: first person, third person, a storyteller, an anonymous voice, a different voice, or the author as self?
- What events in the story were not written down, but could be understood as happening by reading between the lines?
- Were you able to see the events of the story through the eyes of the characters?
- Did you hope a certain event in the book would not happen, but it did happen?
- Did this book make you think about your own life in a different way?

Considering Emotional Connections
- If you were inside the book, how could you have helped a character?
- Which character would you most like to become?
- Did you know enough about the characters from reading the book to believe in them as if they existed? Would you like to know any of them?
- If you were the author, would you have ended the text in any different way?
- Did anything happen to you just as something happened in the story?
- Was the author able to involve you emotionally? Did you laugh or cry?

- Did you ever feel that you were in the story being told, or did you feel as if you were a spectator or an eavesdropper?
- Which character in the book did you connect with? Do you know why?
- Do any of the characters remind you of someone in your life?
- How does the story make you feel?
- Were you reminded of anything in your own life?

Connecting to Other Life Stories
- How is this story like any other story you know?
- How are the characters, settings, and problems like those in other stories you have read?
- What do you know about the period of history in which the subject of the biography lived?
- Does this person's life remind you of other biographies you have read or of fiction texts?
- How are the problems this person faced like the problems of people in other biographies or fiction books you have read?

Assessing Illustrations
- Was the design of the cover or the book jacket effective? Did it catch your attention?
- What special images, diagrams, or graphics do you remember from the text?
- What is your favorite illustration? Why did you choose it?
- Could you picture what was happening when there were no illustrations?
- What information is provided through illustrations? (Consider drawings, diagrams, maps, charts, and more.)
- Are the illustrations clear and understandable? Are they easy to interpret?
- Are the illustrations explained by labels, legends, and captions when needed?
- Have you read other books by this illustrator? How is this text similar to or different from others the illustrator has done?

Thinking about Structure and Language
- How is information organized (e.g., by topic, in time, by contrasting ideas)?
- Does the total format of the text help you understand the topic better?
- What does the title tell you about this text?
- How do headings and subheadings help you find information in this text?
- What genre does the selection represent? How did you know?
- Is the text a good example of this genre?
- How is this book like other books you have read in this genre?
- What do you find difficult about reading books in this genre?
- What are some interesting words, phrases, and sentences?
- Were words used to create a feeling or picture in your mind?
- Was any of the language especially interesting, vivid, or surprising?
- Was the dialogue realistic? Could you hear people in life saying those words?
- Did the author use description well? Was there enough or too much?
- What did you notice about the style of the writing? How did the book begin: with a question, dialogue, a shocking statement, one word? How did each chapter begin?
- Were there long sentences? short choppy ones?
- Was there a common trick or convention the author used throughout the book? Did you notice any in-jokes?
- Were there examples of slang, different spellings, or strange words or expressions?
- Was the book the right length, too short, or too long? How were the chapters organized — long or short? Was the book divided into sections?

Reader's Choice

- What did you like most about this book? What do you wish there were more of in the story?
- Did you choose to read something by this author because of the type of story or because of the story content?
- Did you have any difficulties with the book? How did you handle them?
- Have you read this book before? Was the second reading different?
- Did you read the book in one sitting or a chapter at a time?
- If you had written the book, how would you have changed it?
- Has this book influenced what you think? what you believe in? your view of the world?
- Have you learned anything about yourself or others from reading this book?
- What passages from the book do you especially remember?
- What quotations would you choose from this book to make a poster for your bedroom wall?
- Would you recommend this book to a younger reader?
- What experiences or life circumstances led you to read about this topic?
- If you were the author, would you change the order of any of the events?
- Would you read other books by this author?
- What other books does this book make you want to read?

Deepening Critical Thinking

- What is the author's background and experience?
- Whose point of view is expressed?
- What does the author, filmmaker, or artist want you to think?
- Whose perspective is found in this text?
- Whose voices are missing, silenced, or discounted?
- Which characters in the text seem to hold all the power?
- Were characters or events portrayed in ways that were unexpected?
- Do you belong to any of the groups in this text?
- What is the world like to the people in this text?
- Were things left out of the illustrations that you thought needed to be included?
- How might alternative perspectives or viewpoints be represented?
- What might you add to the story to make it more complete?
- Can you research the author and his or her perspective?
- What do other sources of information say about these events, characters, and issues?
- Is the information accurate and believable?
- What action might you take from what you have learned?

Connecting to the Author

- Do you know other writings by this author? A series? A sequel? An autobiography? A picture book? Have you read any of them? Can you find patterns in the things the author writes about, in the events of the stories, in the characters, in the style of writing?
- Have you read any information about the author, or seen a videotape of the author speaking?
- Has the author drawn on his or her own life in creating the story?
- What type of research went into writing this book?
- Have you read comments about the author's works, such as reviews or opinions from classmates? Do you know what the author is working on now? What questions would you ask the author about the book or about his or her life?
- What is the author's perspective or stance towards the topic?
- What has the author said that makes you question the accuracy of the information?

Biographies of Contributors

Ernest Agbuya was born in the Philippines and raised in Rexdale. He studied journalism before becoming a teacher; he now lives with his wife Jennifer and his music collection in Toronto. He wears no cape, but sleeps with his socks on, even in summer.

Wendy Agnew is an educator in the Montessori system in Ontario. She engages in teaching and learning with both children and adults, with a dash of theatre on the side. Her doctoral thesis is aptly named: "The Universe Is a Horse."

Bob Barton, when not defending his tomato plants from a plague of raccoons, teaches drama to teachers at OISE and tours as a storyteller in the schools for Prologue for the Performing Arts.

Pauline Beder has been an elementary school teacher, a literacy consultant, a teacher at York and Nipissing universities, and a consultant for various publishers. At time of writing, she was at the (Ontario) Ministry of Education as part of the Literacy and Numeracy Secretariat. Her most cherished role is that of grandmother to her brand-new twin grandchildren.

Kimberly Bezaire is an Early Childhood Education specialist and doctoral candidate at OISE/UT. Her research interests include play in Kindergarten, multiliteracies, and gender studies. She has learned to relish "gross" and "scary" stories with her eight-year-old son, Michel.

Marni Binder is an assistant professor in the School of Early Childhood Education at Ryerson University. Many years of teaching in the inner city has shaped her passion for arts-based education. When she is not writing and lecturing, Marni aspires to be a tango dancer.

Anne Burke is assistant professor of literacy education at Memorial University, where she teaches new literacies and technology. An avid reader of children's books, she enjoys travel and is becoming an expert playing the Wii video-game system through the tutoring offered by her six-year-old son.

Linda Cameron is a professor of Education at OISE/UT. An expert in language and literacy learning, play, and educational psychology, Linda has taught, researched, and consulted across Canada, the United States, and internationally. She has five grown children and a funny little dog that sings.

Krysten Cameron is a vice-principal in York Region. As a teacher, she was fortunate to have learned and worked with students in Grades 1, 2, 3, 5, and 7; as a Literacy Mentor, she worked and learned with students in Kindergarten to Grade 8. A favorite hobby is shopping with her mom.

Judy Caulfield led a Storytelling Club for junior students in several schools and learned much about story from her students. She now teaches pre-service student teachers at the Ontario Institute for Studies in Education, University of Toronto (OISE/UT) and tells stories in schools and at festivals. She would travel great distances for candy floss!

Maryjane Cruise teaches Kindergarten and drama for the District School Board of Niagara. She is also an award-winning playwright and published choral composer. Her plays are performed widely in Canada and abroad. Her first play, written when she was in Grade 3, was a murder mystery.

Corey Follett has taught English every summer since completing teacher's college five years ago. He enjoys teaching literature through social justice issues. He has yet to find a student who hasn't taught him something about himself. A Newfoundlander, he is afraid of the ocean and doesn't eat seafood.

Konrad Glogowski has taught English in Grades 7 to 12 and worked as an e-learning consultant. His research interests include adolescent literacy and communities of practice. Most recently, Konrad worked in South Africa and Kenya as English team leader with Teachers Without Borders.

Christopher Grady taught at the Art League of Long Island and the Washington English School in Taiwan before moving to Toronto. He currently resides in Locker 815 at the Toronto bus terminal with his wife and two cats.

Stephen Hurley has been involved in public education for 25 years, working as a classroom teacher, a curriculum consultant, and a teacher educator. In his newest role as father, he is in a different position. School is in and son Luke is the teacher!

Eddie George Ing specializes in teaching Primary Behaviour in Toronto. He is an award-winning coach of his school's hockey team. Eddie's proud family includes a 2006 Guinness record holder and a former NHL goaltender.

Selia Karsten is a lecturer at OISE and a pioneer in web-based teaching and learning. Her constructivist learning environments emphasize creativity and promote student self-actualization while building skills with computer applications. Her cat, PeepEye, is a bi-color masked beauty.

Cathy Marks Krpan is an international speaker and award-winning author. A former elementary educator, Cathy teaches pre-service and graduate courses at the University of Toronto. At dawn, she can usually be seen carefully loading bins of teaching materials into her car.

Crystal May, through her 19 years of teaching, has held as her guiding principle that each task should increase the students' desire to learn. At time of writing, she has a class of 30 girls only as a follow-up to a gender literacy study she completed.

Amy Mohr has been an elementary school teacher, with most of her experience with Grades 7 and 8. Currently, she is an itinerant Literacy/Numeracy teacher. She loves spending time with her dog, Hunter.

Tiina Moore has taught drama at primary, secondary, and tertiary levels for over 30 years. Her early teacher education in Story Drama in Toronto has stood her in good stead across three continents. Now at ELTHAM, College of Education, in Australia, she uses process drama to frame interdisciplinary studies.

John Myers is a curriculum instructor at OISE. He has taught students from Grade 3 to adults in three provinces and three countries for three decades. He has three children and three grandchildren.

Milica O'Brien is an ESL teacher and librarian at Queen Victoria Public School, in the heart of Parkdale, Toronto, where she was born and raised. On blustery winter days, Milica tries to solve mysteries like how does the gooey caramel filling end up in the centre of the chocolate bar?

Joan O'Callaghan, according to Benny the cat, is an instructor at OISE/UT, in the Intermediate and Senior Pre-service programs. She enjoys reading, writing (especially mysteries), live theatre, cooking, knitting, and time with friends and family.

Brian Okamoto teaches Grade 5 at Queen Victoria Public School in Toronto; he also plays the piano and spends his free time bemoaning the demise of good posture, good government, and good manners.

Shelley Stagg Peterson is an associate professor at OISE/UT. A former elementary teacher in Alberta, Shelley teaches, researches, and writes about literacy; she also grows out-of-control zucchini on her farm.

Ken Pettigrew is the vice-principal of Greensborough Public School in the York Region District School Board. As the father of twin toddlers, *critical* literacy takes on a whole new meaning — somehow, daddy never seems to get Goldilock's voice right.

Lynda Pogue shares her knowledge, wit, and humor through art, writing, speaking, and teaching. She knows that talk is the foundation for literacy and her international experience has strengthened her resolve to help students to enter the story with body, mind, and heart.

Nancy Prest, now a Literacy Instructional Coach, has taught Grades 1 through 4. She loves the medieval theme in Grade 4; she even carried it to her wedding, with parchment invitations, minstrel songs in the church, pewter goblets at the feast, and even tunics and tights for the groom and best man.

Krzysztof Rakuc is a new teacher excited about reaching boys with graphic novels. He is an ex-comic book junkie.

Rich Roach is a former mentor artist with LTTA and co-creator of a virtual music program for the Royal Conservatory of Music. Rich enjoys using the Arts to teach his elementary classes in Niagara. He loves his family, music, theatre, poetry, Cypriote archaeology, Latin, and long nature walks.

Leslie Stewart Rose is a lecturer at OISE. Her teaching focuses on inquiry-based learning and how music education can work as a catalyst to inspire social awareness, critique, and action. In her spare time, Leslie is a tree farmer.

Gary Rusland is currently at Valley Park Middle School, where he teaches Grade 8 Science and Grade 6 Special Education Core. He grew up in the wilds of Eastern Ontario and completed two university degrees. He's a big fan of unorthodox lessons and creative curriculum interpretation.

Barb Smith, first a swim and gymnastics instructor in Grade 8, later became a teacher, a consultant, and a lecturer at the University of Saskatchewan and McGill's Faculty of Education; she is now vice-principal (Academic) at The Sterling Hall School. She loves kayaking around the shores of Lake Bolger.

Beverly Strachan has been a classroom teacher, instructional leader, and project leader of the Toronto District School Board's Early Years Literacy Project. She is now a coordinator and instructor in the Initial Teacher Education program at OISE. She lives with her husband on a houseboat.

Larry Swartz is a literacy and drama instructor at OISE/UT. He has been a classroom teacher, consultant, and workshop presenter. When his nose isn't in a kid's book, you might find Larry sipping a latte, working out at the gym, or watching a theatrical production.

Stephanie Tan is a recent OISE graduate, with primary, junior, and instrumental music qualifications. Stephanie enjoys helping students create graphic texts and loves to coach and play volleyball.

Terry Thompson is a literacy coach in Texas, where he trains teachers and works with young readers and writers from Kindergarten to Grade 5. He also holds a degree in psychotherapy and cognitive coaching, and consults with classroom teachers and literacy specialists. He still loves comic books.

References and Resources

Aronson, E., N. Blaney, C. Stephan, J. Sikes, and M. Snapp. 1978. *The Jigsaw Classroom.* Beverly Hills, CA: Sage.

Bandura, A. 1986. *Social Foundations of Thought and Action: A Social Cognitive Theory.* Englewood Cliffs, NJ: Prentice Hall.

Baron, R. A., D. Byrne, and G. Watson. 1998. *Exploring Social Psychology.* 2nd edition. Toronto: Allyn and Bacon.

Beers, K. 2003. *When Kids Can't Read: What Teachers Can Do.* Portsmouth, NH: Heinemann.

Beers, K., R. E. Probst, and L. Rief, eds. 2007. *Adolescent Literacy: Turning Promise into Practice.* Portsmouth, NH: Heinemann.

Berg, P. J., M. K. Devlin, and V. G. Gedaly-Duff. 1992. "Bibliotherapy with Children Experiencing Loss." *Issues in Comprehensive Pediatric Nursing* 23:37–50.

Binder, M. 2002. "Visual Literacy in the Primary Inner City Classroom." *ORBIT* 32 (3): 40–42.

_____. 2004. "The Importance of Child Art as a Foundation for Teaching and Learning." In *The Arts Go to School,* ed. by D. Booth and M. Hachiya (pp. 35–38). Markham, ON: Pembroke Publishers.

Bomer, R., and K. Bomer. 2001. *For a Better World: Reading and Writing for Social Action.* Portsmouth, NH: Heinemann.

Booth, D. 2001. *Reading & Writing in the Middle Years.* Markham, ON: Pembroke Publishers.

_____. 2002. *Even Hockey Players Read: Boys, Literacy and Learning.* Markham, ON: Pembroke Publishers.

Booth, D., and B. Barton. 2000. *Story Works: How Teachers Can Use Shared Stories in the New Curriculum.* Markham, ON: Pembroke Publishers.

Booth, D., and M. Hachiya. 2004. *The Arts Go to School.* Markham, ON: Pembroke Publishers.

Booth, D., and L. Swartz. 2004. *Literacy Techniques for Building Successful Readers and Writers.* 2nd edition. Markham, ON: Pembroke Publishers.

Botelho, Maria J., and Masha K. Rudman. Forthcoming. *Critical Multicultural Analysis of Children's Literature: Mirrors, Windows and Doors.* Mahwah, NJ: Lawrence Erlbaum Associates.

Brewer, M. B. 1991. "The Social Self: On Being the Same and Different at the Same Time." *Personality and Social Psychology Bulletin* 17:475–82.

Buhrow, B., and A. Upczak Garcia. 2006. *Ladybugs, Tornadoes, and Swirling Galaxies. English Language Learners Discover Their World through Inquiry.* Portland, ME: Stenhouse Publishers.

Canadian Society of Children's Authors, Illustrators and Performers (CANSCAIP). 2008. *What's New.* Downloaded 30 September 2008 from: http://www.canscaip.org.

Cowhey, M. 2006. *Black Ants and Buddhists.* Portland, ME: Stenhouse Publishers.

Cummins, J. 2006. "Multiliteracies, Pedagogy, and the Role of Identity Texts." In *Teaching for Deep Understanding,* ed. by K. Leithwood et al. Thousand Oaks, CA: Corwin Press.

Daniels, H. 2002. *Literature Circles: Voice and Choice in Book Clubs and Reading Groups.* Portland, ME: Stenhouse Publishers.

Dean, D. 2008. *Genre Theory: Teaching, Writing, and Being.* Urbana, IL: National Council of Teachers of English.

Deaux, K. 1993. "Reconstructing Social Identity." *Personality and Social Psychology Bulletin* 19:4–12.

Dorn, L. J., and C. Soffos. 2005. *Teaching for Deep Comprehension: A Reading Workshop Approach.* Portland, ME: Stenhouse Publishers.

Edwards, C., L. Gabdini, and G. Forman. 1993. *The Hundred Languages of Children: The Reggio Emilia Approach to Early Childhood Education.* Norwood, NJ: Ablex Publishing.

Egan, K. 2005. *An Imaginative Approach to Teaching.* San Francisco: Jossey-Bass.

Eisner, E. W. 1998. *The Kind of Schools We Need: Personal Essays.* Portsmouth, NH: Heinemann.

Engel, S. 2005. "The Narrative Worlds of 'What is' and 'What if'." *Cognitive Development* 20 (4): 514–25.

Fairclough, Norman. 1992. *Discourse and Social Change.* Cambridge, UK: Polity Press.

Ferguson. Marilyn. 1982. *The Aquarian Conspiracy. Personal and Social Transformation in the 1980s.* London: Granada.

Freire, P. 2001. *Pedagogy of Freedom: Ethics, Democracy and Civic Courage.* 2nd edition. (P. Clarke, Trans.). New York: Rowman and Littlefield. (Original work published 1998).

Gallagher, Kelly. 2004. *Deeper Reading: Comprehending Challenging Texts, 4–12.* Portland, ME: Stenhouse Publishers.

Gallas, K. 2003. *Imagination and Literacy: A Teacher's Search for the Heart of Learning.* New York: Teachers College Press.

Gardner, H. 1991. *The Unschooled Mind: How Children Think and How Schools Should Teach.* New York: Basic Books.

Gee, J. 2001. "A Sociocultural Perspective on Early Literacy Development." In *Handbook of Early Literacy Research,* ed. by S. B. Neuman and D. K. Dickinson (pp. 30–42). New York: Guilford Press.

Glogowski, K. 2008. "Tracing the Emergence of a Blogging/Writing Community: Critical Transformations in a Grade Eight Classroom." Unpublished doctoral dissertation. Toronto: University of Toronto.

Greene, M. 2001. *Variations on a Blue Guitar: The Lincoln Center Institute Lectures on Aesthetic Education*. New York: Teachers College Press.

Hall, Stuart. 1996. "Who Needs 'Identity'?" In *Questions of Cultural Identity*, ed. by S. Hall and Paul du Gay (pp. 1–17). Thousand Oaks, CA: Sage.

Harvey, S., and A. Goudvis. 2007. *Strategies That Work: Teaching Comprehension for Understanding and Engagement*. 2nd edition. Portland, ME: Stenhouse Publishers.

Hill, B. C., K. L. S. Noe, and J. A. King. 2003. *Literature Circles in Middle School: One Teacher's Journey*. Norwood, MA: Christopher-Gordon Publishers.

Internet School Library Media Center. n.d. *Index to Author & Illustrator Internet Sites*. James Madison University website. Downloaded 30 September 2008 from: http://falcon.jmu.edu/~ramseyil/biochildhome.htm.

Hume, K. 2008. *Start Where They Are — Differentiating for Success with the Young Adolescent*. Toronto: Pearson Education Canada.

Jenkinson, S. 2001. *The Genius of Play: Celebrating the Spirit of Childhood*. Gloucestershire, UK: Hawthorn Press.

Jourdain, R. 1997. *Music, the Brain and Ecstasy: How Music Captures Our Imagination*. New York: Avon Books.

Kavanaugh, R. D. 2006. "Pretend Play." In *Handbook of Research on the Education of Young Children*, 2nd edition, ed. by B. Spodek and O. N. Saracho (pp. 269–78). New York: Lawrence Erlbaum.

Keene, Ellin Oliver. 2008. *To Understand: New Horizons in Reading Comprehension*. Portsmouth, NH: Heinemann.

Lattimer, H. 2003. Thinking *through Genre: Units of Study in Reading and Writing Workshops 4–12*. Portland, ME: Stenhouse Publishers.

Leithwood, K., P. McAdie, N. Bascia, and A. Rodrigue. 2006. *Teaching for Deep Understanding*. Thousand Oaks, CA: Corwin Press.

Luke, Allan, and Peter Freebody. 1999. "A Map of Possible Practices: Further Notes on the Four Resources Model." *Practically Primary* 4 (June): 5–8.

Marks Krpan, C. 2001. *The Write Math*. New York: Pearson Education.

Markus, H., and P. Nurius. 1986. "Possible Selves." *American Psychologist* 41:954–69.

Martin, R. 2007. *The Opposable Mind: How Successful Leaders Win through Integrative Thinking*. Boston: Harvard Business School.

McLaughlin, M., and G. L. DeVoogd. 2004. *Critical Literacy: Enhancing Students' Comprehension of Text*. New York: Scholastic Inc.

Miller, D. 2008. *Teaching with Intention: Defining Beliefs, Aligning Practice, Taking Action, K–5*. Portland, ME: Stenhouse Publishers.

Moffett, J. 1988. *Coming on Center: Essays in English education*. 2nd edition. Portsmouth, NH: Boynton/Cook Publishers.

Nicholls, J., M. Opitz, M. P. Ford, and M. D. Zbarackie. 2006. *Books and Beyond: New Ways to Reach Readers*. Portsmouth, NH: Heinemann.

Pajaras, F. 1996. "Assessing Self-Efficacy Beliefs and Mathematical Problem Solving of Gifted Students." *Contemporary Educational Psychology* 21: 325–44.

Pardeck, J. A., and J. T. Pardeck. 1993. *Bibliotherapy: A Clinical Approach for Helping Children*. Langhorne, PA: Gorden and Breach.

Peterson, S. S. 2006. *Writing across the Curriculum: Because All Teachers Teach Writing*. Winnipeg, MB: Portage & Main Press.

———. 2008. *Writing across the Curriculum: All Teachers Teach Writing*. Rev. edition. Winnipeg, MB: Portage & Main Press.

Pinnell, G. S., and P. L. Scharer. 2003. *Teaching for Comprehension in Reading Grades K–2*. New York: Scholastic Professional Books.

Podlozny, A. 2000. "Strengthening Verbal Skills through the Use of Classroom Drama: A Clear Link." *Journal of Aesthetic Education* 34 (3–4): 239–75.

Reeves, A. R. 2004. *Adolescents Talk about Reading: Exploring K.L.S., Resistance to and Engagement with Text*. Newark, DE: International Reading Association.

Robb, L. 2004. *Nonfiction Writing from the Inside Out*. New York: Scholastic Professional Books.

Rosenblatt, Louise M. 1978. *The Reader, the Text, the Poem: The Transactional Theory of the Literary Work*. Carbondale, Ill: Southern Illinois Press.

Routman, R. 2003. *Reading Essentials: The Specifics You Need to Teach Reading Well*. Portsmouth, NH: Heinemann.

Rubenstein, R., and D. Thompson. 2002. "Understanding and Supporting Children's Mathematical Vocabulary Development." *Teaching Children Mathematics* 60 (4): 107–11.

Scott, R. McQuirter. 2008. *Knowing Words — Creating Word-Rich Classrooms*. Toronto: Nelson Thomson.

Serafini, F., and S. Youngs. 2008. *More (Advanced) Lessons in Comprehension: Expanding Students' Understanding of All Types of Texts*. Portsmouth, NH: Heinemann.

Spence, C. M. 2008. *The Joys of Teaching Boys: Igniting Writing Experiences That Meet the Needs of All Students*. Markham, ON: Pembroke Publishers.

Steele, B. 1998. *Draw Me a Story: An Illustrated Exploration of Drawing-as-Language*. Winnipeg, MB: Portage and Main.

Stein, C. 2007. "Let's Talk: Promoting Mathematical Discourse in the Classroom." *Mathematics Teacher* 101 (4): 285–89.

Thompson, T. 2008. *Adventures in Graphica: Using Comics and Graphic Novels to Teach Comprehension, 2–6*. Portland, ME: Stenhouse Publishers.

Tovani, C. 2004. *Do I Really Have to Teach Reading? Content Comprehension, Grades 6–12.* Portland, ME: Stenhouse Publishers.

Vygotsky, L. S. 1978. *Mind in Society. The Development of Higher Psychological Processes.* Cambridge, MA: Harvard University Press.

Weedon, Chris. 1997. *Feminist Practice & Poststructuralist Theory.* 2nd edition. Malden, MA: Blackwell.

Wiggins, G., and J. McTighe. 2005. *Understanding by Design.* 2nd edition. Alexandria, VA: Association of Supervision and Curriculum Development (ASCD).

Wilhelm, J. D. 2001. *Improving Comprehension with Think-Aloud Strategies.* New York: Scholastic Professional Books.

_____. 2002. *Action Strategies for Deepening Comprehension.* New York: Scholastic Professional Books.

_____. 2007. *Engaging Readers & Writers with Inquiry.* New York: Scholastic Inc.

Zipes, Jack. 1983. *The Trials and Tribulations of Little Red Riding Hood: Versions of the Tale in Sociocultural Context.* South Hadley, MA: Bergin & Garvey Publishers.

Other Resources Referred to within This Book

Applegate, K. 2007. *Home of the Brave.* New York: Feiwel and Friends.

Barde, B. (prod.); R. Benger (dir.). 2004. *Daughters of Afghanistan.* [Videorecording] produced by Take 3 Productions in association with Radio Canada and Le Reseau de l'Information (RDI); CBC Newsworld.

Baryshnikov, Mikhail. 2007. *Because . . .* New York: Atheneum.

Browne, A. 1997. *Willy the Dreamer.* Cambridge: Candlewick Press.

Canadian Broadcast Corporation. 2007. "Canadian Women for Women in Afghanistan: Alaina Podmorrow." *CBC The National.* Posted on YouTube website 4 December 2007. Downloaded 30 September 2008 from: http://www.youtube.com/ watch?v=K8oBKiVr2TU.

Central Intelligence Agency (CIA). n.d. *World Fact Book.* CIA.gov website. Downloaded 30 September 2008 from: https://www.cia.gov/library/publications/ the-world-factbook/.

D'Aulaire, Ingi. 1962. *D'Aulaire's Book of Greek Myths.* Garden City, NY: Doubleday Books for Young Readers.

Eastman, P. D. 1960. *Are You My Mother?* New York: Beginner Books.

Ellis, D. 2000. *The Breadwinner.* Toronto: Groundwood Books/Douglas & McIntyre.

Granowsky, A. 1994. *Snow White: The Unfairest of Them All.* London: Bt Bound.

Granowsky, A. (and W. Edelson and J. K. Manning, illus.) 1996. *Help Yourself, Little Red Hen!* Orlando, FL: Steck-Vaughn.

Jarvis, D. H. 2005. *Virtual Art Museums & Galleries.* Resource compilation last updated 11/07/2005. Downloaded 30 September 2008 from: http://www.csea-scea.ca/VirtualMuseums.pdf.

Malyon, John. 2007. *Artcyclopedia. The Guide to Great Art on the Internet.* Downloaded 30 September 2008 from: http://www.artcyclopedia.com/.

Paulsen, G. 1993. *Nightjohn.* New York: Delacorte Press.

Porter, P. 2005. *The Crazy Man.* Toronto: Groundwood Books.

Revolutionary Association of the Women of Afghanistan (RAWA). 2008. "Some of the Restrictions Imposed by Taliban on Women in Afghanistan." RAWA.org website. Downloaded 30 September 2008 from: http://www.rawa.org/rules.htm.

Rylant, C. 1990. *Soda Jerk.* New York: Orchard Books.

Scieszka, J. 1989. *The True Story of the 3 Little Pigs!* New York: Viking Penguin.

Thomson, S. L. (and R. Gonsalves, illus.). 2005. *Imagine a Day.* New York: Atheneum Books.

_____. 2005. *Imagine a Night.* New York: Atheneum Books.

_____. 2005. *Imagine a Place.* New York: Atheneum Books.

Thornhill, J. 2006. *I Found a Dead Bird: The Kids' Guide to the Cycle of Life and Death.* Toronto: Maple Tree Press.

Yerxa, L. 2006. *Ancient Thunder.* Toronto: Groundwood Books.

Young, E. 1989. *Lon Po Po: A Red Riding Hood Story from China.* New York: Philomel Books.

Yusufali, Sultana. 1998. "My Body Is My Own Business." *The Toronto Star* (17 February), C1. Available at: http://www.geocities.com/Heartland/ Fields/2704/article10.html.

Index